NICHOLSON

THE ORDNANCE SURVEY GUIDE TO THE WATERWAYS

3: NORTH

Series editor: David Perrott

Robert Nicholson Publications

Also available in this series:

Nicholson/Ordnance Survey Guide to the Waterways **1. South**
Nicholson/Ordnance Survey Guide to the Waterways **2. Central**
Nicholson/Ordnance Survey Guide to the Broads & Fens
**Nicholson/Ordnance Survey Guide to the River Thames (including the River Wey and
  Basingstoke Canal)**
Nicholson/Ordnance Survey Inland Waterways Map of Great Britain

*The indication of a towpath in this book
does not necessarily imply a public right
of way. If you are in any doubt, check
before you proceed with the latest published
Ordnance Survey map.*
Pathfinder Series (1:25 000 scale or 2½ in to
1 mile). These OS walker and rambler maps show the
countryside in great detail, including rights
of way in England and Wales.
Landranger Series (1:50 000 scale or about 1¼ in
to 1 mile). This OS series covers the country
in 204 sheets and is ideal for detailed
exploring by car or on foot.

First published 1983 by **Robert Nicholson
Publications**, 16 Golden Square,
London W1R 4BN and **Ordnance Survey**,
Romsey Road, Maybush, Southampton SO9 4DH.

4th edition 1989
Revised 1990

Nicholson is an imprint of Bartholomew –
the Cartographic Division of the Collins Publishing Group.

We thank the following CAMRA representatives and
branch members (and others whose names are unknown
to us) for their help in recommending real ale pubs:
Stephen Bray, Macclesfield and East Cheshire; A. Bruce,
West Lancs; R. J. Hall, North Notts; Paul Hannon,
Keighley and Craven; P. W. Marsh, Wigan; John
Thornton, Leeds; Chris Watkinson and Mick Kinton,
Nottingham. Also Glyn Davies.

Special thanks are due to Gerry Turner of British
Waterways, Susan Stevens of Shire Cruisers and Liz and
Tony Robertson-Suggett.

Cover photograph: Derek Pratt

Great care has been taken throughout this book
to be accurate, but the publishers cannot accept
any responsibility for any errors which appear.

Typeset by Rowland Phototypesetting Ltd,
Bury St Edmunds, Suffolk
Printed in Great Britain by
Scotprint Ltd, Musselburgh

Ordnance Survey ISBN 0 319 00169 5
Nicholson ISBN 0 948576 25 1

83/4/45

INTRODUCTION

The canals and navigable rivers of Britain were built as a system of new trade routes at a time when roads were virtually non-existent. After their boom period in the late 18th and early 19th centuries, they gradually declined in the face of fierce competition from the new railway companies, and large-scale commercial carrying ended by the time of the Second World War, when many of the routes had slipped into decay and ruin. It is true that in a few areas goods continue to be carried profitably to this day, but for the majority of canals it was the new traffic of pleasure boats that provided the impetus for rescue and restoration.

The founding of the Inland Waterways Association by L.T.C. Rolt and Robert Aickman in 1946 brought together enthusiasts from all over the country who were to campaign to save and restore these 2000 miles of navigable waterways that are so much a part of our history. During the past few years an amazing transformation has taken place. British Waterways, local councils, and IWA volunteers working with various job creation schemes have tidied up great lengths of town and city canal, and much of the dereliction that was once commonplace has been replaced with gardens and parkland.

There is something for everyone in the canals: engineering feats like aqueducts, tunnels and flights of locks (all of which amazed a world that had seen nothing like it since Roman times); the brightly decorated narrowboats which used to throng the waterways; the wealth of birds, animals and plants on canal banks; the mellow, unpretentious architecture of canalside buildings like pubs, stables, lock cottages and warehouses; and the sheer beauty and quiet isolation that is a feature of so many canals.

A special feature of this new edition is the many new or expanded pub entries, giving details of real ales as recommended by CAMRA. So use this book to discover the waterways for yourself; it is one of five volumes covering the South, Centre and North of England and Wales; the rivers Thames and Wey, and the Basingstoke Canal; and the Norfolk Broads, Ouse, Nene and Middle Level Navigations. A full-colour Nicholson/Ordnance Survey Inland Waterways Map is also available to help you plan your route.

CONTENTS

Planning map 4
How to use this guide 6
Locks and their use 7
General cruising information 10
Planning a cruise 13
Aire & Calder Navigation 15
Calder & Hebble Navigation 20
Huddersfield Broad Canal 28
Bridgewater Canal 29 & 37
Rochdale Canal 35
Chesterfield Canal 41
Erewash Canal 49

Fossdyke & Witham Navigations 55
Lancaster Canal 69
Leeds & Liverpool Canal 81
Macclesfield Canal 113
Peak Forest & Ashton Canals 121
River Trent 131
Trent & Mersey Canal 149
Weaver Navigation 159
North East Waterways 167
British Waterways offices 169
A brief history of British canals 170
Index 174

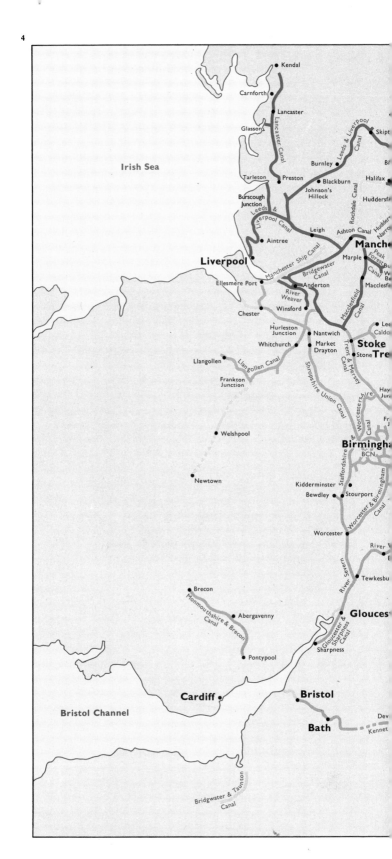

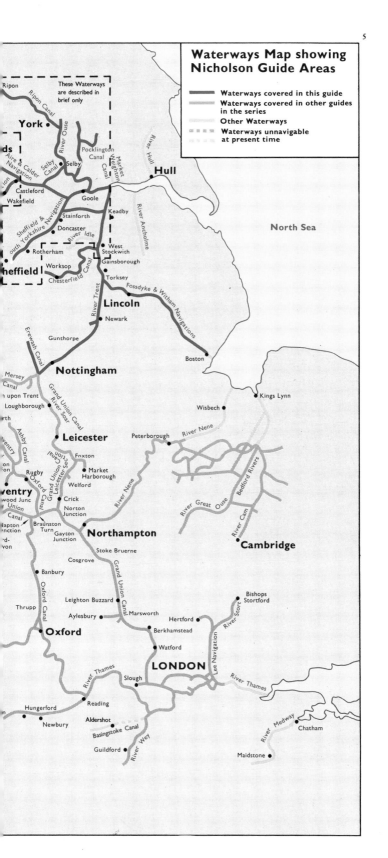

Waterways Map showing Nicholson Guide Areas

━━━ Waterways covered in this guide
━━━ Waterways covered in other guides in the series
━━━ Other Waterways
▬ ▬ ▬ Waterways unnavigable at present time

Ripon

These Waterways are described in brief only

Ripon Canal

York

River Ouse

ds

Aire & Calder Navigation

Selby Canal • Selby

Pocklington Canal

Market Weighton Canal

River Hull

Hull

Castleford

Wakefield

Goole

Keadby

Stainforth

River Ancholme

North Sea

Sheffield & South Yorkshire Navigation

Doncaster

River Idle

West Stockwith

Rotherham

heffield

Worksop

Chesterfield Canal

Gainsborough

Torksey

River Trent

Lincoln

Newark

Fossdyke & Witham Navigations

Mersey Canal

Erewash Canal

Gunthorpe

Nottingham

Boston

Kings Lynn

upon Trent

Loughborough

Grand Union Canal

River Soar

Wisbech

rth

Ashby Canal

Leicester

Peterborough

River Nene

ventry

Foxton

Rugby

Grand Union Canal Leicester Section

Market Harborough

Welford

River Nene

wood Junc

Crick

Union Canal

Norton Junction

River Great Ouse

Bedford Rivers

River Cam

lapton nction

Braunston Turn

Gayton Junction

Northampton

Cambridge

d- von

Cosgrove

Stoke Bruerne

Banbury

Oxford Canal

Grand Union Canal

Leighton Buzzard

Bishops Stortford

Thrupp

Aylesbury

Marsworth

Hertford

River Stort

Oxford

Berkhamstead

Lee Navigation

Watford

LONDON

River Thames

Slough

River Thames

Hungerford

Reading

n

Newbury

Aldershot

Basingstoke Canal

Guildford

River Wey

River Medway

Chatham

Maidstone

HOW TO USE THIS GUIDE

The maps are drawn at a scale of two inches to one mile. Adjacent to each map section is a description of the countryside and places of interest together with a commentary on the course of the canal or river. Details of the boatyards and pubs marked are also given, adjacent to each map, and are arranged in order from the top of the page to the bottom.

Symbols and abbreviations used in the text:

ⓑ Boatyard or boatyard services
Ⓡ Refuse disposal
Ⓢ Sewage or 'Elsan' disposal
Ⓦ Water
Ⓟ Petrol
Ⓓ Diesel
Ⓔ Electric boat recharging
🍺 Public house
✕ Restaurant
❢ Licensed to sell alcohol
L Open for lunch
D Open for dinner
EC Early closing
MD Market day
IWA International Waterways Association
NT National Trust

Symbols used on maps:

ⓑ Boatyard or boatyard services

🍺 Public house

R Refuse disposal

S Sewage or 'Elsan' disposal point

W Water point

28 8′ 8″   Locks, with number and 'rise'. The symbol points uphill.

Staircase locks.

197   Bridge and its number. Many are named.

Tunnel – often described in the text.

Aqueduct – often described in the text.

Winding hole – turning point for boats longer than the ordinary width of the canal (it's pronounced as in the wind that blows). Canal junctions are also good places to 'wind'.

Towing Path

Weir.

Scale and north point
The strip maps are drawn at 2 inches to 1 mile. North is indicated on each map.

Navigational notes
These appear where necessary to point out potential hazards, navigational limits or other vital information.

Boatyards
Services listed are those usually available; do not, however, expect a hire base to stop what they are doing on fleet 'turn around' day (usually Saturday) to help you – *they will be extremely busy*. Any other day you are sure to be made to feel welcome. Remember also that moorings get filled very quickly, so do not assume that there will be space for your boat. Always ask.

A feature of these guides is the 'milestone' which appears on every map thus:

22¼M   22L
Napton
Oxford
27M   17L

This performs many useful functions. It reminds you of your direction of travel – in this example **up** the page is towards Napton, **down** the page is towards Oxford; it denotes distances and indicates the number of locks between the milestone and strategic points (usually junctions) along the waterway – in this example, Napton is 22¼ miles (M) with 22 locks (L) from the 'milestone', and Oxford is 27 miles and 17 locks from the milestone. By deducting the miles and locks on one milestone from those on the next, distances from page to page can be accurately estimated. Using the 'lock-miles' system (see **Planning a cruise**, page 13) the time your journey will take can be calculated, and with a little experience based on your speed of travel and lock operation, your own time formula can be arrived at.

Where this device occurs on a map it simply means that the actual route of the waterway would not fit neatly onto the page, so the cartographer has 'bent' the map, using two north points. The navigator on the water, or the walker on the bank, will notice nothing amiss. Distances in this book should be measured along the thick blue line only, not including these gaps.

LOCKS AND THEIR USE

The different locks and their attendant machinery are a source of endless fascination for all waterway users. Understanding why they are there and the principle upon which they work will help you in their use.

A lock is a device for transporting craft from a higher water level to a lower level, or vice versa, for example when a canal crosses a range of hills. It consists of a box with gates at each end, and a separate means of letting water in at the top (higher level) and out at the bottom (lower level). This is controlled by paddles. These paddles may simply open and shut holes in the gates (gate paddles), or they may open and shut underground culverts (ground paddles). A windlass (carried on the boat) is used to wind the paddles open and shut. Whilst locks differ in detail, the following instructions will apply in the case of the vast majority of *narrow* canal locks. Some extra points regarding wide locks are covered later.

A typical narrow lock

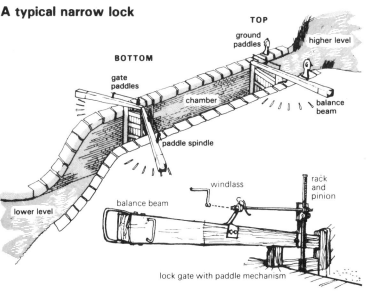

lock gate with paddle mechanism

How to go through a lock

PRELIMINARIES

Stop the boat well outside the lock and secure it. If members of your crew can get off the boat before the lock (at the narrow point under a bridge for example) and run ahead to prepare the lock, this will save time.

GOING UP IN A LOCK (LOCKING UP)

Lock empty – ie water at lower level

Open bottom gate(s)
Drive boat in
Close bottom gate(s)
Check bottom paddles closed
Keep boat near to the bottom of lock
Open top paddles to fill lock
Open top gate(s) when lock is full
Drive boat out
Close top gate(s)
Close top paddles

Lock full – ie water at higher level

Check top gate(s) and paddles closed
Open bottom paddles to drain lock
Open bottom gate(s)
Drive boat in
Close bottom gate(s) and paddles
Keep boat near to the bottom of lock
Open top paddles to fill lock
Open top gate(s) when lock is full
Drive boat out
Close top gate(s)
Close top paddles

GOING DOWN IN A LOCK (LOCKING DOWN)

Lock full – ie water at higher level	Lock empty – ie water at lower level
Open top gate(s)	Check bottom gate(s) and paddles closed
Drive boat in	Open top paddles to fill lock
Close top gate(s)	Open gate(s)
Check top paddles closed	Drive boat in
Keep boat near to the bottom of the lock	Close top gate(s) and paddles
Open bottom paddles to empty lock	Keep boat near to the bottom of the lock
Open bottom gate(s)	Open bottom paddles to empty lock
Drive boat out	Open bottom gate(s)
Close bottom gates and paddles	Drive boat out
	Close bottom gate(s) and paddles

If you have to drain or fill a lock in order to enter it, make sure there is no boat approaching that could usefully use the lock before you. Always try to conserve water, which is being continually passed down the canal from its summit and thus requires constant replenishment at a higher level.

SOME GENERAL DO'S AND DONT'S AT LOCKS

Do not leave your windlass slotted onto the paddle spindle – if something slips it could be thrown off and cause injury.

Always leave all gates and paddles closed when you leave, but look out for notices which may give other instructions for the proper operation of a particular lock.

Always wind the paddles down – letting them drop is bad practice, and causes damage.

Beware of protrusions in the side walls of the lock chamber that may damage the boat, and don't use fenders in narrow locks – they may jam.

When opening and closing lock gates, keep to the landward side of the balance beam.

Don't rush around at locks, especially in wet weather, when the sides are slippery. Never jump across partly opened gates.

Always make the safety of the crew and boat your prime concern and remember that if things do start to go wrong, you can stop everything by closing the paddles.

There is no reason why your children, wearing buoyancy aids and properly supervised, should not help at locks – it is all part of the fun, after all – but impress upon them the potential dangers, and establish some common-sense rules. You have no authority over other people's children, and their participation should be discouraged. Great difficulties could ensue should they be injured in any way.

Beware of fierce top gate paddles, especially in wide locks.

Don't leave your windlass behind; hundreds are lost this way each year.

WIDE LOCKS

Taking a narrowboat (7ft beam) through a wide lock (14ft) can present special difficulties, especially when locking up. If all the top paddles were to be opened fully at the same time, the boat would be buffeted considerably. The diagram below illustrates one method of ensuring a smooth passage. The stern line held ashore will provide added security.

Locking up in a wide lock
(a suggested technique)

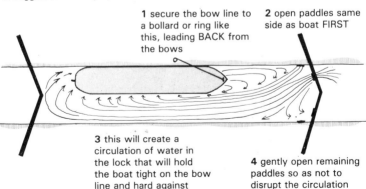

1 secure the bow line to a bollard or ring like this, leading BACK from the bows

2 open paddles same side as boat FIRST

3 this will create a circulation of water in the lock that will hold the boat tight on the bow line and hard against the side of the lock

4 gently open remaining paddles so as not to disrupt the circulation already established

STAIRCASE LOCKS

Where the top gates of one lock are the bottom gates of the next. Usually there is a board nearby giving operating instructions – read it carefully and make sure you understand it before you start. And remember: in a narrow staircase you can't pass a boat coming the other way.

Even young children can help, if properly supervised, but you must make sure life jackets are worn all the time when near the water. *David Perrott.*

GENERAL CRUISING INFORMATION

The majority of the waterways covered in this book are controlled by British Waterways. All craft using its canals must be licensed and those using its rivers must be registered. Charges are based on the length of the boat and a canal craft licence covers all the navigable waterways under its control. Permits for permanent mooring on the canals are also issued by British Waterways. Apply in each case to the local area office; addresses are given on page 169. British Waterways will also supply a list of all its rivers and canals. Other river navigation authorities relevant to this book are mentioned where appropriate.

Getting afloat

There is no better way of discovering the joys of canals than by getting afloat. The best thing is to hire a boat for a week or a fortnight from one of the boatyards on the canals (each boatyard has an entry in the text, and most of them offer craft for hire; brochures may be easily obtained from such boatyards) or go on one of the trip boats for a couple of hours, or longer.

General cruising

Most canals are saucer-shaped in section and so are deepest in the middle. Very few have more than 3–4ft of water and many have much less. Try to keep to the middle of the channel except on bends, where the deepest water is on the *outside* of the bend. When you meet another boat, the rule is to keep to the right, slow down, and aim to miss the approaching boat by a couple of yards: do not steer right over to the bank or you will most likely run aground. The deeper the draught of the boat, the more important it is to keep in the middle of the deep water, so this must be considered when passing other boats. If you meet a loaded working boat, keep right out of the way. Working boats should always be given precedence, for their time is money. If you meet a boat being towed from the bank, pass it on the outside rather than intercept the towing line. When overtaking, keep the other boat on your starboard, or right, side.

Speed

There is a general speed limit of 4mph on most British Waterways canals. This is not just an arbitrary limit: there is no need to go any faster, and in many cases it is impossible to cruise even at this speed. Canals were not built for motor boats, and so the banks are easily damaged by excessive wash and turbulence. Erosion of the banks makes the canal more shallow, which in turn makes running aground a more frequent occurrence. So keep to the limits and try not to aggravate the situation. It is easy to see when a boat is creating excessive turbulence by looking at the wash – if it is 'breaking' or causing large waves, you are going too fast and should slow down.

Slow down also when passing moored craft, engineering works and anglers.

Slow down when there is a lot of floating rubbish on the water: old planks and plastic bags may mean underwater obstacles that can damage a boat or its propeller if hit hard. Try to drift over obvious obstructions in neutral.

Slow down when approaching blind corners, narrow bridges and junctions.

Running aground

The effective end of commercial traffic on the narrow canals has resulted in canals being shallower than ever. Running aground is a not uncommon event, but is rarely serious, as the canal bed is usually soft. If you run aground, try first of all to pull the boat off by gently reversing the engine. If this fails, use the pole as a lever against the bank or some solid object, in combination with a tow rope being pulled from the bank. Do not keep revving the engine in reverse if it is obviously having no effect. Another way is to get your crew to rock the boat from side to side while using the pole or mooring lines. If all else fails, lighten your load; make all the crew leave the boat except the helmsman, and then it will often float off quite easily.

Remember that if you run aground once, it is likely to happen again as it indicates a particularly shallow stretch – or that you are out of the channel. If you are continually bumping the bottom in a shallow stretch, it may be that you are going too fast, causing the boat to 'dig in' at the back. Going less fast may make things more comfortable.

In a town it is not uncommon to run aground on sunken rubbish; this is most likely to occur near bridges and housing estates. Use the same methods, but be very careful as hard objects can very easily damage your boat or propeller.

Remember that winding holes are often silted up – do not go further in than you have to.

Mooring

All boats carry metal stakes and a mallet. These are used for mooring when there are no rings or bollards in sight, which is usually the case. Generally speaking you may moor anywhere to British Waterways property but there are certain basic rules. Avoid mooring anywhere that could cause an obstruction to other boats; do not moor on a bend, in a winding hole or a narrow stretch; do not moor abreast boats already moored. Never moor in a lock, and do not be tempted to tie up in a tunnel or under a bridge if it is raining. Pick a stretch where there is a reasonable depth of water at the bank, otherwise the boat may bump and scrape the canal bed – an unpleasant sensation if you are trying to sleep. For reasons of peace and quiet and privacy it is best to moor away from main roads and railway lines.

Never stretch your mooring lines across the towpath; you may trip someone up and face a claim for damages.

There is no need to show a riding light at night, except on major rivers and busy commercial canals.

Beware of mooring at unrecognised sites in cities – you may attract the unwelcome attention of vandals.

So long as you are sensible and keep to the rules, mooring can be a pleasant gesture of individuality.

Knots

A simple and easy way of securing a rope to a bollard or mooring stake is to use a couple of round turns and a half hitch or two made with a loop and pulled tight. This can be released quickly by pulling the loose end, which will have been left tidily coiled.

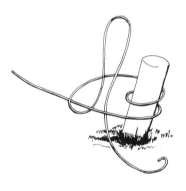

When leaving a mooring, coil all the ropes up again. They will then be out of the way, but ready if needed. Many a sailor has fallen overboard after tripping on an uncoiled rope.

Fixed bridges

At most bridges the canal becomes very narrow, a means of saving building costs developed by the engineers. As a result, careful navigation is called for if you are to avoid hitting either the bridge sides with the hull, or the arch with the cabin top. As when entering a lock, the best way to tackle 'bridgeholes' is to slow down well in advance and aim to go straight through, keeping a steady course. Adjustments should be kept to a minimum for it is easy to start the boat zig-zagging, which will inevitably end in a collision. One technique is to gauge the width of the approaching bridgehole relative to the width of the boat, and then watch one side only, aiming to miss that side by a small margin – say 6in; the smaller you can make the margin, the less chance you have of hitting the other side of

the bridge. If you do hit the bridge sides when going slowly it is not likely to do much damage; it will merely strengthen your resolve to do better next time.

Moveable bridges

Swing and lift bridges are an attractive feature of some canals and cannot be ignored as they often rest only 2 or 3ft above the water. They are moved by being swivelled horizontally, or raised vertically. Operation is usually manual, although some have gearing to ease the movement. There are one or two mechanised versions; these have clear instructions at control points. Before operating any bridge make sure that approaching road traffic is aware of your intention to open the bridge. Use protective barriers if there are any and remember to close the bridge again after you.

Some *lift bridges are very unstable*, and could close while your boat is passing underneath, with disastrous consequences. For this reason it is prudent to have your strongest (or heaviest) crew member hold it open until the boat is clear. Many swing bridges are very heavy to operate, and require two strong people to move them.

Tunnels

Many people consider a canal incomplete without one or two tunnels, and certainly they are an exciting feature of any trip. Nearly all are easy to navigate, although there are a few basic rules:

Make sure your boat has a good headlight in working order and *always* use it.

If it is a narrow tunnel (ie 7ft) make sure there is no boat coming the other way *before* you enter. Craft of 7ft beam can pass in some wide tunnels – slow right down when you meet to lessen the almost inevitable bump.

In most tunnels the roof drips constantly, especially under ventilation shafts. Put on a raincoat and some form of hat before going in.

A notice on the tunnel portal will give its length, in yards, and will say whether unpowered craft are permitted to use it.

Where there are restrictions on time of entry, and one-way systems, these must be adhered to. To meet head on half way through a long narrow tunnel would create great difficulties.

Care of the engine

Canal boats are generally powered by either diesel, petrol or two-stroke engines. If you have a hire craft, the boatyard will give you instructions for your daily maintenance, which will no doubt include some or all of the following:

Every day before starting off, you should:

Check the oil level in the engine.
Check the fuel level in the tank.

If your engine is water-cooled, check that the filter near the intake is clean and weedfree. Otherwise the engine will over-heat, which could cause serious damage.

Check the level of distilled water in the battery, and ensure that it is charging correctly.

Lubricate any parts of the engine, gearbox or steering that need daily attention.

Check that the propeller is free of weeds, wire, plastic bags and any other rubbish. The propeller and the water filter should be checked whenever there is any suspicion of obstruction or overheating – which may mean several times a day.

Pump the bilges every day.

When navigating in shallow water, keep in mind the exposed position of the propeller. If you hit any underwater obstruction put the engine into neutral immediately. When running over any large floating object put the engine into neutral and wait for the object to appear astern before re-engaging the drive.

Fuel

Petrol engines and petrol/oil outboards are catered for by some boatyards and all road-side fuel stations. Fuel stations on roads near the canal are shown in the guide, and these should be considered when planning your day's cruise. Running out is inconvenient; remember you may have to walk several miles carrying a heavy can.

Diesel-powered craft, and narrowboats in particular, can usually cruise for over two weeks before needing to be refilled. Those using diesel-powered hire craft rarely need to be concerned about fuel. Those with their own boats, however, should bear in mind that boatyards are few and far between on some parts of the network, and should a diesel-powered boat run out of fuel, the system will need to be bled before the engine can run again. Most boatyards sell marine diesel (indicated Ⓓ in the text), which is cheaper than the road fuel.

Electrically powered boats

These are becoming very popular on the inland waterways, in view of their quietness and lack of environmental pollution. Indicated Ⓔ under the **BOATYARD** heading are those establishments known to offer recharging facilities – polite enquiry by electric boat users will certainly reveal more. If you are lucky enough to be using this form of power, please note the following:

All boats using this information are assumed to have a battery charger on board and 50 metres of cable fitted with standard 13 amp terminals.

It is essential for the safety of the boater, the owner of the supply and the general public that a proper residual current circuit breaker (RCD) be carried by the boat and fitted between the boat's cable and the supply unless the supply is already so protected. The RCD must be tested for correct operation before battery charging starts.

Water

Fresh water taps occur irregularly along the canals, usually at boatyards, British Waterways depots, or by lock cottages. These are marked on the maps in the guide. Ensure that there is a long water hose on the boat (British Waterways taps have a ½-inch slip-on hose connection). Fill up every day.

Lavatories

Some canal boats are fitted with chemical lavatories which have to be emptied from time to time. Never empty them over the side or tip them into the bushes. Use the sewage disposal points marked on the map Ⓢ (for which you will need a British Waterways key) or those located at boatyards. Many boats now have pump-out toilets, which must be emptied with a special machine – usually at boatyards and indicated in the text. This symbol at the canalside indicates just such a 'pump-out station' (although not all boatyards with the facility display it). Expect to have to pay.

Some British Waterways depots and boatyards have lavatories for the use of boat crews; again, you may need your British Waterways key.

Litter

Some canals are in a poor state today because they have long been misused as unofficial dumps for rubbish, especially in towns. Out of sight is only out of mind until some object is tangled round your propeller. So keep all rubbish until you can dispose of it at a refuse disposal point, indicated Ⓡ on the map, or at a boatyard equipped to deal with it.

By-laws

Although no-one needs a 'driving licence' to navigate a boat, boat users should remember that they have certain responsibilities to others on the waterways. Prospective navigators are advised to obtain a copy of the by-laws relevant to the waterways on which they are to travel.

Stoppages

Although the British Waterways and other navigation authorities plan their maintenance for the winter months, it often becomes necessary to carry out repairs during the cruising season. Many of the structures on the canal system are beginning to show their age (especially the tunnels) and repairs are a lengthy and costly affair, sometimes resulting in stoppages lasting many years. A long dry spell can lower water levels and restrict lock operation, and a canal embankment can, of course, breach at any time.

To avoid disappointment it is wise to check that your planned route is clear before you set off, and that there are no time restrictions on locks that may upset your schedule. Those using hire craft may be able to get this information from their boatyard, although some are surprisingly lax. It is best to check for yourself by phoning the British Waterways office (listed on page 169) or the relevant navigation authority. News of any last minute stoppages is available on 'Canalphone', as a recorded message. Phone (071-)723 8486 for the North and Midlands, or (071-)723 8487 for the South and Midlands.

PLANNING A CRUISE

It is wise when planning a cruise to establish a means of calculating the time it takes to travel any given length of canal. This ensures that you can reliably work out whether you will reach a shop or pub before closing time. And of course for those who have hired their boat for a fixed period, it is vital to return to the starting point in time.

The time taken to navigate any canal depends, of course, on the average cruising speed of your boat and the amount of time it takes to negotiate the locks along the way. Remember that there is in any case an overall legal speed limit of 4 mph on all canals. In practice, 3 mph is a realistic canal cruising speed for most boats and 2 mph is the maximum which can be achieved on shallow canals, such as the Peak Forest.

To the uninitiated, 3 mph may sound an unbearably slow rate of progress through the countryside; but a few hours of gentle cruising on a fine day is usually enough to convert most people to this pace. For only by proceeding at walking pace can you appreciate the peace and beauty of the countryside, watch the bird life, and see the scurry of voles, rats and other creatures as they suddenly notice the slowly approaching boat.

The length of time taken to work through a lock depends on several things: whether the lock is full or empty, wide or narrow, deep or shallow. It depends on the number and size of the paddles that control the sluices, on the presence or otherwise of other boats near the lock, and of course on the number and competence of the boat crew. Most people take between 10–20 minutes on average to work through a typical lock – or, to put it another way, they may take as long to get through a lock as they would have taken to travel another mile at 3 mph. Herein lies the basis for a simple method of estimating time required to travel along a given length of canal: take the number of miles to be travelled and add half the number of locks to be negotiated on the way. This gives the number of lock-miles. Divide this by three, and the result is the approximate length of time it will take, in hours. Thus if you intend to travel 30 miles, and there are 12 locks along the way, the calculation is as follows: 30 + 12 divided by 3 (mph) = 14 hours. So this particular journey will take you around 14 hours, assuming your average cruising speed to be 3 mph and assuming you take about 20 minutes to get through each lock (if they are all narrow locks in good condition then you may well better this time). The length of your journey and the number of locks can easily be calculated using the 'milestones' that appear on every map in this series of guides. To refine the system, simply tailor it more closely to the actual cruising speed of your boat and the efficiency of your lock-operating technique.

An excellent fortnight's trip, for example, would be the circuit formed by the River Soar and Trent & Mersey, Coventry, Oxford and Grand Union (Leicester Section) canals. This is 152 miles and 100 locks long (about 84 hours cruising time), and takes you through some of the very best parts of Leicestershire. You will see the Foxton staircase locks, Braunston Tunnel, the delightful canal village of Shardlow, and have time to explore the lock-free Ashby Canal (22 miles long – 2 days there and back) or the meandering course of the unspoilt Market Harborough arm, 5 miles long.

For just a one week holiday, a good round trip with plenty of contrasts could encompass the Staffs & Worcs north of Aldersley Junction, the Trent & Mersey from Great Haywood to Fradley, the Coventry to Fazeley Junction, then the Birmingham & Fazeley to Farmers Bridge returning along the Birmingham Canal Main Line. With 75 miles and 79 narrow locks, this should take no more than 50 hours cruising time. You will enjoy the old locks and bridges of the Staffs & Worcs as it follows the pretty valleys of the rivers Penk and Sow, culminating at Tixall Wide. After a visit to Shugborough Hall you continue past the eccentric footbridge at Drayton Manor before starting the long climb to Farmers Bridge. There's a choice of routes on the Birmingham Canal Main Line to complete the circuit.

These are just two examples of the many circular cruising routes available – a glance at the planning map on pages 4 and 5 will reveal many more. Of course, there is also much to be said for a straight out and back cruise – it will all look different when you are coming the other way, and you can arrange to re-visit that favourite pub again. The whole secret is to *allow plenty of time*, for shopping, for exploring and for gentle cruising. Many a holiday has been spoilt by becoming a race against time. The most comprehensive source of information for planning a waterways cruise is Nicholson's *The Ordnance Survey Inland Waterways Map of Great Britain*.

See also 'Stoppages' in the **General cruising information** section.

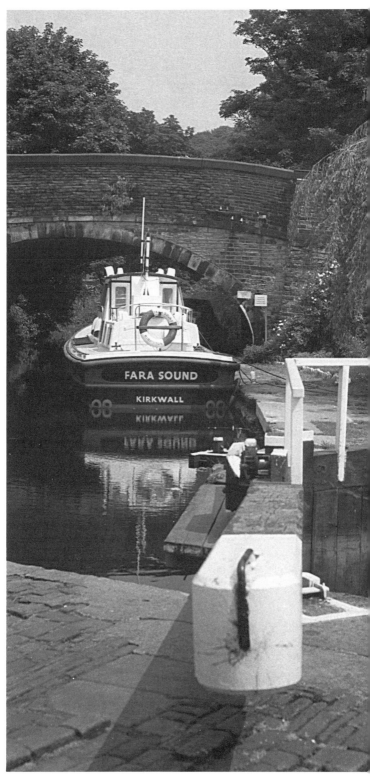

Above Salterhebble Locks. *David Perrott.*

AIRE & CALDER
Leeds to Wakefield
CALDER & HEBBLE
HUDDERSFIELD
BROAD CANAL

Maximum dimensions

Aire & Calder
River Lock to Leeds Lock
Length: 143'
Beam: 17'
Headroom: 12'
Leeds Lock to Castleford
Length: 200'
Beam: 20'
Headroom: 12'
Castleford to Wakefield
Length: 140'
Beam: 17'
Headroom: 12'

Calder & Hebble
Wakefield to Broad Cut
Length: 120'
Beam: 17'
Headroom: 12'
Broad Cut to Sowerby Bridge
Length: 57' 6" (or 60' narrowboat)
Beam: 14'
Headroom: 9' 6"

Huddersfield Broad Canal
Length: 57' 6" (or 60' narrowboat)
Beam: 14'
Headroom: 9' 6"

Mileages

LEEDS to:
Castleford: 10 miles, 6 locks
Wakefield: 17½ miles, 12 locks
Cooper Bridge: 30½ miles, 28 locks
Sowerby Bridge: 37 miles, 41 locks

Huddersfield Broad Canal: 3¾ miles, 9 locks

The River Aire was first made navigable to Leeds in 1700, and rapidly became a great commercial success, taking coal out of the Yorkshire coalfield and bringing back raw wool, corn and agricultural produce. Improvements were then made to the difficult lower reaches, with first Selby and later Goole becoming Yorkshire's principal inland port. The opening of the New Junction Canal in 1905 further secured its suitability for commercial traffic, which today still amounts to some 2½ million tonnes, mainly coal and petroleum.

The construction of the Aire & Calder resulted in pressure to improve the Calder above Wakefield. After much opposition, the Calder & Hebble was built, with boats finally reaching Sowerby Bridge in the 1770s. Never as successful as the Aire & Calder, it did, however, benefit from trade coming in from the Huddersfield Broad Canal and later, in 1811, from the Huddersfield Narrow. Commercial traffic ended in 1981, when the last coal barges unloaded at Thornhill Power Station. Becoming increasingly popular and yet still uncrowded, the waterways covered here have much to offer, with great industrial interest and, in many places, considerable charm.

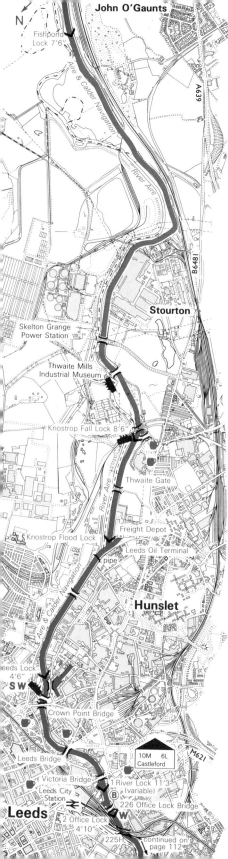

Leeds

The great Aire & Calder Navigation joins the Leeds & Liverpool Canal at River Lock, in the centre of Leeds by the City Railway Station. The area above the lock is now an attractive canal centre, with boatyards, canal warehouses and a crane; trees, moored craft and some handy shops, including an off-licence. Heading east, the waterway passes under three substantial bridges, generally hemmed in by tall buildings and warehouses with much new building and development, particularly housing. Industry predominates below Leeds Lock, although the lock itself is quite handsomely situated – overlooked by tall Victorian warehouses and accompanied by a houseboat. Keep right to avoid the weir at Leeds Lock. Boaters should take the centre channel at Knostrop Flood Lock, through the gates which are usually open (they are closed when the river level rises after prolonged heavy rain, effectively closing the navigation), avoiding the river and a weir to the left, and the basin of Leeds Oil Terminal to the right. Passing the Leggett Freightway Group Depot the navigation enters an artificial channel, with the River Aire to the north, which is to persist for a little over 7 miles until the river is rejoined below Kippax Lock. At Knostrop Fall Lock use the larger of the two locks, indicated by lights. Both are overshadowed by an impressive railway viaduct, an excellent example of civil engineering which dominates the landscape in this shallow river valley. Passing the new Thwaite Mills Industrial Museum and Skelton Grange Power Station (the fuel for which is no longer delivered by boat), a no man's land of closed collieries and landscaped spoil heaps is entered. The towpath is diverted at Fishpond Lock, a lonely outpost, to avoid a small wooded area now maintained as a local nature reserve.

Navigational notes
1. All the locks on the Aire & Calder operate mechanically, and are controlled by lock keepers, so progress through them is quick. Obey the traffic light signals.
2. Remember that this is a river navigation. Many of the locks are accompanied by large weirs, so keep a sharp look out for the signs which direct you safely into the locks.
3. When the river level rises after prolonged heavy rain, the flood gates will be closed. Pleasure craft should stay put until they are advised by a lock keeper that it is safe to proceed.
4. This is a commercial waterway, used by 600-tonne tanker barges and push-tow coal barges. Keep a look-out for them, and give them a clear passage. Moor carefully, using bollards or fixed rings rather than mooring stakes, since the wash from these craft can be substantial.

The towpath
The indication of a towpath alongside this waterway does not entail the existence of a public right of way. Indeed the towpath generally on the Aire & Calder to Castleford is often badly overgrown and incomplete. Where there is some evidence of a path it has been marked on the map – but many diversions may be necessary. It is hoped that this situation will improve in the not too distant future.

Leeds
W. Yorks. EC Wed. MD Tue, Fri, Sat. All services. A vast industrial city that was a wool centre in the Middle Ages and has continued to grow to prosperity under the textile and clothing trades; indeed Marks & Spencer started business here with a stall in the market. Montague Burton also became established here building what was to become, by 1921, the largest clothing factory in the world. However the last few years have brought substantial changes, with old industries being replaced by new, and the atmosphere is one of growth and prosperity.
The great Town Hall in Victoria Square (walk north from Victoria Bridge and turn left at Great George Street) stands as a magnificent monument to Victorian civic pride. Recently

continued on page 112

cleaned, it was designed by Cuthbert Brodrick and opened in 1858. Looking at the Corinthian columns on all sides and the clock tower some 255ft high, it is hard to believe that Brodrick was only 29 years old when he submitted his plans. As a measure of this man's self confidence, note that he also designed the organ, installed in 1859, which itself weighs almost 70 tons, has 6,500 pipes and stands 50ft high. The light and airy Corn Exchange (north of Leeds Bridge along Call Lane) built in 1861 is also Brodrick's work. Always the cultural centre of Yorkshire, the city hosts an international concert season and an international piano competition. It has several splendid theatres including The Grand in Briggate, modelled on La Scala, Milan; the City Varieties, the oldest surviving music hall in the country; and the Leeds Playhouse repertory theatre. There are several splendid parks and rich museums, and excellent shopping facilities including the ornate Victorian Queens and County arcades. Headingley, the home of Yorkshire cricket and a test match venue attracts an enthusiastic following in the area, and of course the city's association football and rugby teams are known world-wide. Boaters should try to spend a day here if they possibly can – there are good moorings on the Leeds & Liverpool Canal by Office Lock, or above Leeds Lock.

See also page 112 for information on Armley Mills Industrial Museum and Abbey House Museum.
Tourist Information Centre 19 Wellington Street, Leeds (462454). Walk west from the front of City Station. The usual mine of free information and the first place you should visit. For just 10p you can obtain a guide to all the museums and galleries in West Yorkshire, and for a further 60p the useful *Museum of Leeds Trail Guide* is a must.
Art Gallery and Henry Moore Sculpture Centre The Headrow, Leeds (462495). Walk north from Victoria Bridge. A large collection of mainly 19thC paintings, drawings and prints. Sculpture by Henry Moore, Barbara Hepworth and Jacob Epstein. *Open all day Mon–Sat, & Sun afternoons*. Free.
City Museum Calverley Street, Leeds (462465). Walk north from Victoria Bridge. Archaeology, natural history, ethnography, coins – exactly what you would expect in a large city museum. *Closed Sun & Mon*. Free.
Leeds – Settle – Carlisle Line From Leeds City Station. The 70 miles from Settle to Carlisle is said to be one of the most memorable rail journeys in the world, so this would make an excellent day trip away from the boat. *Every Sat & Sun from May–Oct* there are free guided walks from trains on the line. Coach tours around the Yorkshire Dales also connect. Details from leaflets at the station or Tourist Information Centre.

Middleton Railway Tunstall Road, Leeds (645424, evenings). Built in 1758 to link Leeds with the Middleton Colliery, this is considered to be the world's oldest railway. It operates at *weekends Easter–Sep* from the industrial suburb of Hunslet, where steam engines were once built.
Thwaite Mills Industrial Museum Thwaite Lane, Leeds (496453). A canalside flint and china stone-grinding mill built in 1872 and powered by two waterwheels until 1975, when they were washed away, bringing closure a year later. Visitors are able to see the working conditions in the mill, as well as a Marshall engine and various artefacts. *Phone for opening times*.

BOATYARDS

⑧ **Yorkshire Hire Cruisers** 26 Canal Wharf, Leeds (456195). [S] [W] Pump-out, gas, hire craft, mooring, toilets, restaurant trip boat. Basin café *open daily*.

PUBS AND RESTAURANTS

A fine city such as Leeds has many pubs and restaurants. The following are a selection of those fairly close to the navigation.
✗🍴 **Bibi's Pizzeria** 7–8 Mill Hill, Leeds (430905). Off Boar Lane, close to the station. A jolly Italian restaurant. *L & D. Closed Mon*.
✗🍴 **Gandhi** 68 New Briggate, Leeds (451608). North of Leeds Bridge. An upstairs restaurant doing the usual range of curries very well. *L & D daily*.
✗🍴 **Whan Hai** 20 New Briggate, Leeds (435019). Good value for money in a Pekinese restaurant. *L & D. Closed Mon*.
🍺 **Grove** Black Row, Leeds. South of Victoria Bridge. Small traditional pub with a choice of rooms. John Smith real ale, *lunchtime* food (*Mon–Fri only*). Folk music some evenings.
🍺 **Adelphi** Hunslet Road, Leeds. South of Leeds Bridge. A superbly restored and very grand Edwardian pub, with lots of etched glass and mahogany. Tetley's real ale, food *lunchtime* (*Mon–Fri*). This is the closest pub to the Tetley's brewery.
🍺 **Whitelock's** Turk's Head Yard, Briggate, Leeds. North of Leeds Bridge. An unspoilt Edwardian pub, one of the first buildings to have electricity. Youngers real ale, excellent fresh traditional food *lunchtime and evenings until 19.30* (*Sun snacks only*).
🍺 **Duck & Drake** Kirkgate, Leeds. North of Crown Point Bridge, near the church. Simply decorated pub with an open fire and a choice of 15 real ales. Food *lunchtime*, live music *Wed, Thur & Sun*.
🍺 **Old Red Lion** Thwaite Gate, Leeds. Down-to-earth Tetley's real ale pub, with a fish & chip shop opposite.
🍺 **Crooked Billet** Thwaite Gate, Leeds. Comfortable Tetley's real ale pub with beams and brasses. Food, garden.

iver Lock, Leeds. *David Perrott*.

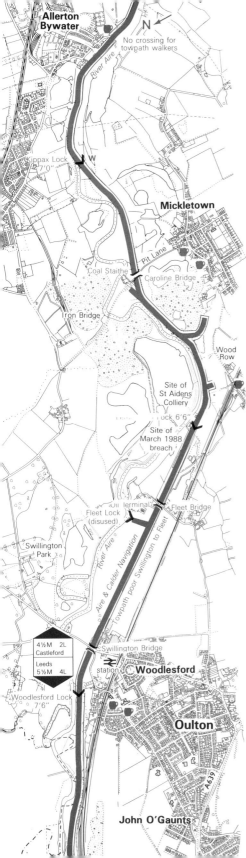

Woodlesford

The navigation continues along its straight
course with the River Aire just to the north, its
meanderings having endowed it with a series of
oxbow lakes. All around are the remains of
disused coal workings, some landscaped into
smooth grassy banks, others a gaunt pale grey.
At Woodlesford a path up from the lock leads
to two pubs, a post office, café and shops.
Further up the hill there is a useful delicatessen
and wine merchant. Just before Fleet Bridge an
arm branches off to the north. A disused lock
here once used to connect with the river.
Enclosed by the arm is an oil terminal – notice
how the storage tanks have been colonised by
house martins. The river by Fleet Lock still
shows evidence of the disastrous breach which
occurred in March 1988 when the ground
separating it from the adjacent St Aidens
open-cast mine collapsed and the water poured
in. Apparently the river below the breach
flowed backwards for half a day, such was the
volume of water consumed, and the workforce
only just managed to rescue the large cranes. As
we go to press there are plans being discussed to
pump it out, although it would seem an
impossibly expensive task. Only three months
after the disaster this vast expanse of water had
already acquired a resident duck population.
Surely a solution based on wildlife and
recreation will prove the better option. At
Caroline Bridge a modern staithe loads regular
trains of compartment barges with coal for the
huge Ferrybridge Power Station downstream.
Rejoining the river at Kippax Lock (use the
larger one with lights and a gantry) the mining
village of Allerton Bywater appears. There is a
welcome waterside pub here, but make sure
you moor securely if you stop, since passing
commercial craft cause a considerable wash.

The towpath
From Fishpond Lock to Kippax the towpath is
generally good. Unfortunately there is no
means of crossing to The Boat pub.

Woodlesford
W. Yorks. PO, tel, stores, garage, station. Good
moorings above the lock, and nearby pubs
make this a popular stopping place for boaters.
Temple Newsam House (Leeds 647321).
Walk north from Swillington Bridge, fork left
after the river – 2 miles. A superb
Tudor/Jacobean house in 900 acres of parkland.
Magnificent Georgian and Regency interiors.
*Open 10.30–18.15 (20.30 Wed, May–Sep; dusk
in winter). Closed Mon.* Charge.
Mickletown
W. Yorks. PO, tel, stores. Claimed by the locals
to be the second largest village in England –
although no one seems to know which is the
largest – Mickletown has clearly had its
problems since the neighbouring colliery
closed. The next-door village of Wood Row is
very close by, and the pub, store and post box
there can be easily reached via a path from
Lemonroyd Lock.
Allerton Bywater
W. Yorks. Stores, tel. With its winding gear still
standing above the roof-tops, this is one of the
few mining villages still active as such. Coal was
once loaded from wagons onto barges from a
small staithe here.

PUBS
Two Pointers Woodlesford. Up the hill
from the lock. A smart pub serving real ale.
Patio.
White Hart Woodlesford. Just past the Two
Pointers. A snug and comfy Tetley's real ale
pub. Food, family room, garden. Post office,
shops and Chinese take-away close by.
United Kingdom Wood Row. Up the path
from Lemonroyd Lock, just over the level
crossing. A Tetley's real ale local with a nice
garden. Food.
Old Bay Horse Mickletown. Turn right out
of Pit Lane, up from Caroline Bridge (do not
moor anywhere near the staithe). A lovely,
cosy, traditional Tetley's real ale pub with fine
lace curtains and a piano. Garden with swings.
Boat Riverside, Allerton Bywater. An
attractive Bass Yorkshire pub with a waterside
garden. Take care when mooring here, since
passing commercial craft cause a considerable
wash.

Castleford

There is a waterways 'crossroads' at Castleford.
Navigators heading towards Sowerby Bridge
should turn right here and *must on no account go
straight across* – since that way leads to the huge
Castleford Weir. To the left, through the Flood
Lock, are a sanitary station and good moorings,
beyond which lies the route to Goole, Hull,
Sheffield, York and ultimately the North Sea.
The large commercial craft which trade to
Leeds emerge from here, so take care. Entering
the River Calder, navigators will notice that its
course here has been straightened, as the oxbow
lakes either side will testify. After ducking
under a large road bridge and two railway
bridges a path which gives access to two fine
pubs at Whitwood can be seen to the south.
Your nose will also tell you there is a large
sewage works here. Pressing on, the large, deep
mechanised Woodnock Lock is reached. This
replaced the earlier Fairies and Altofts locks
(now disused) to the south. By comparing the
sizes of the locks, an impression of the
improvements carried out on the navigation
during the last 100 years can be gained. Beyond
the large motorway bridge is King's Road Lock
(also mechanised) and paths from here lead to
Altofts, although there is little reason to walk
the half mile or so, except for supplies.

Navigational note
Boaters must on no account take the river
course towards the weir at Castleford Junction.
Make sure you are clear about where to go
before you get there.

The towpath
The path on this section is generally very poor
and overgrown.

Castleford
*W. Yorks. EC Wed. MD Mon, Fri, Sat. All
services.* Once the Roman settlement of
Lagentium, now a busy industrial town which
has grown up at this important waterways
junction. The British Waterways Area
Engineer's Office can be seen by the Flood
Lock, and Allinsons water mill is situated by
the huge weir – here they produce their popular
stoneground flour.
Castleford Museum Carlton Street, Castleford
(559552). Changing exhibitions of local
interest, including recent finds from the Roman
town of Lagentium. *Open 14.00–17.00 Mon–
Fri. Free.*
Altofts
W. Yorks. PO, tel, stores, station. Originally a
mining village and now a suburb of Wakefield,
with a pick-your-own fruit farm at the western
end, but little else. There was once a pub by the
river, but it is now a private house. There are
still two pubs in the village.

PUBS
Old Mill Just south of Castleford Junction,
at the Barnsdale Road Bridge. Superbly kept
Theakstons bitter (real ale) in a friendly local.
Food, garden, children's playpark at the rear
and post office and stores close by.
Griffin Opposite The Old Mill. Comfortable
pub offering food and John Smith real ale.
Outside drinking area.
Bridge Inn Whitwood. A most interesting
pub, newly built but with old bricks and
timbers. There is a lofty ceiling over the bar,
with more intimate drinking and eating areas
off to the sides. Good bar meals, friendly staff
and Theakstons real ale. Patio.
New Wheatsheaf Whitwood. Large,
brightly-decorated traditional pub, where
someone clearly takes a great pride in their
flower arrangements. Tetley's real ale, food,
carvery restaurant, garden.
Between these two pubs is the Castleford &
Whitwood Greyhound Racing Stadium
(Castleford 559940), where there are races *every
Mon, Wed & Fri at* 19.30.

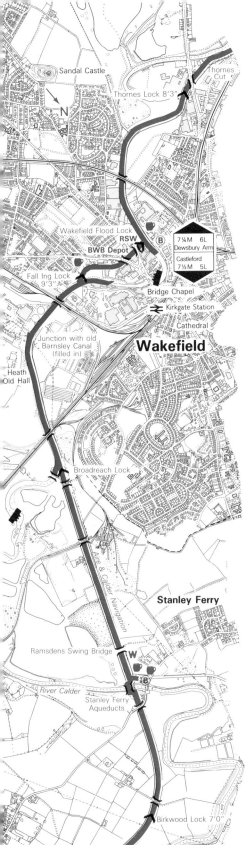

Wakefield

Birkwood Lock is the last mechanised lock
when travelling upstream. At Stanley Ferry the
canal is diverted over the new aqueduct, which
stands alongside the original and was opened in
1981. The original aqueduct was thought to be
at risk from the large craft which can now
navigate here. There is a British Waterways
repair yard immediately before the aqueduct,
and a fine new marina, with a pub and a
museum immediately after. This has been built
in a defunct loading basin. After Ramsden's
Swing Bridge (operated by a keeper at time of
writing) the navigation continues in a dead
straight line, passing Broadreach Flood Lock
and Heath Old Hall before turning west to join
the Calder & Hebble at Fall Ing Lock. There
are craft moored here by an old loading chute,
picnic area and convenient pub. Below
Wakefield Flood Lock the river is navigable for
a short distance towards the weir, giving access
to a boatyard. Leaving Wakefield you pass
under a splendid curving brick railway viaduct
known locally as 'the 99 arches'. A careful
count will reveal only 95. At Thornes Lock
only one of the two chambers is now in use –
you will need a Calder & Hebble 'handspike' to
operate this, and subsequent locks. Here the
navigation enters a short cut.

Navigational notes
1. Take heed of the notices and flood indicator
boards at the locks. Pleasure craft should only
proceed if the water level is in the *green* sector.
2. Most locks on the Calder & Hebble have a
unique type of paddle gear, consisting of a
small perforated wheel which is turned using a
'handspike'. These are obtainable from
boatyards on the navigation, and from
Castleford Lock. Or a piece of 3″ × 2″
hardwood, 3ft long, will do just as well.
3. When coming downstream (from Sowerby
Bridge direction) keep a sharp look out for the
entrance to Wakefield Flood Lock. There is a
large weir on the river, a short distance beyond
the boatyard, by the bridge.

Stanley Ferry Aqueduct
It is a good idea to moor at Stanley Ferry
Marina and walk to the road bridge for a full
view of this fine structure – a trough suspended
from a two-pin cast-iron arch – built on the
same principle as the Sydney Harbour Bridge,
which it predates by 100 years. Nearly 7000
tons of Bramley Fall stone and 1000 tons of cast
iron were used in its construction. The first
boat to pass across it was the 'James', a
schooner of 160 tons drawn by three grey
horses, on 8th August 1839. The 700 men who
worked on it were fed at the nearby public
houses, one of which, The Ship, still stands.
Designed by George Leather, the strength of
the structure was severely tested when, soon
after opening, the largest flood for 20 years
caused the river below to actually flow into the
trough. The towpath is carried on a separate
wooden breakwater designed to protect the
aqueduct during such floods. The concrete
aqueduct was built in 1981, and the original,
though still in water, has a new life – as a tourist
attraction.

Wakefield
*W. Yorks. EC Wed. MD Mon, Tue, Thur, Fri,
Sat. All services.* The city centre is north of the
navigation. The regional capital of West
Yorkshire, it gained city status in 1888 when
the cathedral was granted its charter. Mainly
15thC Perpendicular in style, the cathedral's
247ft spire is a landmark for miles around. On
much smaller scale, but perhaps of equal
interest, is the Chantry Chapel of St Mary, a
rare 14thC example of a bridge chapel, just a
short walk north of Fall Ings, by the weir. The
city itself is set on a hill, and still contains some
quiet streets and dignified Georgian houses,
notably those in St John's Square, with its
delightful church and handsome council
buildings. There has been a settlement at
Wakefield since Saxon times, and the strategic
importance of this site on the River Calder is
confirmed by the remains of the 12thC Sandal
Castle. The Battle of Wakefield, a significant
conflict in the Wars of the Roses, was fought
near here in 1460, and resulted in the death of

Richard, Duke of York. Wakefield's prosperity was founded on the textile and engineering industries, both of which have taken a battering in recent years. However the city has been successful in attracting new industry, such as Coca Cola/Schweppes; and the vast and spectacular Ridings shopping complex has created many new jobs. The Theatre Royal & Opera House provides a lively programme of entertainment, and the Yorkshire Sculpture Park at Bretton Hall displays some important works by Barbara Hepworth and Henry Moore, both local artists.

Tourist Information Centre Town Hall, Wood Street, Wakefield (370211). North west of the cathedral.

Wakefield Museum Wood Street, Wakefield (370211). Local history and archaeology, excavations from Sandal Castle, and the Waterton collection of exotic birds and animals. The building, designed in 1820, was originally a music saloon. *Closed Sun.* Free.

Wakefield Art Gallery Wentworth Terrace, Wakefield (370211). Sculpture by local artists Barbara Hepworth and Henry Moore, plus contemporary paintings, prints and drawings. *Closed Sun.* Free.

Heath Village 2 miles east of Wakefield. A beautifully preserved village with some 18thC merchants' houses amongst other substantial buildings. Heath Hall is a fine Georgian house by John Carr (1753) with carved woodwork and moulded plaster ceilings. The gas-lit pub is a gem (see below).

BOATYARDS

Ⓑ **Stanley Ferry Marina** Ferry Lane, Stanley, Wakefield (290596). Ⓡ Ⓦ Ⓓ Gas, pump-out, shop, chandlery, toilets, mooring, storage, crane, museum, pub & restaurant (see below), telephone.

Ⓑ **West Riding Marine** Thornes Wharf, Thornes Lane, Wakefield (377676). *The following are expected to be available during 1989:* Ⓡ Ⓢ Ⓦ Ⓓ Gas, pump-out, hire craft, slipway, overnight mooring, long-term mooring, shop. Boat building (narrowboats and sea-going vessels), boat and engine repairs, toilets, passenger trip boat.

PUBS AND RESTAURANTS

🍺✗ **Ferryboat Inn** Stanley Ferry Marina. Theakstons real ale in one of the old, well-converted buildings. Tom Pudding Restaurant upstairs.

🍺 **Ship** Stanley Ferry, close to the marina. Comfortable pub with flocked wallpaper. There must have been much merriment here on the day in August 1839 when the new aqueduct opened. Wilson's real ale, children's room, garden with swings, food *lunchtime and evenings Tue–Sat.*

🍺✗ **King's Arms** Overlooking the common, Heath Village (Wakefield 377527). Theakstons real ale in an historic old pub with a gas-lit, wood-panelled bar; full of antiques. Open fire, food *lunchtime and evenings,* garden and restaurant.

🍺 **Graziers** Just south of Fall Ing Lock. Tetley's real ale pub with some outside seating. Take-away food shop opposite.

🍺 **Jolly Sailor** Thornes Wharf, opposite Wakefield Flood Lock.

🍺 **Henry Boon's** Westgate, Wakefield. West of the cathedral. Fine traditional brewery tap for Clark's Brewery. A real ale enthusiasts' pub, with live jazz several times each week.

✗ **Val's Tea Shop** 61 Kirkgate, Wakefield (378996). Traditional breakfasts, sandwiches and cakes, substantial lunches all served by aproned waitresses. *Open 08.30–17.30. Closed Sun.*

Near Fall Ing. *David Perrott.*

Horbury Bridge

The navigation rejoins the River Calder at
Thornes Flood Lock, and passes under the M1
motorway. Ahead is the tall spike of Elmley
Moor television transmitter. The beautifully
kept Broad Cut Low Lock, with its flowers and
trees, marks the start of a 5-mile-long canal
section with 8 locks. There was regular trade on
this stretch until 1981, when West Country
barges took coal from the British Oak Colliery
to Thornhill Power Station. Remains of loading
staithes can be seen opposite the Navigation
Inn. The navigation now becomes more
intimate and enclosed, and is indeed quite
pretty at The Wyke. There are good moorings
at Horbury Bridge, and a post office and farm
shop are close by. A short arm here used to
connect with the river – the remains of a lock
can still be seen. Beyond the bridge a tree-lined
cutting leads to Figure of Three Locks. There
are two locks on the navigation with another
now disused, behind the lock-keeper's house,
which used to connect with the river. Is it this,
or the fact that the river here makes the shape
of a '3', which gives these locks their unusual
name? Experts seem unable to agree. The
towpath from Broad Cut to Dewsbury is good,
having been improved by the local authority,
the Manpower Services Commission and BWB
in 1986–7.

Horbury
W. Yorks. EC Wed. PO, tel, stores. A small
town up a steep hill from the bridge,
overlooking the Calder Valley. The most
attractive feature of Horbury is the delicate
spire of the parish church, designed, built and
paid for by the architect John Carr, a son of the
town. The hymn 'Onward Christian Soldiers'
was written and first sung here; it was
composed by the Reverend S. Baring-Gould as
a marching song for the children to sing on
their way to church.

Yorkshire Mining Museum Claphouse
Colliery, New Road, Overton, Wakefield
(848806). On the A642, a little under 2 miles
south-west of Horbury Bridge (bus service). Go
450ft underground to visit old- and new-style
coalfaces, examine machinery and visit the
pit-head baths, in the company of friendly
ex-miners. Audio visual show, café, shop,
picnic area. Wear warm practical clothes; not
suitable for very young children. *Open
10.00–17.00 Mon–Sun.* Charge.

PUBS
⬤ **Navigation** Broad Cut Top Lock, by the
railway viaduct. Handsome stone-built
canalside pub serving Tetley's real ale. Garden,
food, games area. Good moorings here; post
office and fish & chips just a short distance to
the south. Showers available for a small charge.
⬤ **Bingley Arms** Horbury Bridge. Tetley's real
ale in another fine looking pub.
⬤✕ **Ship** Horbury Bridge (Wakefield 272795).
Comfy local with a restaurant.

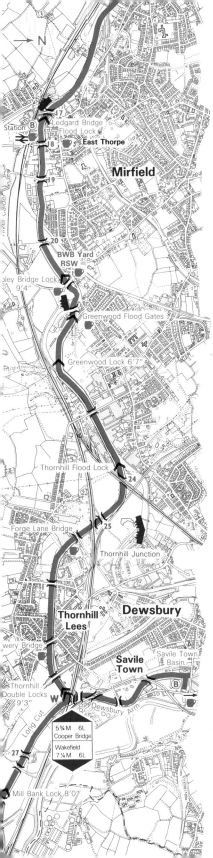

Dewsbury

After Mill Bank Lock look out for a milestone marked 'from FALL INGS 7 miles' on the towpath side, by the next bridge. Thornhill Double Locks mark the junction with the Dewsbury Arm, which branches off to Savile Town Basin. This is a worthwhile diversion, although much of the original charm of the basin was lost when the wooden warehouses were demolished. There are still some attractive buildings left, however, and Robinson's Hire Cruisers maintain a small but very interesting museum in the old stables. Climbing Thornhill Double Locks (good moorings here) the navigation enters a deep secluded cutting spanned by tall bridges, which eventually gives way to an open industrial wasteland (for which there are large-scale redevelopment plans) around the site of Thornhill Power Station, where barges once used to unload coal. Between Thornhill Flood Lock and Greenwood Lock a short, wide, river section intervenes before the navigation enters another artificial channel to the south of Mirfield. There is plenty of interest around the pub and boatyard here, and landscaping and pretty waterside gardens make this a pleasant spot. At Shepley Bridge Flood Lock the river is rejoined. The towpath is generally good on the canal sections, less so, or indeed non-existent, on the river sections.

Navigational notes
1. When coming downstream, look out for the entrance to Ledgard Bridge Flood Lock. A large weir awaits those who miss it.
2. There are landing stages below the locks which you can use, as well as ladders in virtually all the locks.

Dewsbury
W. Yorks. EC Tue. MD Wed, Sat. All services. An industrial town that has long been the focus of the heavy woollen manufacturing area of Yorkshire. The compact and attractive town centre is a mile away from Savile Town Basin.
Dewsbury Arm Extending for ¾ mile to Savile Town Basin, this used to be the main line of the navigation, until the Thornhill Cut made it redundant in the 1790s.
Thornhill
W. Yorks. PO, tel, stores. This old stone-built mining village up on a hill above the canal offers fine views across the valley.
Mirfield
W. Yorks. EC Tue. MD Fri. All services. A useful place to get supplies.

BOATYARDS
British Waterways Shepley Bridge (Mirfield 492151). R S W Toilets, dry dock. 'Handspikes' are made here.
B **Robinson's Hire Cruisers** Savile Town Basin, Dewsbury (467976). R S WD Gas, pump-out, hire craft, overnight mooring, long-term mooring, slipway, winter storage, boat building, boat and engine repairs, crane, excellent museum, toilets.
B **Mirfield Boatyard** 10 Station Road, Mirfield (492007). Below Shepley Bridge Flood Lock. R W emergency D Gas nearby, overnight mooring, long-term mooring, winter storage, crane by arrangement, dry dock, general and emergency repairs, boat building, toilets.

BOAT TRIPS
Calder Lady Trips from Savile Town Basin. Contact Robinson's Hire Cruisers, Dewsbury (467976).
The Princess Mary A traditional river cruise-boat built in 1920, runs regular trips *Sun & B. Hols May–Oct* from Mirfield, plus a waterbus service between Mirfield and Brighouse on *Wed & Sat during Jul & Aug.* Also available for private charter. Details from Mirfield Boatyard, Mirfield (492007).

PUBS AND TAKE-AWAYS
Savile Hotel Turn left out of Savile Town Basin and follow Mill Street East to the traffic lights (5-minute walk). Websters real ale in a large hotel with some nice clocks and a *chaise longue* by the fire. Food, sheltered garden.
X **Agra** Warren Street, Savile Town, Dewsbury (467365). Turn left out of the basin,

left again, over the bridge and bear left. Superb inexpensive Indian take-away. *Open Mon–Thur & Sun, Fri & Sat to 24.30. PO and Asian grocers close by.*

🍺 **Nelson** Scramble up the bank at Brewery Bridge. Food, games room.

🍺 **Perseverance Inn** Thornhill Junction. Canalside pub built in 1905, undergoing renovation at time of writing.

🍺 **Bull's Head** Tetley's real ale pub near Greenwood Flood Gates.

🍺 **Ship Inn** East of Shepley Bridge Lock.

Large, smart and comfortable pub serving food and Whitbread real ale.

🍺 **Swan** Above Shepley Bridge Lock. Smart Tetley's real ale pub with a roadside patio. Food *lunchtime and evenings.*

🍺 **Navigation** Canalside near Shepley Bridge Flood Lock. A fine Whitbread real ale pub dwarfed by the Bass Charrington building next door. Meals *lunchtime and evenings*, garden.

🍺 **Black Bull** North of bridge 18. Imposing Tetley's real ale hotel. Food *lunchtime and evenings* and occasional live music.

Thornhill Double Locks. *David Perrott.*

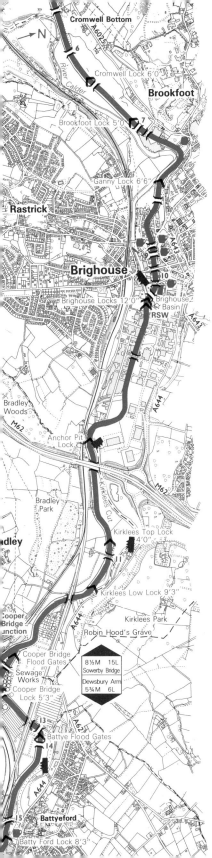

Cooper Bridge

At Battyeford there is a short canal section which rejoins the river opposite a large sewage works. A fine display of roses suggests they are not short of fertilizer! Cooper Bridge marks the junction of the Calder & Hebble with the Huddersfield Broad Canal (*see page 28*), which branches off to the south below the flood gates, overlooked by the tall chimney of Bottomley & Sons. Kirklees Park lies on a hillside to the north before the navigation passes under the M62 motorway and enters a cutting on its approach to Brighouse, completely enclosed by factories. The basin above Brighouse Locks provides good moorings, and the passage through the town is pleasant, with gardens, seats and willow trees. Leaving the town the canal is now more reminiscent of the narrower Midlands canals, indeed there is a pleasant wooded mooring, ideal for a picnic, at Cromwell Bottom. Flooded gravel pits to the north are used for waterskiing. The towpath improves above Brighouse.

Kirklees Park In the grounds are the modest ruins of a priory founded in the 12thC for Cistercian nuns. Most of the stones were incorporated in the construction of Kirklees Hall during the late 16thC. It is believed that Robin Hood died whilst at the priory but before so doing he shot two arrows from the window to mark his burial place. One landed in the River Calder and floated away, the other landed in the grounds of the park. A tablet marks the spot thought to be his grave.
Brighouse
W. Yorks. EC Tue. MD Wed, Sat. All services.
A woollen textile producing village transformed into an important canal port with the building of the Calder & Hebble Navigation. In the 19thC silk and cotton were also spun here. Now there seems to be plenty of thriving new industry. The canal bisects the town, passing very close to the market place. A large Victorian church at the top of the hill is surrounded by trees and flowers.

PUBS

- **Pear Tree Inn** Near Battyeford Lock. Pleasant pub with a real fire and a collection of plates. Websters real ale, family room. Food *lunchtime and evenings.* Moorings at the bottom of its riverside garden.
- **Red Rooster** 123 Elland Road, north of Brookfoot Lock. Real ale enthusiasts' pub, with a real fire as well. Boddingtons, Marstons, Theakstons and guest beers. Garden.
- **New Tavern** Near Brighouse Basin (Brighouse 712755). Comfortable modern pub with a restaurant. Whitbread real ale.
- **Anchor Bridge** Brighouse. Sam Webster's real ale. Being renovated at time of writing.
- **Black Bull** North of the bridge, Brighouse. Whitbread real ale. Excellent food, live music.
- **Prince of Wales** North of the bridge, Brighouse. A handsome black and white half-timbered pub rebuilt in 1926 with timber from 'HMS Donegal', a wood-built battleship launched in 1858. The Tudor-style interior is compromised by two TVs, a juke box and a battery of fruit machines. Sam Webster's real ale.

Sowerby Bridge

A milestone right by Park Nook Lock (*off-licence and grocers nearby*) reveals that you are now 18 miles from Fall Ing, with just a short distance to travel to Sowerby Bridge. Elland Basin, with its tastefully restored buildings and gardens, is worth more than a fleeting glance, however, and makes a good stopping place en route. There are several pubs close by. Have a look at the fine converted warehouse with its covered dock, before pressing on to the three superbly kept and picturesque Salterhebble Locks. The bottom lock here has an electrically-powered guillotine gate operated by the lock-keeper. This was installed when the road was widened in the 1930s. The towpath passes separately through its own narrow tunnel. Immediately after this first lock the canal passes over a small aqueduct before climbing the top two. To the right is the Salterhebble Branch (where the old Salterhebble Basin is being restored), to the left the route to Sowerby Bridge. The canal, now relatively narrow, clings to the side of a wooded hill, its clean water alive with small fish. A conspicuous building to the north is Wainhouse Tower, built in 1875 as a 253ft dyeworks chimney but converted into a viewing tower. A superb example of stonemasonry, it is *opened on Bank Holidays* (400 steps to the top). The buildings close in as the navigation approaches the basins at Sowerby Bridge, where the Rochdale Canal once branched off to cross the Pennines. Perhaps one day soon it will again be possible to make this trip, thanks to various restoration schemes. The towpath throughout this section is excellent.

Elland
W. Yorks. EC Tue. MD Fri. PO, tel, stores, bank. Elland has an enviable position on the steep south side of the Calder Valley, its narrow streets discourage through traffic, and its handsome church and terraces of stone houses give an air of tranquillity. The well-restored canal basin makes an excellent stopping point.
Halifax
W. Yorks. EC Thur. MD Fri, Sat, Sun. All services. Well known as the home of the Halifax Building Society, founded in 1853, which now has ultra-modern offices in Portland Place; it is worth the journey north from the canal to visit this industrial town. The splendid Piece Hall, rebuilt in 1770, is the last remaining manufacturers' hall in the country. Here weavers traded their products, the continuation of an industry that dates back to 1275 in Halifax. Now restored, the hall houses arts and craft shops, a museum, restaurant and the Tourist Information Centre. The parish church of St John the Baptist is Perpendicular in style, battlemented and with a mass of pinnacles, parapets and gargoyles.
Calderdale Industrial Museum Next door to the Piece Hall, Halifax (59031). Steam engines, a Spinning Jenny, a Flying Shuttle loom and toffee wrapping machines, all working. Re-creations of 19thC Halifax, coal mines and clay mines. *Open 10.00–17.00 Tue–Sat, 14.00–17.00 Sun.* Charge.
Shibden Hall Folk Museum Shibden Park, Halifax (52246). A 15thC building with 17thC furniture and extensive folk exhibits. *Open Apr–Sep 10.00–18.00 Mon–Sat, 14.00–18.00 Sun (closes 17.00 Oct, Nov & Mar). Closed Dec & Jan, and Mon–Sat in Feb.* Charge.
Sowerby Bridge
W. Yorks. EC Wed. MD Tue, Fri. All services. Although this is an industrial town, the scale and grandeur of the surrounding landscape dominates the mill chimneys and factory roofs that are dotted about. This rare subservience to nature makes the town human and attractive. The 19thC classical church is in a good position, overlooking the present canal terminus.
Sowerby Bridge Basin
PO, tel, stores. This great canal centre is a classic example of the functional tradition in industrial architecture, and has thankfully survived to be given a new life in restoration, while many other such examples have disappeared. The Rochdale Canal was built to accommodate vessels up to 72ft in length, so goods had to be transhipped here into the

shorter Calder & Hebble craft before they could continue their journey; hence this important centre grew in stature.

Rochdale Canal

One of three canal routes across the Pennines, its 92 wide locks over a distance of 33 miles virtually guaranteed its ultimate commercial failure. Long stretches have now been restored however, including 11 miles (hopefully 15 miles to Littleborough by 1990) starting behind the Kwiksave supermarket in Sowerby Bridge. It is also worth taking the 10-minute train ride from Sowerby Bridge to Hebden Bridge to see the canal there.

BOATYARDS

ⓑ **Shire Cruisers** The Wharf, Sowerby Bridge (Halifax 832712). Facilities either here or in the basin. ⓇⓈⓌⓅⒹ Gas, pump-out, hire craft (also from Hebden Bridge on the restored section of the Rochdale Canal), overnight mooring, long-term mooring, boat building, boat and engine repairs, winter storage, crane by arrangement, shop, toilets.

ⓑ **Sowerby Marine** Sowerby Bridge Basin. (Halifax 832922). Boat sales and chandlery. *Closed Wed.*

BOAT TRIPS

Calder Valley Cruising From Hebden Bridge Marina (train from Sowerby Bridge). Trips along a restored section of the Rochdale Canal, and visits to the Clog Factory. Details from Hebden Bridge 844833.

PUBS AND RESTAURANTS

🍺 **Colliers Arms** Between Elland and Park Nook locks. Traditional canalside pub offering Sam Smith real ale, food *lunchtime and evenings*, an open fire and a waterside garden.

🍺 **Barge & Barrel** Elland Basin. An interesting choice of real ales in a comfortable Victorian style pub. *Lunchtime* food, real fire, garden. Families welcome.

🍺 **Royal** South of Elland Bridge. Websters real ale in an attractive stone-built pub. *Lunchtime* food.

🍺 **Malt Shovels** Next to The Royal. Sam Smith real ale, garden. These two pubs are separated by an extravagant neo-Grecian workshop.

🍺 **Calder & Hebble Inn** East of Salterhebble Locks.

🍺 **Jenny Dee** A new pub at the terminus of the Salterhebble Branch.

🍺 **Punch Bowl Inn** By the Salterhebble Branch.

🍺 **Navigation Inn** By bridge 1. Friendly 17thC canalside pub with a collection of Buckby cans. Tetley's real ale and an extensive bar menu. Garden.

🍺✕ **Moorings** No 1 Warehouse, Sowerby Bridge Basin (Halifax 833940). A good choice of bar food and real ale in this attractive conversion. Wide range of foreign lagers and beers. Restaurant *open Tue–Sat evenings*. Patio, family room.

🍺✕ **Ash Tree** 75 Wharf Street, by the basin (Halifax 831654). A pub/restaurant specialising in Indonesian food (*evenings only*). Good choice of real ale, including Old Mill and Stones. Bar food (*lunchtime*).

🍺 **Engineers** and the **William IV** are also very close to the basin.

Sowerby Bridge Basin. *David Perrott.*

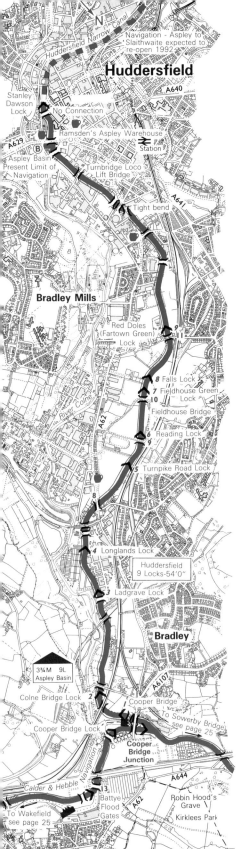

Huddersfield

Also known as Sir John Ramsden's Canal, this navigation was authorised in 1774. It leaves the Calder & Hebble at Cooper Bridge and makes a very rewarding short diversion off the main line. Brick-arched bridges and a succession of locks maintain interest, and although industry is omnipresent, there are plenty of green patches, and a vast expanse of cricket pitches, to bring light relief. After climbing Red Doles Lock, the last of the nine, a tight bend under three bridges brings you to the remarkable Turnbridge loco lift bridge. Dated 1865, you will need a Leeds & Liverpool-type key to unlock it. Aspley Basin is effectively the limit of navigation, although the new Wakefield Road Bridge means that the link with the Huddersfield Narrow Canal has once again been made navigable for craft of 7ft beam. It is well worth exploring this end of the narrow canal, especially to have a look at the warehouse south of the bridge. Built prior to 1778 it is probably the oldest surviving example of such a building, demonstrating an early stage in the development of the large multi-storey warehouses of the 19thC. However, if it is to survive much longer, it will need to be sympathetically restored. The crane beside it dates from the early 19thC. Further along, beyond Huddersfield Polytechnic, is the first restored lock on the narrow canal, which is expected to open as far as Slaithwaite sometime around 1992. The towpath on the Huddersfield Broad Canal is good.

Navigational notes
1. When joining the Huddersfield Broad Canal at Cooper Bridge, take care to avoid the weir on the river just beyond the entrance lock (1).
2. Although there are mooring rings on the Huddersfield Narrow Canal south of Aspley Basin, turning here may be difficult.

Huddersfield
W. Yorks. EC Wed. MD Mon. All services.
Huddersfield is in the best tradition of Victorian industrial towns: all built to a grand scale of dark local stone, in a happy mixture of 19thC styles. The most striking part of the town is around the railway station, built in 1847 with its powerful classical façade of Corinthian columns, considered one of the finest examples of railway architecture. The renowned Huddersfield Choral Society operates from the 19thC Town Hall.
Huddersfield Narrow Canal
One of three Pennine canal crossings, and noted for the length of its summit tunnel at Standedge, fully 5668yds end to end. Authorised in 1794 and completed in 1811, this canal packs 74 locks into its 20 miles between here and Manchester. Active restoration is afoot at both ends.

BOATYARDS
Ⓑ **Aspley Wharf Marina** Aspley Basin, Huddersfield (514123). Ⓢ Gas, slipway, mooring, chandlery. Cruiser and speedboat sales and repairs. *Closed Wed.*

PUBS AND RESTAURANTS
🍺 **White Horse Inn** South of bridge 8. Handy pub by the cricket pitches. Food.
🍺 **Spinners Arms** East of the canal, approaching Turnbridge. Roadside pub serving bar meals.
✕🍷 **Montana Exchange** Aspley Basin, Huddersfield (544250). A modern glitzy cocktail bar/restaurant which barely acknowledges the presence of the canal. However families with children can eat here.
🍺 **Wharf** Just across the busy road from the basin (access along the towpath through the Wakefield Road Bridge is preferable to the traffic). Take-away food close by.
🍺 **College Arms** 33 Queensgate, Huddersfield. Close to the basin. Websters and Wilson's real ales in this unusual pub, formerly the Dog & Gun. Bar meals *lunchtime and evenings.*

BRIDGEWATER CANAL

Maximum dimensions

Length: 70′
Beam: 14′
Headroom: 8′
Draught: 3′

Licences

Estates Officer, Manchester Ship Canal Company, Trafford Road, Manchester. Enquiries: 061-872 7031.
All craft using the canal must be licensed and insured against normal third party risks. Any boat holding a normal British Waterways licence may cruise freely on the Bridgewater for up to 7 days.

Mileage

PRESTON BROOK to
Lymm: 9¾
Waters Meeting, junction with
Leigh Branch: 20½
Hulme Locks Branch: 23¼
CASTLEFIELD JUNCTION, start of
Rochdale Canal: 23½

No locks

DUCIE STREET JUNCTION, start of
Ashton Canal: 25 (Rochdale Canal, 9 locks)

Preston Brook to Runcorn: 5¾, no locks

Leigh Branch: 8½, no locks

The Bridgewater Canal, which received the Royal Assent on 23 March 1759, was the fore-runner of all modern canals, following a route that was independent of all existing natural watercourses. It was built by Francis Egerton, third Duke of Bridgewater, to enable coal from his mines at Worsley to be transported to Manchester and sold cheaply. His engineers were James Brindley and John Gilbert, who designed a lockless contour canal which crossed the River Irwell on a stone aqueduct – a revolutionary concept and one that was ridiculed by many sceptics. However the line was open to Stretford by the end of 1765.

While the canal was under construction, there began the excavation of a remarkable system of underground canals to serve the Duke's mines, reached through two entrances at Worsley Delph. Eventually 46 miles of underground canal were built, some on different levels and linked by an ingenious inclined plane built along a fault in the sandstone. The craft used in the mines were known as 'starvationers', double-ended tub boats which could carry up to 12 tons of coal. This whole system remained in use until the late 19thC.

In 1762 the Duke received sanction to extend his canal to the Liverpool tideway at Runcorn – this was later amended in order to connect with the new Trent & Mersey Canal at Preston Brook. The route between Liverpool and Manchester was opened in 1776, although Brindley did not live to see its completion. In 1795 the Duke, then 60 years old, received the Royal Assent for the final part of the network, which linked Worsley to the Leeds & Liverpool Canal at Leigh. As a result of this enterprise, the Duke spent much of his life heavily in debt, although he finally recouped his investments to die, in 1803, a rich man.

The coming of the railways did not initially affect the prosperity of the canal, the Trustees going to great lengths in Parliament to protect their position. In 1872 the newly formed Bridgewater Navigation Company purchased the canal for £1,120,000, and they in turn sold it to the Manchester Ship Canal Company in 1885. The building of the new Ship Canal meant that Brindley's original stone aqueduct over the River Irwell would need to be replaced. Its successor, the Barton Swing Aqueduct, was no less outstanding than the original, being a steel trough closed by gates at each end, pivoting on an island in the Ship Canal. The weight of water carried by the new aqueduct is 1500 tons.

The Bridgewater Canal is a tribute to its builders in that it continued to carry commercial traffic until 1974 – indeed its wide gauge, lock-free course and frequent use of aqueducts makes many later canals seem retrograde.

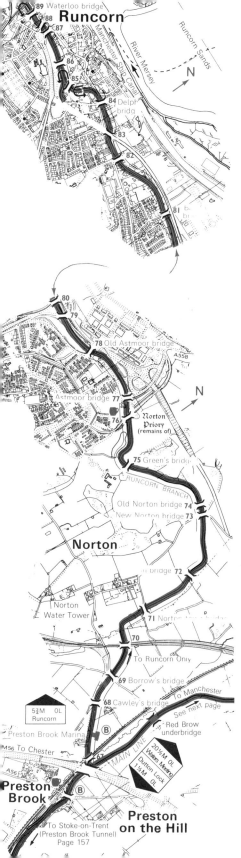

Preston Brook

Although the main line of the Bridgewater was
originally to Runcorn, where it locked down to
the Mersey, this is now a dead end, reached
through the dull acres of the new town's
expanding housing estates, there are, however,
some attractive terraces and elegant iron
bridges to enliven the journey. The locks down
to the Mersey were closed in 1966. The route to
Manchester bears to the right immediately after
the big motorway bridge, and the canal's direct
course to the south of the Mersey affords
interesting views of the Manchester Ship Canal
and industry to the north.

Runcorn
Ches. EC Wed. MD Tue, Thur, Sat. All services
Runcorn's industrial growth began with the
completion of the Bridgewater Canal in the
latter part of the 18thC. The old town is to be
found down by the docks, where the elegant
curved 1092-ft single span of the steel road
bridge (built 1961), with the railway beside,
leaps over the Ship Canal and the Mersey. West
of the bridge, by the Ship Canal, is Bridgewater
House where the 'Canal Duke' spent much of
his time while the docks were being built – it is
now occupied by the Manchester Ship Canal
Company. The massive flight of 10 double
locks which connected the canal to the Mersey
was finally abandoned in 1966, and filled in,
much to the dismay of thousands of industrial
archaeologists and canal enthusiasts. Since 1964
Runcorn has been a 'new town', its rapid
growth being carefully planned. It is interesting
to note that Runcorn, following recent local
government reorganisation, is now part of
Halton (which includes Widnes on the north
bank of the Mersey), an echo of the time
following the Norman Conquest when it was a
dependent manor of the Barony of Halton.
Tourist Information Centre Church Street,
Runcorn (76776).
Norton Priory The remains of a priory c1200,
set in woodland, with a picnic area and
museum. *Open Mon–Wed, Sat, Sun & B. Hol
afternoons in summer – also Thur & Fri in Aug.*
Preston Brook
Ches. PO, tel, stores. A village that grew up to
serve the canal, where goods were transhipped
from the wide beam craft of the north west to
the narrowboats of the Midlands. There is now
little left to remind us of this activity, and a
very different means of transport, the M56
motorway, dominates the area. To the south,
on the Trent & Mersey Canal, is the
1239-yard-long Preston Brook Tunnel (see page
157).

BOATYARDS

Ⓑ **Claymoore Navigation** The Wharf, Preston
Brook. (Runcorn 717273). Ⓡ Ⓦ Ⓓ Pump-out,
gas, hire craft, overnight mooring, long-term
mooring, winter storage, chandlery, boat
fitting, boat sales, repairs, toilets, groceries and
gifts.
Ⓑ **Preston Brook Marina** Preston Brook.
(Runcorn 719081). Ⓡ Ⓢ Ⓦ Ⓓ Gas, overnight
mooring, long-term mooring, slipway,
chandlery, boat sales, toilets, showers.

PUBS

Plenty of pubs in Runcorn, including:
🍺 **Clarendon** Church Street, Runcorn.
🍺 **Egerton Arms** Bridge Street, Runcorn.
🍺 **Barge Hotel** Norton. By bridge 77.
🍺 **Red Lion** Preston Brook.

Daresbury

Industry is far enough away to the north to remain an interesting diversion rather than an ugly intrusion as the canal passes through pleasant countryside, punctuated initially by the tall white tower and pleasant landscaped grounds of the Science Research Laboratory at Daresbury, where nuclear research is carried out. By Moorefield Bridge there is one of the small cranes used to hoist stop planks into position, should a section of the canal need to be drained. The canal frontage at Moore is attractive, with moored boats, a shop and a phone right by the canal, followed by a group of interesting red brick, bow-fronted cottages. A short rural stretch is interrupted by the estate village of Higher Walton, which can be seen among trees, and this is followed by a secluded tree-lined length in a shallow cutting before the outskirts of Stockton Heath are approached. There follows a pleasant example of urban canal, busy with fishermen and walkers. There are useful services at London Bridge.

Stockton Heath
Ches. EC Thur. Shops and services north of London Bridge. An outer suburb of Warrington, England's centre for vodka distilling. A useful place to victual.
Stockton Quay Bridge 15. The terminus of the canal from 1771 to 1776, before the Duke of Bridgewater completed his route from Manchester to Runcorn, and consequently a major transhipment point with stables, yards, wharves, warehouses and a canal company office. Passenger packet boat services also ran from here from 1771 to the mid 1880s, one of the craft being the renowned 'Duchess-Countess'.
Higher Walton
Ches. PO, tel, stores. A pretty, late Victorian estate village among trees. The gardens of Walton Hall are open to the public.
Daresbury
Ches. PO, tel, stores. Half-a-mile up the road from Keckwick Bridge. Appealing village on a hill, where Charles Lutwidge Dodgson, better known as Lewis Carroll, was born in 1832. His father was vicar of Daresbury (pronounced Darzby) and they lived until 1843 in the Old Parsonage, Newton-by-Daresbury, 2 miles south of the church. The home was burnt down in 1883 – the site is now marked by a plaque, standing in an open field on Glebe Farm. The church has a Lewis Carroll memorial window, bright and cheerful, where he is shown with characters from 'Alice in Wonderland'.

BOATYARDS

Ⓑ **Thorn Marine** London Bridge, Stockton Heath. (Warrington 65129). Ⓢ Ⓦ Gas, chandlery, sweets, ice cream. 'Frayed Knot' café and take-away next door.

PUBS

🍺 **London Bridge** Stockton Heath. Canalside.
🍺 **Walton Arms** Higher Walton. Food, garden.
🍺 **Ring o' Bells** Daresbury. Unspoilt old pub.

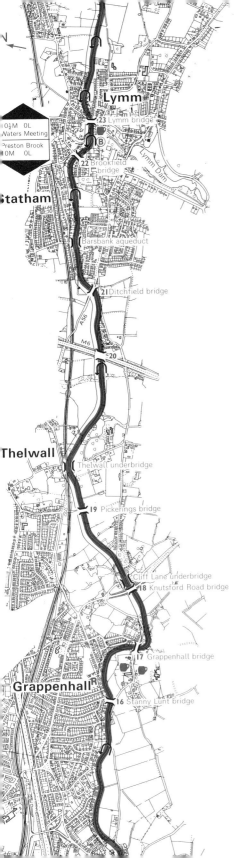

Lymm

Where the canal comes to within a ¼ mile of
the Manchester Ship Canal, the houses of
Stockton Heath merge into those of
Grappenhall crowded to the north, while to the
south the old village survives. The canal makes
a dog-leg turn past Thelwall and under the M6
Motorway south of the vast and infamous
Thelwall Viaduct which climbs laboriously over
the Ship Canal. There are fine views of the
distant Pennines to the north before the canal
makes a very pleasing passage through the heart
of Lymm, whose cobbled streets come down
almost to the water's edge. There are
convenient temporary moorings here.

Lymm
*Ches. PO, tel, stores, banks, fish & chips,
launderette.* The 17thC Lymm Cross, with
replica wooden stocks close by, stands on a rock
outcrop just a few yards from the canal in the
centre of this hilly and attractive little town,
which has retained its intimate character in
spite of its proximity to Warrington. Craft of
the Lymm Cruising Club line the banks, and
there are several fine canalside residences.
Thelwall
Ches. A short walk north from Thelwall
underbridge will bring you to a ferry where, for
a minimal charge, you will be rowed across the
Ship Canal.
Grappenhall
Ches. PO, tel, stores. A fine group of buildings
on cobbled streets survive around the church of
St Wilfred, where the village stocks remain.
There are two pubs.

BOATYARDS

ⓑ **Wharfage Boat Co** Agden Wharf, Lymm
(754900). Ⓡ Ⓢ Ⓦ Ⓓ Pump-out, hire craft,
boat-building, repairs, toilets, groceries and
gifts.

BOAT TRIPS

Lymm Bargee is a 42-seater restaurant
trip-boat, operating from Agden Wharf,
Lymm. Phone Lymm 754900 for details.

PUBS

There are plenty of pubs in Lymm.
🍺 **Golden Fleece** Lymm. Canalside. Food,
garden, children's room.
🍺 **Spread Eagle** Town centre, Lymm.
🍺 **Ram's Head** Grappenhall. Food.
🍺 **Parr Arms** Grappenhall. Food.

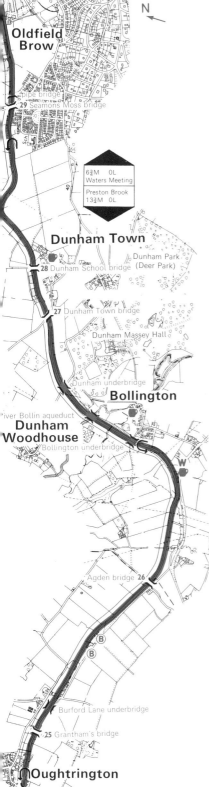

Bollington

The canal leaves Lymm, passes the village of
Oughtrington to the north and a row of smart
new houses to the south, each with a canalside
garden and barking dog, before entering
surroundings which are surprisingly rural.
Rows of moored boats, some in an advanced
state of decay, announce the presence of
two useful boatyards. The fields then gently
fall away into the valley of the River Bollin,
which the Bridgewater crosses on a large
embankment, with fine views of the
Manchester Ship Canal and Dunham Park, the
last greenery before Sale and Manchester. The
Bollin Aqueduct is a new concrete and steel
construction, built to replace the original stone
trough which breached disastrously in August
1971 and resulted in a 2-year closure. It cost
£125,000 to repair. *PO, stores, fish and chips* are
south of Seamons Moss Bridge.

Dunham Town
Gt Manchester. PO, tel, stores. A small scattered
farming village.
Dunham Massey Hall Until recently the seat
of the Earl of Stamford, now owned by the
National Trust. The beautiful 18thC house
stands in a wooded park, with deer and an
Elizabethan mill. Access is via Bollington, over
the footbridge near the Swan with Two Nicks.
Open daily except Fri, Apr–Oct. Restaurant &
shop. Admission charge.
Bollington
Ches. A compact and attractive village, with a
fine old pub.
Oughtrington
Ches. PO, tel, stores. A good place for supplies.

BOATYARDS

Ⓑ **Lymm Marina** Warrington Lane, Lymm
(2945). Ⓓ Gas, long-term mooring, slipway,
chandlery, boat sales.
Ⓑ **Hesford Marine** Warrington Lane, Lymm
(4639). ⓌⒹ Gas, moorings, slipway, crane,
chandlery, winter storage, boat building, boat
and engine sales and repairs, toilets.

PUBS

🍺 **Bay Malton** By Seamons Moss Bridge.
Food, bowling green, overnight mooring, Ⓡ.
🍺 **Axe & Cleaver** Dunham Town. Food,
garden.
🍺 **Swan with Two Nicks** Bollington. Fine old
pub with good food.
🍺 **Ye Olde No 3** Bollington Wharf. Food,
garden.

Sale

Beyond Seamons Moss Bridge the buildings
close in on the canal, and the countryside
disappears from view. Among the derelict
buildings and graffiti stands the superb
Victorian Linotype Factory, dated 1897, where
metal printing type was manufactured. Moored
by Timperley Bridge are assorted craft of the
Sale Cruising Club. The electric suburban
railway closes in from the south east and escorts
the canal all the way through Sale and on into
Stretford – as the trains hurry by you can enjoy
a more relaxing 3 mph. There are two
convenient canalside pubs before the canal is
crossed by the M63 motorway, and then itself
crosses the River Mersey. A large expanse of
graves heralds the entrance to Stretford,
followed by the moorings of the Stretford Boat
Club.

Sale
Gt Manchester. EC Wed. All Services. A
residential suburb of Manchester, transformed
from a farming community by the building in
1849 of the Altrincham to Manchester Railway
– hence most of its buildings are Victorian or
later. St Martin's Church is, however, 18thC
and has a hammerbeam roof. The clock tower
of the town hall, built in 1914, is a prominent
landmark. There are shops close to Sale Bridge
(35). The northern part of Sale merges into
Ashton Upon Mersey, unremarkable except as
the birthplace of Stanley Houghton
(1881–1913) who wrote 'The Dear Departed'
in 1908 and 'Hindle Wakes' in 1912.
Altrincham
Gt Manchester. EC Wed. A few black and white
half-timbered buildings remain in the market
square of what was once a small market town.
Later in the 18thC it became a textile
manufacturing centre, and is now, inevitably, a
dormitory town.

PUBS
🍺 **Bridge Inn** Canalside at Dane Road Bridge
Shop & launderette nearby.
🍺 **Railway** Canalside at Sale Bridge. Food.

Edge Lane bridge 38

N

Hawthorn Lane aqueduct

Mersey aqueduct

M63

37

2M   0L
Waters Meeting

Preston Brook
18½M   0L

Ashton Upon Mersey

Dane Road bridge 36

Sale bridge 35

Marshland bridge 34

Sale

Timperley bridge 33

32

31

Broadheath

Altrincham

Broadheath bridge 30

Linotype factory

Manchester

At Waters Meeting the original main line of the
canal is joined – to the north west is Barton,
Leigh and the connection with the Leeds &
Liverpool Canal which crosses the Pennines to
Leeds; to the east is the centre of the
Manchester & Rochdale Canal, which itself, as
the name implies, once crossed the hills to
Rochdale before it fell into disuse. The
Bridgewater's route is now hemmed in by
factory walls and fences, passing close to the
Manchester United football ground. The
floodlights of this famous football club tower
above the canal, which passes between the
ground and the massive (and empty) docks of
the Ship Canal. Old Trafford cricket ground,
the home of Lancashire Cricket Club and a Test
Match venue is a little further south. The Ship
Canal is now very close – more empty docks are
passed before Hulme Lock Branch, which
connects the two canals, is reached. There are
moorings here on a narrow isthmus isolated
from the surrounding factories and roads – it is
not particularly attractive, and trains pass
frequently high above, but it is a safe spot to
spend the night before tackling the locks of the
Rochdale and Ashton canals (after Castlefield
Junction the next safe mooring is Fairfield
Junction). The Bridgewater ends and the short
navigable stretch of the Rochdale begins at
Castlefield Junction – the first of the nine wide
locks is just after the bridge. The gear is
anti-vandal locked so you will need to use the
British Waterways anti-vandal key. The canal
now creeps between the backs of tall buildings
festooned with steaming pipes and beneath
elaborate railway arches, all of which have a
certain faded grandeur. Tantalising glimpses of
Victorian buildings invite exploration, but
there is really nowhere to leave an unattended
boat. You can, however, moor for a rest at the
picnic area above the second lock. Finally the
canal crawls under an 18-storey office block
where a lock lurks amidst concrete pillars. The
Rochdale Canal Office is next to the top lock, so
if you haven't already done so, you must pay
your licence fee. Sharp right and sharp left
turns bring you to the start of the Ashton
Canal, and the climb to Fairfield Junction (see
page 129).

Manchester
All services. It is a pity that Manchester does
little to welcome canal travellers. The provision
of safe moorings would allow navigators to visit
what is one of Britain's finest Victorian cities, a
monument to 19thC commerce and the textile
boom. There is an incredible wealth of
Victorian buildings still surviving in spite of
redevelopment – the Town Hall and the
surrounding streets being a particularly rich
area (north of Oxford Street Bridge). St Peter's
Square, by the Town Hall, was the site of the
'Peterloo Massacre' in 1819, when a meeting
demanding political reform was brutally
dispersed by troops carrying drawn sabres.
Eleven people were killed and many more were
injured. The Free Trade Hall, home of the
Hallé Orchestra, is a little further along the
road. Built in 1856 on the site of the original
Free Trade Hall, it was badly damaged in
World War II, but was subsequently rebuilt to
its original Palladian design. The old Central
Station has now been converted into a £20
million conference and exhibition centre. There
is theatre, ballet and cinema, art galleries, a
wealth of interesting buildings and the superb
North Western Museum of Science and
Industry in Grosvenor Street. Victorian
shopping arcades, many pubs with an excellent
choice of good beer, many excellent restaurants
– one being an Indian tandoori house, in
Sackville Street, between the sixth and seventh
lock up, all a short walk from the canal. What a
pity that most navigators feel safest if they
charge through as quickly as possible.
Tourist Information Centres In Portland
Street, not far east of Ducie Street Junction
(061-247 3694), and in the Town Hall (061-236
1606).

Manchester Ship Canal
The Harbour Master, The Port of Manchester,
Manchester Ship Canal Co, Dock Office,
Manchester (061-872 2411). The canal was
opened in 1894 at a cost of £15½ million and
carries ships up to 15,000 tons displacement. It
is 36 miles long and connects the tidal Mersey
at Eastham to Manchester. The Weaver
Navigation, the Bridgewater and the
Shropshire Union connect with it.
Pleasure craft wishing to navigate on the Ship
Canal must complete an application form
demanding stringent standards of
seaworthiness (and third party insurance for
£50,000), and return it to the Harbourmaster at
the above address at least 48 hours before
entering the canal.

LICENCES

Rochdale Canal Company 75 Dale Street,
Manchester (061-236 2456). By the top lock. A
licence must be purchased for these important
2 miles of canal, which are usually open during
the cruising season from *09.00–19.00 every day*.

PUBS AND RESTAURANTS

There are many fine pubs in Manchester.
Peveril of the Peak Great Bridgewater
Street, Manchester. A superbly restored
building close to the old entrance to the now
abandoned Manchester & Salford Junction
Canal. Wilson's and Websters real ale and good
lunchtime bar snacks. Children welcome,
outdoor drinking area.
Crown Deansgate, Manchester.
Comfortable and well appointed pub offering a
good choice of *lunchtime* meals and snacks at all
times, Wilson's and Websters real ale. Handy
for the Castlefield Heritage Centre and
museums.
Kathmandu Tandoori 42–44 Sackville
Street, Manchester (061-236 4684). An
excellent and reliable Indian restaurant,
decorated with Kama Sutra murals. *L & D.
Closed B. Hols.*
Ordsall Ordsall Lane, Salford. West of
Hulme Locks. A good basic city pub with many
others close by. Wilson's real ale, *lunchtime*
meals and snacks at all times. Children
welcome.

The Rochdale Canal passes through the heart of Manchester, hemmed in by high walls and tall buildings.
David Perrott.

Worsley

This is a very interesting section of canal, well worth visiting. What was the original line of the canal leaves Waters Meeting through the vast Trafford Park Industrial Estate to cross the Manchester Ship Canal on the impressive Barton Swing Aqueduct (*open 09.00–17.00 every day*). There is a useful boatyard just to the north of the aqueduct – the closest canal services to the city centre. Curving through the suburbs of Salford the navigation reaches the village of Worsley and the entrance to the underground mines which provided its *raison d'être*. It is now possible for small shallow-draughted craft to navigate into the Delph to view the entrance tunnels where iron ore colours the water bright ochre. After Worsley the M62 motorway and its attendant slip roads cross the canal, which then heads west through parkland on its way to Leigh.

Worsley
Gt Manchester. EC Wed. PO, tel, stores, garage.
Originally an estate village dating from the 18th–19thC, now recognised as the birthplace of British canals. Coal had been mined in Worsley since the 14thC, originally from the surface, and later by sinking shafts. It is thought that a drainage sough, common in underground workings, may have provided the germ of the idea for an underground canal network to bring the coal out. John Gilbert, the Duke of Bridgewater's agent, probably designed the system, which included an inclined plane on a 1 in 4 gradient. Work started at the same time as the building of the canal to Manchester, and eventually 46 miles of tunnels were hewn out. A particular kind of double-ended tub boat was used underground, called a 'starvationer', carrying up to 12 tons of coal. The old canal basin at Worsley Delph, with its entrance tunnels to the mines, is still intact, and full length narrowboats can enter the wind – smaller craft can navigate the entrance tunnels. The basin is overlooked by Worsley Old Hall (now a restaurant), the half-timbered Court House and the Lantern Gallery. The church, by George Gilbert Scott, 1846, has a spire decorated with crockets and gargoyles – inside there is a rich collection of monuments to the Dukes of Bridgewater.

Salford
Gt Manchester. Although now merged with Manchester, Salford was granted its charter 80 years before that of its now larger neighbour. It has a fine new university, built in 1967, and a Roman Catholic cathedral dating from 1855. It is, however, most widely known as being the subject of many paintings by the artist L. S. Lowry (1887–1976). It is less widely known that he gained his inspiration by walking the streets of Salford for many years as a rent collector, only painting in the evenings and at weekends – a fact to which he would never willingly admit. There is a wonderful collection of his paintings in Salford Art Gallery, Peel Park.

Eccles
Gt Manchester. EC Wed. All services. Monks Hall Museum, Wellington Road, contains an important collection of Nasmyth machine tools and relics. *Closed Sun.*

Patricroft
Gt Manchester. All services. Here are the Bridgewater Mills, established in 1836 by Nasmyth, who invented the steam hammer. Now a Royal Ordnance factory.

Barton upon Irwell
Gt Manchester. PO, tel, stores, garage. In an interesting position overlooking the two canals. The richly decorated Catholic church is by Pugin, 1867.

Barton Aqueduct
One of the wonders of the waterways, it carries the Bridgewater Canal over the Manchester Ship Canal. Designed by Sir Edward Leader Williams, it was built in the early 1890s. Gates seal off the 234ft-long 800-ton section that swings at right angles to the Ship Canal over a central island. It replaced Brindley's earlier aqueduct over the Irwell. The aqueduct operates *daily 09.00–19.00 Mon–Thur, to 21.00 Fri–Sun.*

BOATYARDS

Ⓑ **Worsley Dry Docks** The Boatyard, Worsley. (061-793 6767). 🅦 Moorings, dry dock. Egerton Narrow Boats operate from here.

Ⓑ **Lorenz & Co** 26 Worsley Road, Worsley. (061-794 1441). Based just north of the Barton Swing Aqueduct at Barton Yard. 🅡🅦🅓 🅟 and gas close by). Boat building and repair, engine repairs, overnight moorings. The closest boatyard to the centre of Manchester.

Ⓑ **Brinks Boats** The Old Boatyard, Worsley. (061-728 1184). 🅦 (opposite) 🅓 Pump-out, gas, hire craft.

BOAT TRIPS

Lorenz & Co Address as above. Run regular summer Sunday afternoon trips from Worsley; other trips from Timperley and Manchester by arrangement.

Castlefield & Tiller Operate public trips on *Sun & B. Hols* from Worsley and Castlefield. Also private charter. Phone 061-748 2680 for details.

PUBS AND RESTAURANTS

🍺 **Bridgewater Hotel** Worsley. Canalside.

✕🍷 **Worsley Old Hall** Old Lane, Worsley. (061-799 5644). Choose from a French à la carte restaurant, or a 17thC-style Jacobean banquet. James Brindley stayed in this building while working on the new canal. *L (not Sat) & D (not Sun)*.

🍺 **Wellington Inn** 37 Worsley Road, Patricroft. Friendly canalside local offering Greenall Whitley real ale and *lunchtime* bar food. Children allowed in lunchtime (ask). *Opens 19.00 Sat.*

🍺 **Bridgewater Packet House** By bridge 47. A cosy corner pub serving Boddingtons real ale and *lunchtime* bar meals. *Opens 19.00 Sat.*

🍺 **Dutton Arms** Barton Road, Barton. A large canalside pub which features original plans for the Manchester Ship Canal. Boddingtons real ale and *lunchtime* bar meals. Children allowed in at lunchtime (ask).

🍺 **King's Head Hotel** 535 Barton Lane, Eccles. Near the swing aqueduct. Large open-plan pub offering good home-cooked food at *lunchtime*. Boddingtons real ale, outside drinking area. *Opens 19.00 Sat.*

Worsley, on the Bridgewater Canal. Iron ore colours the water bright ochre here. *Derek Pratt.*

Leigh

After the excitement of Barton and Worsley, the canal now passes through open farmland towards the mill town of Leigh, and its junction with the Leeds & Liverpool Canal. Raised canal banks beyond Boothshall Bridge reveal the problems of subsidence in this area, caused by mine workings. The colliery village of Astley Green is passed, and an industrial wasteland is entered. Soon the mill chimneys of Leigh appear, and the canal becomes the Leeds & Liverpool beyond Leigh Bridge. The familiar stop plank cranes of the Bridgewater finish here, and signs announce you are back in British Waterways territory. Wigan is 7¼ miles away (*see page 92*).

Leigh
Gt Manchester. EC Wed. All services. Once the archetypal mill town, most of the tall buildings and chimneys have now been demolished. In the market place you can see the fine Edwardian baroque Town Hall, built 1904–7, facing the battlemented church of St Mary.
Astley Green
Gt Manchester. PO, tel, stores. Canalside mining village dominated by a gaunt red brick Victorian church.

PUBS

🍺 **Bull's Head** Butts Bridge, Leigh. Canalside local serving John Smith real ale and *lunchtime* meals. Garden, accommodation.
🍺 **Foundry** 276 Chapel Street, Butts Bridge, Leigh. Autograph hunters' pub run by ex-England footballer, Alex Lindsay. Greenall Whitley real ale.
🍺 **Railway Hotel** Twist Lane, Leigh. A beer enthusiast's pub offering Tetley, Walkers, Jennings and Ind Coope Burton real ales. *Opens 12.00 & 19.00 (sometimes later)*.
🍺 **Bridge Inn** 7 St Helens Road, Leigh. The licensee of this large, quiet and comfortable pub is a waterways enthusiast. Greenall Whitley real ale and a good range of *lunchtime* food.
🍺 **George & Dragon** King Street, Leigh. A recently refurbished pub with a wide choice of food at *lunchtime*. Greenall Whitley real ale. Can be busy in the evening.
🍺 **Cart & Horses** Town Lane, north of bridge 59. Holt's real ale in a friendly pub.
🍺 **Boat House Inn** By bridge 58.

The Chesterfield Canal at Clayworth. *Derek Pratt.*

CHESTERFIELD

Maximum dimensions

Length: 72′
Beam: 7′
Headroom: 7′ 6″
(Craft of 8′ 6″ beam *may* be able to proceed as
far as Clayworth, depending on the height of
the superstructure).

Mileage

WEST STOCKWITH to
Drakesholes Tunnel: 6½
Hayton: 12
Retford Lock: 15¼
Oberton Lock: 22¼
WORKSOP Town Lock: 25½

Locks: 16

The Chesterfield Canal was surveyed and large-ly built by James Brindley, who did not survive to see its opening. He called a public meeting in Worksop in 1769 to launch his project, which was estimated to cost £100,000 and to take 4 years to build. Its object was to provide trade outlets for the industries based on lead, coal and other resources in the Chesterfield area. Up until then, products from the area had to go by pack mule to Bawtry and then down the River Idle to West Stockwith on the Trent.

Construction of the canal was authorised by Act of Parliament in 1771, and work started in July that year. Owing to the difficulty of building the 2895yd tunnel at Norwood, the work exceeded the 4-year estimate and the navigation was not opened until the 12 September 1777. Meanwhile the estimated cost of £100,000 rose to an actual £152,000 as a result of fraudulent dealings by the Company's agent John Varley and the main contractor, Hugh Henshall (James Brindley's brother-in-law). Traffic built up steadily to a peak of over 200,000 tons in 1848, but in that year the canal was bought by the Manchester & Lincoln Union Railway (later the Great Central). Traffic immediately began to fall off, and 10 years later was down to 110,000 tons. Mining subsidence hastened the decline of the waterway – Norwood Tunnel was particularly vulnerable – and the heavily locked section from Worksop to Chesterfield was unnavigable by 1896. By 1906, only 40 boats were left working the canal, and by 1939 a mere 20,000 tons were carried annual-ly. The navigation was temporarily resuscitated by the transport of munitions during the War, but came to an end in the 1950s, when the small traffic from Walkeringham brickworks (near Gringley) to the Trent finished.

During the 1960s voluntary working par-ties undertook an extensive programme of res-toration, and now the navigation is in good condition for pleasure craft. The restored sec-tion, saved in the nick of time from complete decay, runs from Worksop to West Stockwith, and has 16 locks.

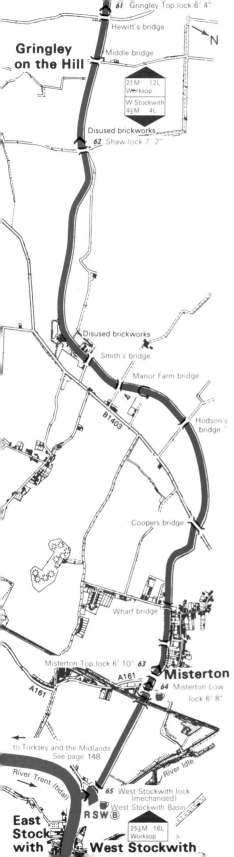

61 Gringley Top lock 6' 4"

Hewitt's bridge

Gringley on the Hill

Middle bridge

21M	12L
Worksop	
W Stockwith	
4½M	4L

Disused brickworks

62 Shaw lock 7' 2"

Disused brickworks

Smith's bridge

Manor Farm bridge

B1403

Hodson's bridge

Coopers bridge

Wharf bridge

Misterton Top lock 6' 10" **63**

A161 **Misterton**

A161 **64** Misterton Low lock 6' 8"

to Torksey and the Midlands
See page 148

River Trent (tidal)

River Idle

East Stock with

65 West Stockwith lock (mechanised)

R S W Ⓑ West Stockwith Basin

| 25½M | 16L |
| Worksop | |

West Stockwith

West Stockwith

The church spire of East Stockwith stands opposite the entrance to the Chesterfield Canal, just downstream of a sharp bend in the River Trent. The lock here is power-operated. Just above the lock is a basin housing a boatyard, a boat club, a slipway (apply to the lock keeper), and plenty of moored pleasure boats. A pub is nearby. This is obviously an excellent safe mooring to keep a sea-going boat. Leaving the basin for the gradual 15-lock rise to Worksop, the navigator must notice the tremendous contrast between the great tideway of the River Trent and this little canal, picking its way through the countryside. At Misterton there are two locks close together, with a canalside pub at the bottom. The canal's passage through the village is a pleasant one. At the new Cooper's Bridge the canal emerges into quiet farmland, heading south towards and then along the ridge of low hills that is capped by the village of Gringley. There are two disused brickyards along here – they supplied the canal with its last commercial traffic, sending bricks to Stockwith for the Trent Navigation. The yards were closed down in 1948. The course of the canal is entirely rural and pleasant, passing well established but often decaying farm buildings that are mostly built of the rich red brick that is so common in north Nottinghamshire. At Gringley top lock the little old lock cottage has a delightful garden, with creepers, climbing roses and flowers on the towpath.

Navigational note
The river lock at West Stockwith basin is power-operated. The operation of the lock is dependent on the height of the tide, but a passage can usually be made 2½ hrs before to 4½ hrs after high water.

Gringley on the Hill
Notts. PO, tel, stores, garage. Situated along the top of a ridge of hills, the village is about a mile's walk up from the canal. Its high situation is emphasised by the tower of the old windmill. Gringley is a quiet and attractive place with plenty of handsome, mellow houses – and a butcher's shop. The pretty stone church commands the village. Its most striking aspect inside is probably the north side of the nave, whose arches are leaning drastically outwards. A small rise on a level with the church tower gives a good view – over the flat lands to the north and the hills of Nottinghamshire to the south. On a clear day the pinnacles of Lincoln Cathedral can sometimes be seen, nearly 20 miles to the south east.

Misterton
Notts. PO, tel, stores, garage, banks (with irregular hours). Although attractive from the canal, this village is not really very fascinating. The two pubs are in the older part, which surrounds the curiously shaped church; a stubby spire stands heavily beside its rather low, flat nave roof. It was rebuilt in the 19thC after being struck by lightning. The village also has a thriving Methodist church, like most of the places in this area. (John Wesley came from nearby Epworth.)

West Stockwith
Notts. PO, tel, stores. An interesting riverside village at the junction not only of the Chesterfield Canal with the Trent but also of the River Idle with the Trent. The Idle was once a busy navigation up to Bawtry, so West Stockwith must have been a very prosperous port in days gone by. The village extends along the west bank of the River Trent, although bank raising measures over the years have shut out a view of the river from ground level. The houses are old, and remind one of a typical coastal village. The plain 18thC brick church preserves the illusion. East Stockwith is just across the river, tantalisingly out of reach. The two communities used to be connected by a ferry, but as so often on this river, the ferry has vanished. In a way, the total lack of communication with the other village, only 50yds away, serves to enhance the magical sense of remoteness that Stockwith possesses – especially when one sees the big barges appearing round the bend on every tide,

churning past the two villages and then as quickly disappearing again.

BOATYARDS

ⓑ **Milethorne Marine** The Yacht Basin, West Stockwith, nr Doncaster. (Gainsborough 890450). R S W D E Pump-out, gas, hire craft, overnight mooring, long-term mooring, winter storage, slipway, dry dock, chandlery, books and maps, boat building, boat and engine repairs, boat sales, boat fitting, toilet.

PUBS

🍺 **White Hart** Gringley on the Hill.

🍺 **Blue Bell** 1 mile from the canal, in Gringley. Bass real ale in a pub which *opens evenings only Mon–Fri.*

🍺 **White Hart** Misterton, near the church.

🍺 **Windmill** Misterton, near the church. *Fish & chips* nearby.

🍺 **Packet Inn** Canalside at Misterton Low Lock. Darley Thorne real ale and meals *lunchtime and evening.*

🍺 **Crown** Canalside, at West Stockwith Basin Real ale.

🍺 **Red Hart** West Stockwith. By the junction of the rivers Idle and Trent.

Drakeholes Tunnel on the Chesterfield Canal. *Derek Pratt.*

15¾M 11L
Worksop

W Stockwith
9¾M 5L

Clayworth

This is a thoroughly delightful stretch of canal.
Leaving Gringley Top Lock, the navigation
goes along the bottom of the ridge of hills,
before turning sharply south east and heading
for Drakeholes Tunnel (154yds). All the way
from Gringley to Drakeholes the canal is
heavily overhung by trees. Plenty of wildlife
lives here near the water's edge, especially
coots, moorhens, water rats, and bats. It is very
secluded, but the intimate feeling of the thickly
wooded cutting preceding the tunnel has been
ruined by the construction of a large road
bridge. The tunnel is cut through rock and is
mostly unlined. At the south end one emerges
to find a sharp corner at a mooring site, where
there is also a turning place for full-length
narrowboats, and a slipway owned by the
Retford & Worksop Boat Club. A handsome
pub stands nearby. Leaving Drakeholes, the
canal is still accompanied by woods as it reaches
Wiseton Park, passing the stern features of a
bearded man on the parapet of Old Man
Bridge. The canal then skirts the Park's kitchen
garden and heads off through a wooded cutting
to Clayworth. The straight road that crosses the
canal at Gray's Bridge is of Roman origin. The
navigation circles round the village, ending up
with a sharp turn to the right at Clayworth
Bridge. The white building by the bridge used
to be a pub (The White Hart). It is now a boat
club base, so a good lookout for other boats
should be maintained when negotiating the
bridge.

Clayworth
Notts. PO, tel, stores. A quiet and pleasant
village extending along a single main street.
The houses are of all periods, the new blending
well with the old. The Retford & Worksop Boat
Club is based at the old pub at Clayworth and
welcomes visitors to the clubhouse. There are
good moorings and a water tap here. In the old
days a passenger boat used to run every
Saturday from this pub to Retford, so that the
villagers of Clayworth, Hayton and
Clarborough could take their produce to
Retford Market. The goods were loaded into
the 'packet' boat on the Friday night, then the
people would return early on the Saturday
morning, leaving at 06.30 to reach Retford by
08.30. The boat used to return in the evening
when the market closed.

Wiseton
Notts. PO, tel. A superbly elegant estate village
set in a landscaped park, still clearly fulfilling
its original manorial function. Trees and grass
separate the various buildings, of which the
large stable with its handsome clock tower is
the most significant. The hall, a modern red
brick building which replaced the original in
1962, is well hidden behind high walls.

BOAT TRIPS

Norwood Packet Public trips *every 2nd & 4th
Sun in the month Apr–Sep*, and private charter,
from Drakeholes Basin. Details from
Chesterfield 37705.

PUBS

🍺 **Brewers Arms** Clayworth.
🍺✕ **Blacksmiths Arms** Clayworth.
🍺 **Griff Inn** An unusual shaped pub by
Drakeholes Tunnel. Bass and Websters real ale
and meals *lunchtime and evenings, but closed
Mon.*

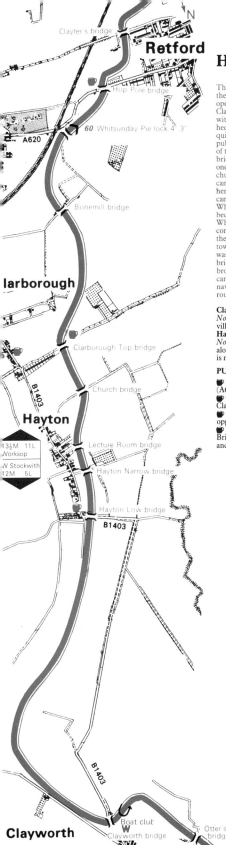

Hayton

The canal now leaves the woods and low hills to
the north and heads southwards through more
open farmland towards Retford. From
Clayworth to Hayton there is a 2-mile stretch
without a single bridge, only green fields and
hedgerows accompanying the navigation on its
quiet course. Approaching Hayton, there is a
pub by the bridge but otherwise the only signs
of the village are a succession of old farms and
bridges – one of them extremely narrow. Near
one of these bridges is the very ancient stone
church. At Clarborough Wharf there is another
canalside pub, with good moorings. South of
here the railway embankment draws near as the
canal arrives at the first lock for 9 miles.
Whitsunday Pie Lock is apparently so called
because a local farmer's wife baked a vast pie on
Whit Sunday for the navvies who had that day
completed construction of the lock. This lock is
the last wide lock on the canal as one travels
towards Worksop. The cottage near the lock
was built this century, of bricks fired at the
brickyards near Gringley and, naturally,
brought to this site by canal boat. Yet another
canalside pub is soon encountered, before the
navigation begins to follow its circuitous course
round East Retford.

Clarborough
Notts. PO, tel, stores, garage. An unexciting
village straggling along the main road.
Hayton
Notts. Tel. A quiet farming village, stretching
along the road parallel to the canal. The church
is near the canal and dates from 1120.

PUBS

🍺 **Hop Pole Inn** Canalside, at Hop Pole Bridge
(A620). Real ale, food, garden.
🍺 **Gate** Clarborough. Canalside, near
Clarborough top bridge.
🍺 **Kings Arms** Clarborough. *Fish & chips*
opposite.
🍺 **Boat Inn** Canalside, near Hayton Low
Bridge. Bass, Whitbread and Stones real ales,
and meals *at all times*.

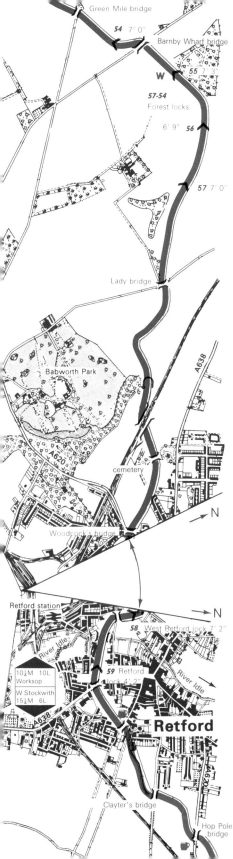

Retford

The canal's twisting passage through Retford is
outstandingly pleasant – though not by design.
It just happens that almost all the way through
the town, the canal is accompanied by green –
either grazing fields, or common land, or water
meadows (however unkempt), or at the west
end of the town by a long and treelined
cemetery. In the town centre one encounters
the first of the narrow locks, with a large canal
warehouse beside it. West of here the canal
crosses three minute aqueducts, then a double
bend and an old iron foot bridge lead to West
Retford Lock, overlooked by large trees and
old houses. Beyond the main road bridge the
canal is still lined by trees and bushes as it
invades the very middle of the extensive
cemetery. The busy East Coast railway line
crosses here, and while the navigation now
begins to meander through open farmland, the
noise of the frequent express trains thundering
along the track takes a long time to recede. In
the open countryside along here are the four
Forest Locks. At the third one up is a British
Waterways permanent mooring site; and there
is a water point right beside the top gate. The
straight road crossing at the nearby Barnby
Wharf Bridge was a Roman highway. It was, in
fact, the original course of the Great North
Road; but 200 years ago the citizens of Retford
got the road diverted to pass through their
town, thereby increasing its importance and
prosperity. They must now be equally relieved
to have rid themselves of it again.

East Retford
Notts. EC Mon, Wed. MD Sat. All services. A
market town with good railway connections
(passenger services in four directions) and light
industry. There is a funfair held on *23 March*
and a sheep fair on *2 October*. The market
square is the only area of any interest in
Retford, and this is indeed superb, with lots of
cheerfully uneven Georgian terraced houses
jumbled up with lesser, newer buildings. All
are put to shame by the flamboyant Town Hall,
built in 1868. In front of it is a stone called the
Broad Stone, and when a plague raged in the
town many years ago people making cash
transactions would put their coins into a
vinegar-filled vessel on this pedestal. The
vendor picking the money out of the vinegar
thus ran less risk of catching the disease from
the purchaser, it was thought.
East Retford Church A splendid cruciform
structure of great dignity and elegance, all set
about with battlements, pinnacles, and fine
foliate ornament. The nave is tall, and
incorporates a generous clerestory giving light
to the interior, while there is a peal of 10 bells in
the tower. Outside, the church is guarded by a
mean-looking black 24-pounder cannon,
captured at Sevastopol in 1855.
Bassetlaw Museum 40 Grove Street, Retford
(706741). Local history, archaeology,
applied art and social history of north
Nottinghamshire. *Open 10.00–17.00 Mon–Sat.
Closed Sun & B. Hols.*

PUBS
- **White Hart Hotel** The Market Place,
Retford (703671). *L & D daily.* Ancient
coaching establishment.
- **Clinton Arms** Retford, not far from Retford
Lock.
- **Hop Pole** Retford. Canalside.
- **Packet Inn** Canalside, at Gas House Bridge,
Retford. This used to be the terminus for the
weekly market boat from Clayworth.
- **Ship** Wharf Road, Retford.

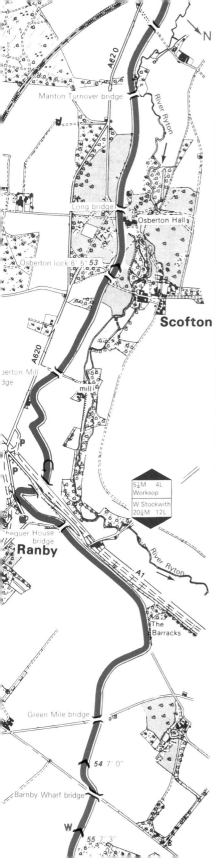

Osberton Park

Leaving Forest Top Lock, the canal now
wanders westwards before turning sharply
south as it meets the noisy A1 road. There used
to be a big army barracks here during the
1914–18 War, but now only a small cottage
survives as a reminder. The road follows the
canal very closely for over ½ a mile, and its
presence is deafening. Fortunately a thick
hedge serves to screen it. At Ranby the canal
begins once again to follow a winding course,
passing under the A1 before making for the
haven of Osberton Park. The little lock here,
where the towpath crosses over, introduces one
of the most attractive stretches of the whole
canal, passing through a country estate, which
looks as carefully maintained now as it
doubtless did in the 18thC. The canal goes
straight past the stables at Osberton Hall.
Manton railway viaduct, consisting of low but
heavily braced red brick arches dwarfs the little
accommodation bridge over the canal. Nearby
the long-standing pit heaps of Manton Colliery
have been landscaped and grassed.

Osberton Hall Built in 1806 by James Wyatt
and enlarged and altered in 1853 (Private).
Scofton
Notts. This is the tiny estate village for
Osberton Hall. It looks decayed now, but the
old stable block is impressive. It is, of course,
surmounted by a clock tower. The church,
built in 1830, has been completely restored, at
great expense. All the roof lead has been
renewed, the windows have been rebuilt, a new
red carpet has been laid, and central heating has
been installed. The inside of the church now
looks brand new, and for the visitor is a
refreshing sight.
Ranby
Notts. Tel, garages (on A1). A small rambling
village which manages to retain some charm in
spite of being practically on top of the A1. The
willow trees that line the canal bank near the
village are the gesture of a local tree-loving
landowner. There is a pub on the canal, the
only one for miles in either direction.

PUBS

🍺 **Chequers** Ranby. Canalside.

Worksop

Leaving Manton Colliery the canal now negotiates two locks before reaching Worksop. The canal's course into Worksop is fairly open, as the towpath is also a minor public road. There is a canal pub along here, and a good place to tie up for the Canal Tavern is at either side of the old Pickford's warehouse that straddles the canal. One can still see the trapdoors above the water where the goods used to be hauled straight up out of the boats. The British Waterways yard is just through the warehouse, and this is a remarkable oasis of privacy and quiet in the town centre. Worksop Town Lock is by the yard. Just beyond the lock, the navigation is very narrow for a short stretch. The remaining 20 miles of the canal to Chesterfield is no longer a through navigation although parts have been restored, and a trip boat operates on the summit level near Kiveton Park station. At the turn of the century there was little trade on the canal and the 3100yd tunnel on the summit level at Norwood collapsed because of mining subsidence. There is an attractive walk along the towpath of the old canal, and there are good railway connections from Worksop and Retford with the canalside stations of Kiveton Park and Shireoaks. The unnavigable section of the canal still feeds water into the navigable section.

Navigational note
The winding hole above Worksop Town Lock is suitable for full length (70ft) craft.

Worksop
Notts. EC Thur. MD Wed, Sat. All services. An unlovely town in the centre of the north Nottinghamshire coal field – which has contributed much to the present prosperity and ugliness of the area. Old buildings of note in Worksop are the Priory and its gatehouse.
The Priory Near Prior Well Bridge. The church dates from the 12thC, although it suffered badly under Henry VIII's policy towards monasteries. Much rebuilding has taken place since then: in fact in 1970–2 the superstructure was added to, incorporating a new spire. There are interesting paintings and monuments inside the church, and a gruesome relic from Sherwood Forest – a skull with the tip of an arrow embedded in it.
14thC Gatehouse This was given to the priory under a trust by the Duke of Newcastle.
Tourist Information Centre Queen's Buildings, Potter Street, Worksop (475531).

Within a few miles of the town there are some interesting places and some beautiful countryside to visit, although a car or a bicycle is needed to reach them. All around are the surviving woods of Sherwood Forest, while to the south of the town is the area called the Dukeries, each of the adjacent estates of Thoresby, Clumber and Welbeck having been owned by a duke. Welbeck is now an army college, Thoresby Hall and Park are open to the public. Clumber House was demolished in 1938 but the Park, owned by the National Trust, is one of its most visited properties. There are superb avenues of trees in this park. Three miles west of Worksop is an outstanding building well worth visiting. This is the tiny Steetley Chapel, which has been described by one expert as 'the most perfect and elaborate specimen of Norman architecture to be found anywhere in Europe'. There is a delightfully elaborate triple rounded porch and a beautiful apse. The windows are very narrow, so the interior is dark.

BOATYARDS

British Waterways Worksop Yard (Worksop 472788). R S W.

PUBS

🍺 **Fisherman's Arms** Church Walk, Worksop. 100yds south of the BWB yard. Home's real ale.
🍺 **French Horn** Potter Street, Worksop. ⅓ mile south of Town Lock. Stones real ale in a large basic pub.
🍺 **King's Head** Victoria Square, Worksop. 100yds north of Town Lock. Home's real ale and snacks in a refurbished pub.

EREWASH

Maximum dimensions

Trent Lock to Tamworth Road Bridge
Length: 78'
Beam: 14' 3"
Headroom: 7' 4"
Tamworth Road Bridge to Langley Mill
Length: 72'
Beam: 14' 3"
Headroom: 6'

Mileage

TRENT LOCK to
Sandiacre Lock: 3¼
Hallam Fields Lock: 5½
LANGLEY MILL: 11¾

Locks: 15

The Erewash is one of five canals built towards the end of the 18thC to carry coal from the pits of the Nottinghamshire/Derbyshire coalfield to the towns of the East Midlands. Completed in 1779 by the engineer John Varley, its success encouraged the promotion and construction, during the following decade, of the Cromford, Nottingham, Derby and Nutbrook Canals. The Erewash Canal is navigable for its entire 11¾-mile length from the River Trent to Langley Mill. Unlike its neighbours, the Cromford and Nottingham canals, the Erewash never came under railway control but remained independent until its absorption into the Grand Union system in 1932.

Nationalisation of the canals in 1947 brought the Erewash Canal under the administration of the British Transport Commission and in 1962 this body closed to navigation the upper section from Gallows Inn to Langley Mill. The need to supply water to the lower section for navigation and industry, however, meant that the upper section had still to be maintained, and boats were allowed to navigate

it upon application to the Commission and subsequently to its successor, the British Waterways Board. With the cessation of narrowboat carrying in 1952, such boats had been few, but the growing interest in pleasure boating resulted in more and more craft venturing up the canal from the popular River Trent. With increased use the canal gradually improved, and the news that the major portion of it was to be designated a 'remainder' waterway in the impending 1968 Transport Act was received locally with dismay. A public meeting led to the formation of the Erewash Canal Preservation and Development Association (ECPDA), a body consisting of representatives of boating and fishing interests, residents and local authorities. The need to convince local authorities of the value of the canal as an amenity was recognised at a very early stage and the association's efforts eventually met with success when in 1972 Derbyshire and Nottinghamshire County Councils agreed to share the cost, with the British Waterways Board, of the restoration of the canal to 'cruising waterway' standards.

Sandiacre Lock. *David Perrott.*

Long Eaton

The Erewash Canal leaves the Trent Navigation
at Trent Lock, a fascinating waterway junction.
A long line of moored boats, including several
houseboats nestling in the shade of the willow
trees, stretches from this junction for nearly ½
mile. To the south can be seen the towers of
Ratcliffe Power Station, peeping over the top of
Red Hill. At the two railway bridges is the
concealed entrance to an interesting basin,
known as Sheet Stores Basin, this was an
important railway depot where the tarpaulin
sheets for covering railway wagons were made
and repaired. (Nowadays, synthetic materials
have rendered tarpaulin obsolete in this field).
The basin was used for transhipment of coal
between boats and trains; now it is full of
pleasure boats, for a boatyard and a boat club
are based here. North of this basin one sees the
first of many canalside gardens that use the
canal as a perfect background. Approaching
Long Eaton, the canal passes under the A453
and then runs right beside it, a pleasant,
tree-lined urban boulevard. The centre of Long
Eaton is conveniently close. North of Long
Eaton Lock the old lace mills with their
ornamental capped chimneys overshadow the
navigation. To the east is the little River
Erewash, which despite its name is not joined
by the canal at any point. At Sandiacre is the
only surviving lock cottage on the Erewash
Canal (now the base of the ECPDA), and this
lock is particularly significant because the
Derby Canal used to branch off here. The
Derby Canal Company shared this toll office
until 1832, when they built their own lock
house on the opposite bank of their canal, by
the bridge. North of the big concrete bridge
carrying the A52 is Sandiacre; just through the
bridge is a delightfully landscaped free
overnight mooring, with a properly kept lawn,
flower beds and young trees. All services are
nearby. Nearly a mile further on is Pasture
Lock, in a pleasant setting between the partly
hidden railway sidings and some water
meadows. The towpath is in excellent condition
along the whole length of the navigation.

Navigational note
Trent Lock should always be left *full*, with the
top gates open, except when there is much
traffic about. This will ensure that any flotsam
coming down the canal is able to escape over
the bottom gates.

Derby Canal
The closure of the Derby Canal ended Derby's
link with the navigable waterways which dated
back to the time when the Danes sailed up the
River Derwent to found the settlement of
Deoraby. Navigation of the Derwent was never
easy – the absence of navigation works and,
later, the construction of water mills were
obviously a great handicap – but it was not until
1796, with the completion of the canal, that
navigation on the river ceased. The main line of
the Derby Canal commenced at Swarkestone on
the River Trent. Four locks, which like all the
rest were built to take Upper Trent barges,
lifted the canal to a junction with the Trent &
Mersey Canal. A ¼-mile section of this canal
was then used with the Derby Canal
recommencing just before Swarkestone Lock.
The main line then continued into Derby,
where it crossed the Derwent on the level, and
terminated at Little Eaton. A 9-mile-long
branch ran from Derby to connect with the
Erewash Canal at Sandiacre, and a short
navigable feeder connected with the upper
Derwent. The southern section (from Derby to
the Trent) was an early casualty due to the
double tolls payable on the Trent & Mersey,
and the abandonment of the length to Little
Eaton followed in 1935. The rest of the canal
survived until 1964, when a Warrant of
Abandonment was granted to the Derby Canal
Company.

Long Eaton
Derbs. EC Thur. MD Fri, Sat. All services. The
town is an important junction for canals,
railways and roads, and has little intrinsic
character of its own. Its prosperity was based
on the lace trade – nearby Nottingham has for a
long time been the national centre of this
industry. Long Eaton has an annual festival in
May.

Trent Lock

An important waterway junction and a long-established boating centre. For motorists, Trent Lock is at the dead end of a narrow lane – but they flock there, for it has great charm and two fine pubs. Sailing clubs on the Trent fill and confuse the scene here; while across the river the steep wooded slopes of Red Hill are overlooked by the steaming towers of Ratcliffe Power Station. The busy railway line to the south disappears into the hill via two splendid blackened portals. Boats navigating the Trent in this rather complicated area should beware of straying too near Thrumpton Weir.

BOATYARDS

ⓑ **Wyvern Marine** Sheet Stores Basin, Field Farm Road, Long Eaton (726539). Ⓡ Ⓢ Ⓦ Overnight mooring, long-term mooring, crane, slipway, boat building, DIY repair facilities, toilets, licensed club.

ⓑ **Mills Dockyard** Trent Lock, Long Eaton (733657). Ⓦ Overnight mooring, long-term mooring, winter storage, dry dock, chandlery, boat building, boat and engine repairs.

ⓑ **Davisons Sawley Marina** Trent Lock, Long Eaton (734278). Ⓡ Ⓢ Ⓦ Ⓓ Pump-out, gas, day hire boats, overnight mooring, long-term mooring, winter storage, chandlery, café, toilet, showers.

ⓑ **Davisons** Trent Lock, Long Eaton (734278). Ⓔ Overnight mooring, dry dock, boat building, boat and engine repairs, toilet. *Closed Sat & Sun.*

PUBS

🍺 **Barge Inn** On the B6540 south of Long Eaton Lock. Friendly games-orientated pub with a skittle alley and several pool tables. Shipstone's real ale.

🍺 **Navigation Inn** Trent Lock. Large popular pub with a fine riverside garden. Home's real ale and *lunchtime* food.

🍺✕ **Steamboat Inn** Trent Lock, on the Erewash Canal. (Long Eaton 732606). Built by the canal company in 1791, when it was called the Erewash Navigation Inn, it is now a busy and popular venue. The bars have been handsomely restored and decorated with suitably nautical objects. The real ale is brewed on the premises and includes a dark mild, a bitter and a stronger brew aptly called the 'Destroyer'. Bar and restaurant meals *lunchtime and evenings*. Garden, playground, children welcome.

The Steamboat Inn, Trent Lock. *David Perrott.*

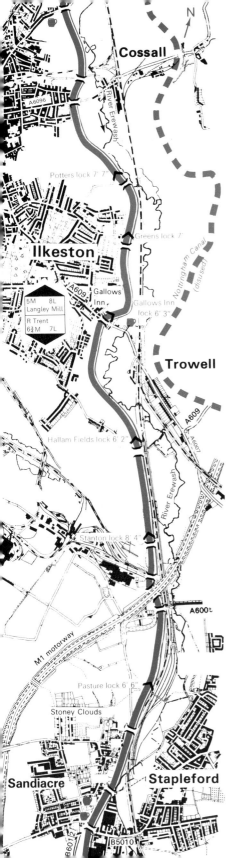

Ilkeston

At Stanton Gate the MI motorway looms up
and then crosses the canal on its way to
Sheffield. The outskirts of Ilkeston loom up on
the left side while, across the shallow Erewash
valley, the course of the disused Nottingham
Canal appears from the east, twisting along the
contours of the hillside. Like the Erewash
Canal, its course is generally northerly, but the
two waterways do not meet until Langley Mill.
Meanwhile the Erewash Canal passes extensive
low-lying playing fields before reaching the pub
at Gallows Inn Lock with PO and stores
nearby. North of Gallows Inn, the canal passes
housing estates on one side and water meadows
and a main line railway on the other. The town
of Ilkeston is on the hillside on the west side of
the canal. In spite of its proximity to these
built-up areas, the canal is relatively unspoiled,
and surprisingly rural.

Cossall
Notts. Tel. Cossall is a refreshing contrast to
Ilkeston, an attractive village built on top of a
hill, spreading gently down to the Nottingham
Canal. A narrow street winds among the
houses, all of which seem to be surrounded by
pretty gardens. The church contains an
oak screen made by village craftsmen: in the
churchyard is a memorial to a soldier killed at
Waterloo. The remains of a moat are to be
found just to the east.
Ilkeston
Derbs. EC Wed. MD Sat. Cinema. A market
and textile town, with a compact main square.
The parish church of St Mary dates from 1150
and has an unusual 14thC stone screen. The
annual 3-day fair is held in the Market Place in
Oct.
Sandiacre
Derbs. PO, tel, stores, garage, bank. These
services are all conveniently near the canal, but
there is not much of interest in this outskirt,
apart from the handsome mill by the canal, and
the church, which is set on a rise called 'Stoney
Clouds' (clearly visible from the canal at
Pasture Lock). The church features some
original Norman work inside, including
carvings. The font is 600 years old.
Nutbrook Canal
This little branch off the Erewash Canal used to
lead for 4½ miles almost parallel to the
Erewash Canal and slightly west of it. But it has
been unnavigable since 1895 and is now totally
abandoned. The short section that used to pass
through the old Stanton Ironworks was filled in
in 1962 and is now quite untraceable.

PUBS

Gallows Inn Canalside at Gallows Inn Lock.
Nicely refurbished pub run by an
ex-professional footballer. Shipstone's real ale,
food *lunchtime and evening.*
White Cow Nottingham Road, Ilkeston.
Shipstone's real ale and *lunchtime* food in a
friendly and comfortable pub.
Needlemakers Arms Kensington Street,
Ilkeston. A cheerful local offering Shipstone's
real ale and *lunchtime* food.
Warren Arms Derby Road, Stapleford.
Ansells real ale in a modernised coaching inn.
Lunchtime food.
Old Cross Stapleford, 1 mile east of B5010
bridge. Named after the Saxon cross which
once stood in the churchyard opposite, this
atmospheric pub dispenses Shipstone's real ale.
Plough Canalside, Sandiacre. North of the
main road bridge. Fine canalside garden with
good moorings. *Lunchtime food Mon–Sat.*
Red Lion Hotel (Nottingham 399069). By
the Padmoor moorings, Sandiacre. Large
canalside pub and steak bar serving Kimberley
real ale. Food *lunchtime and evenings (booking
required for steak bar)*, garden, children's room.
Music at weekends.

Langley Mill

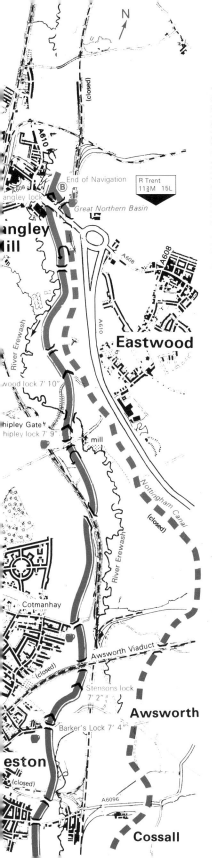

The northernmost section of the Erewash Canal
is more isolated than the rest, and is definitely
more rural and attractive. As the tentacles of
Ilkeston are left behind, a big trestle viaduct
across the valley is passed; the inconspicuous
River Erewash and beyond it the Nottingham
Canal continue to wind their ways northwards.
There are two splendid old canal buildings
beside Shipley Lock – one was a stable and the
other a slaughterhouse for worn-out canal
horses. Just above the lock, the River Erewash
creeps under the canal, which is carried above it
on a very small aqueduct. Since this river is the
county boundary between Derbyshire and
Nottinghamshire, the canal now enters
Nottinghamshire. Beyond the next very
pleasant rural stretch is Langley Mill, where
the canal terminates at the Great Northern
Basin beyond the final lock. Boatmen who have
navigated the whole of the Erewash to this
point are invited to call at the cottage just above
the old junction in order to obtain a free
facsimile of the old Erewash Canal Company's
bylaws.

Great Northern Basin
This restored basin once formed the junction of
the Erewash, Cromford and Nottingham
canals. A feeder enters here from Moorgreen
reservoir. Since it passes through a coal field on
its way to the basin, it brought down a lot of
coal silt – which over the years filled up the
Great Northern Basin. Now the Erewash Canal
Preservation & Development Association has
restored the basin and lock, so that boats may
reach a good mooring site with an enjoyable
pub beside it. The Nottingham and Cromford
canals can never be restored here, for their
closure was necessitated by mining subsidence
– although substantial lengths of both canals are
still in water, away from Langley Mill. The
Cromford Canal Society runs horse-drawn trips
from Cromford Wharf during the summer
(Wirksworth 3727). Both canals pass through
an interesting mixture of heavily industrial
surroundings and quiet open countryside. The
northern 5 miles of the Cromford Canal, from
Ambergate to Cromford (a length still in water)
is strongly recommended to all walkers,
country lovers and especially industrial
archaeologists. Explorers will find all kinds of
exciting things, including two aqueducts and a
fine old pumping station regularly in steam
(Wirksworth 3727 for details).
Langley Mill
Derbs. EC Wed. Near the head of the Erewash
Canal, with the little Erewash river going past
it. Langley Mill stoneware pottery is made here
in a very modern works.
Eastwood
Notts. EC Wed. PO, tel, stores, garage, bank.
Up on the hill east of the Great Northern Basin,
this mining town is best known as the
childhood home of D. H. Lawrence. He was
born at 8a Victoria Street, and the early part of
'Sons and Lovers' is set in the town. At the Sun
Inn a meeting in 1843 between local coal
owners and iron masters led to the construction
of the Midland Railway.

BOATYARDS

Ⓑ **Langley Mill Boat Co** Great Northern
Basin, Langley Mill (760758). RSWDE
Overnight mooring, long-term mooring, winter
storage, slipway, dry dock, crane, boat
building, boat and engine sales and repairs,
toilet.

PUBS

🍺 **Great Northern** At Great Northern Basin
(the railway company were once owners of the
canal). An excellent local pub serving
Kimberley real ale and food *lunchtime and
evenings.* Canalside garden.
🍺✕ **Shipley Boat Inn** (Langley Mill 530313).
100yds west of Shipley Lock. A very handsome
pub/restaurant. Castle Eden real ale. Garden
with swings. *Bar lunches daily, D Tue–Sat.*
🍺 **Bridge Inn** Awsworth Road, Ilkeston.
Canalside pub with a large garden. Ind Coope
real ale and meals *lunchtime and evenings.*
🍺 **Bridge Inn** Bridge Street, Cotmanhay. Small
canalside local offering Kimberley real ale and
snacks. Garden with swings.

Great Northern Basin, the terminus of the Erewash Canal. *David Perrott.*

FOSSDYKE & WITHAM

Maximum dimensions

Fossdyke Navigation (Torksey to Lincoln)
Length: 75′
Beam: 15′ 3″
Headroom: 12′
Witham Navigation (Lincoln to Boston)
Length: 75′
Beam: 15′ 3″
Headroom: 9′ 2″

Mileage

TORKSEY to
Saxilby: 5½
Brayford Pool, Lincoln: 11
Bardney: 20½
Southrey: 23¼
Kirkstead: 26¾
Dogdyke: 31¼
Anton's Gowt: 40¼
BOSTON Grand Sluice: 42¾

Locks: 3

The Fossdyke Navigation was built in about 120 AD by the Romans, and is the oldest artificially constructed waterway in the country which is still navigable. It was designed to connect the River Witham (made navigable by the Romans) to the Trent and the Humber. The two navigations were used by the Danes when they invaded England, and later by the Normans to carry stone to build Lincoln Cathedral. Subsequently the Fossdyke and the Witham navigations became the responsibility of various riparian landowners, and of the church. They gradually deteriorated and by the beginning of the 17thC were virtually impassable. But King James I transferred the Fossdyke to the Corporation of Lincoln, and from that time conditions improved. Acts of Parliament were passed in 1753 and 1762 for straightening and dredging both navigations, and in 1766 the Grand Sluice at Boston was built, to protect the Witham from the damaging effects of tides and floods. In the 18thC and 19thC further improvements were made, many related to the extensive drainage systems carried out throughout the Fenlands. Thus over a period of centuries the two navigations came to assume the wide, straight course that is so characteristic of them today.

In 1846 the navigations were leased to the Great Northern Railway Company, and immediately their revenue began to fall. Railway competition continued, and by the end of the 19thC both navigations were running at a loss. After a period of dormancy the Witham and Fossdyke navigations became established cruising waterways, as pleasure boats replaced the last surviving commercial operators.

Today their isolation and total lack of development attracts many, while their survival preserves the pleasures of visiting Lincoln by boat; also Boston is one of the vital links between the inland waterway system and the open sea.

The famous Glory Hole in Lincoln. *Derek Pratt.*

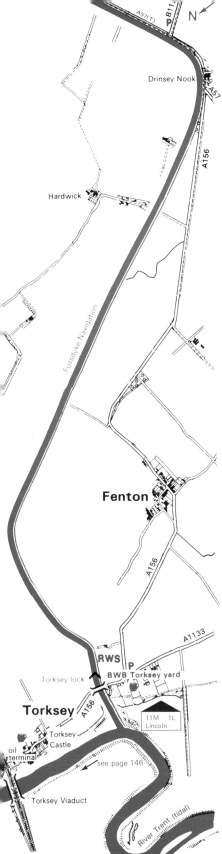

Torksey

The Fossdyke Navigation dates from Roman
times and is the oldest artificial navigation in
Britain. It leaves the tidal Trent at Torksey, ½
mile south of the railway viaduct. The lock may
be operated only by the resident keeper, who
should, if possible, be given notice of arrival
(Torksey 202). The lock may be used at nearly
all states of tide. Although the village is some
way to the north, there are plenty of services
available at the lock, including a grocery/
chandlery, a garage and a pub. There is a good
restaurant in the village. A great number of
pleasure boats are moored above the lock.
Leaving Torksey the canal twists slightly before
settling down to a series of long, wide, dead
straight reaches flanked by high banks. This
sets the pattern for the course of the navigation
all the way to Boston, which is 44 miles but
only two locks from Torksey. The long straight
reaches make the navigation somewhat
unexciting, as the banks prevent boatmen from
seeing much of the countryside; but the canal is
quiet and pleasant, and the green banks
harbour plenty of wildlife, while cattle browse
by the water. At Hardwick there used to be a
ferry across the canal. At the end of a very long
straight a busy main road joins, and the canal
completely loses its privacy. They curve
together towards Saxilby, passing a garage and
an AA telephone box.

Torksey
Lincs. PO, tel. Once a Roman port, but now a
small riverside village quite separate from the
thriving settlement centred on the lock. The
main feature is the ruined castle, whose gaping
Tudor façade is best seen from the Trent. The
17thC pub houses a restaurant. A short distance
north of the railway is the site of Torksey
Pottery, now completely vanished. It was
established in 1802 by William Billingsley, a
noted porcelain decorator who previously had
worked at Pinxton. Although an excellent
decorator, Billingsley was not a sound business
man, and the pottery closed down after 3 years.
Examples of his work can be seen in Lincoln's
Usher Art Gallery.

BOATYARDS

British Waterways Torksey Yard at Torksey
Lock. (Torksey 202). R S W

PUBS

🍺 **White Swan** Torksey. Near the lock. Also a
caravan and camping site.
🍺✗ **Hume Arms** Torksey (613). An attractive
old pub with two bars, situated 300yds from the
junction of the Fossdyke and Trent
navigations. A la carte menu with lots of fish
specialities. *L & D every day.*
🍺 **Carpenters Arms** Fenton.

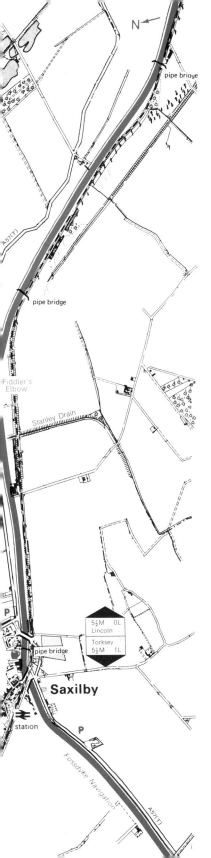

Saxilby

The main road clings to the canal all the way
into Saxilby, where it disappears behind
houses. It seems strange that the railway bridge
in Saxilby is the first one since Torksey, 5½
miles away to the north west. Emerging from
the railway bridge one finds the main street of
this attractive village laid out right beside the
navigation. The canal is below the level of the
street, but there are plenty of excellent
moorings, and two pubs just across the road.
Unfortunately the railway makes quite a lot of
noise. Leaving Saxilby, the canal is rejoined by
the busy main road, the A57, which runs right
beside it again for 1½ miles. As the road finally
moves away, the Gainsborough–Lincoln
railway line moves in to take its place on the
other bank, although separated from the canal
for much of the way by a low hedge. After a few
industrial works on the way out of Saxilby, the
canal is entirely in countryside, green and flat.
For most of this stretch, the towers of the
mighty Lincoln Cathedral are clearly visible in
the distance. As usual the canal's course
consists mainly of a series of dead straight
reaches broken up by occasional corners.

Saxilby
*Lincs. PO, tel, stores, garage, bank, station, fish
& chips.* The presence of the Fossdyke Canal
has clearly determined much of the layout of
the village, although the siting of the church
over ½ mile to the north has obviously
provided another focal point, and as a result
Saxilby extends between the two. All the
buildings in the main street face the waterway,
which is a welcome change for canal veterans,
and a line of cherry trees completes the scene.
The church is pretty, and has a generous
Perpendicular clerestory. Inside the church are
the alabaster figures of a knight and his lady;
they date from the 14thC, but are badly
defaced.

PUBS
🍺 **Sun** Saxilby. Canalside. *Fish & chips*
nearby.
🍺 **Ship** Saxilby. Canalside, near the Sun.
🍺 **Anglers Hotel** Saxilby.
🍺✕ **Bridge Hotel** Saxilby (Lincoln 702266).
Near the canal.

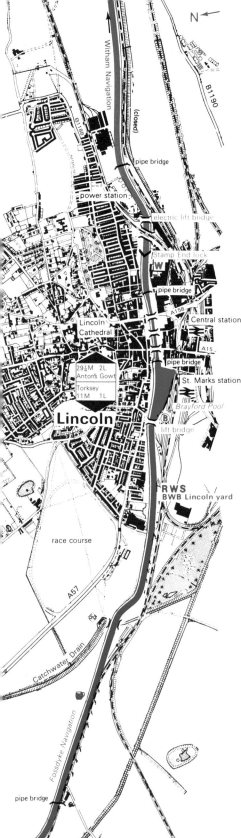

Lincoln

This is in parts a fascinating stretch of
waterway. The approach of Lincoln is marked
by the magnificent towers of the cathedral on
the hill. Passing the remarkable isolated Pye
Wipe pub on the canal bank, the Fossdyke
bends briefly as it reaches Lincoln Racecourse,
which is edged by trees. Then a long line of
moored pleasure boats leads to a lift bridge
operated by British Rail. This bridge is
normally left open at night and at weekends – at
other times, just hoot. Beyond this bridge, the
navigation widens out dramatically into the vast
expanse of water known as Brayford Pool.
There is a boatyard here and boat clubs.
Boatmen should resist the temptation to cruise
all over this lake, since much of it is heavily
silted: it is advisable to keep to the north side.
Continuing straight through the pool, boatmen
will see the River Witham flowing in as an
unnavigable stream at the south corner, and
from here onwards (eastward) the Fossdyke
Canal is replaced by the Witham Navigation.
Leaving Brayford Pool, one passes under the
new concrete bridge; here the channel becomes
extremely narrow and goes straight through the
heart of old Lincoln, passing through the
famous and well-named 'Glory Hole', an
ancient half-timbered building astride the
navigation. Lincoln High Street runs over the
heavily vaulted bridge that carries this house.
East of the Glory Hole the navigation continues
its narrow course along a pleasantly landscaped
stretch before the channel widens out, passing
the old flour mills that once used barges for
shipping the grain. Further on are Stamp End
Lock and sluices: the lock keeper lives across
the road, and will come to operate the lock and
its swing footbridge. The top gate has no
paddles, for it is simply raised *à la guillotine* into
a steel framework to let the water rush in and
the boats pass underneath. Beyond the next
railway bridge is another, larger bridge with a
headroom of about 5ft. An operator should be
summoned by sounding your horn. One moves
out into uncluttered, flat landscape and
wonders at the difference between the
Fossdyke Canal and the River Witham. To the
west is Lincoln Cathedral, standing proudly on
the hill above the town.

Navigational note
Water levels on the River Witham can change
rapidly – leave some slack in your lines when
mooring, and use the anchor as an added
precaution.

Lincoln
All services. Lincoln is a very fine city, with a
vast amount for the visitor to see. Once the
Celtic settlement of Lindon, it became Lindum
Colonia, a Roman town; and many Roman
remains have been discovered. Plenty of these
traces can be seen around the town. The old
part of Lincoln is of course grouped around the
cathedral, which sits on a hill to the north of the
river, overawing the city and the surrounding
countryside for miles. There are some splendid
rows of houses in the Close and just outside it,
where the steep and narrow cobbled streets
have remained unchanged for centuries, and
motor traffic can hardly penetrate.
Lincoln Cathedral This very splendid building
dominates the city and should certainly be seen
by visitors to Lincoln. The original Norman
cathedral was begun in about 1074, but a fire
and an earth tremor in the next century made
two extensive restorations necessary. The
present triple-towered building is the result of
rebuilding in Early English style begun in 1192
after the second disaster, although the
magnificent central tower (271ft high) was not
finished until 1311. The vast interior contains
an abundance of fine stone monuments and
wood carvings, and in the Cathedral Treasury is
one of the original copies of the Magna Carta.
Lincoln Castle Built as a stronghold for
William the Conqueror in 1068, it stands on the

crest of the hill close to the cathedral. Over 6 acres of lawns and trees are enclosed by the thick walls, the two towers and the Cobb Hall – a 14thC addition. The Observatory Tower and the old keep were built on separate mounds on the south side of the castle. The keep is now a mere shell, but the Observatory Tower is in good repair and there is an excellent view of the surrounding area from the top. Cobb Hall, a lower battlemented tower, was built in the north east corner of the castle and was a place of imprisonment and execution.

Brayford Pool
This great sheet of water separates old Lincoln from industrial Victorian Lincoln. It joins the Fossdyke Canal to the Witham Navigation, and provides the navigator with a welcome relief from the long straight stretches of navigation on either side of Lincoln.

BOATYARDS

British Waterways Lincoln Yard Fosse Bank South, Lincoln (20148). R S W.
Ⓑ **Lincoln Marina, James Kendall & Co** Brayford Pool, Lincoln (26896). R W D Gas, overnight mooring, long-term mooring, winter storage, slipway, dry dock, chandlery, boat sales, toilets, licensed bar.

PUBS

🍺✕ **Green Dragon** Broadgate, Lincoln (24950). By main road bridge 300yds east of the Glory Hole. Medieval pub beside River Witham.
🍺 **Royal William IV** North east corner of Brayford Pool. Old pub.
🍺✕ **Pye Wipe Inn** Canalside, 2 miles west of Lincoln. Very isolated pub, with moorings. Terrace overlooking the Fossdyke.

Lincoln Cathedral.

N ←

Five Mile House

24M   1L
Anton's Gowt

Lincoln
5¼M   1L

Washingborough Fen

Fiskerton

Cherry Willingham

B1190

Washing borough

Greetwell Hall

Washingborough

Leaving Lincoln, the River Witham heads due east in a series of straight, wide reaches. The landscape is similar to that seen from the Fossdyke, but the river follows the bottom of a wide valley. Right beside the navigation is a railway line which accompanies the river for most of the way to Boston, but is now open only as far as Bardney. There are no passenger trains, but closed riverside stations along the way remind the traveller of the former service. To the west, the towers of Lincoln Cathedral are visible from the river for about 10 miles out of Lincoln. Overhead, RAF transport planes approach the landing strip at Waddington airfield, 5 miles south of Lincoln. There are several villages on the hills overlooking the Witham; to the south is Washingborough, all trees and chimneys, while opposite is Greetwell Hall and its little stone church. Further east is the unappealing sprawl of Cherry Willingham, and then Fiskerton. At the end of this section is the old Five Mile House station: this is, predictably, exactly 5 miles from Lincoln Cathedral. The former ferry service has been replaced by a steel footbridge.

Fiskerton
Lincs. PO, tel, stores, garage. The name of this village comes from 'fisher's town', for in the old days it was a fishing village. Once, fishing boats could sail right up to Fiskerton Church on the tide. Later, the fens here were drained and the river diverted into its present straight course. Since then Fiskerton has stood back from the river. However when the river breached its banks in 1962, the water once again reached the church. The village is full of new housing. The church is curious, having the only round tower in Lincolnshire.
Washingborough
Lincs. PO, tel, stores, garage. A pretty village on the south side of the Witham valley. There are some attractive stone terraced cottages and many trees. This has clearly become a smart commuter village.

PUBS
🍺 **Carpenter's Arms** Fiskerton.
🍺 **Five Mile House** Fiskerton (in the village, not on the river).
There are several pubs in Washingborough.

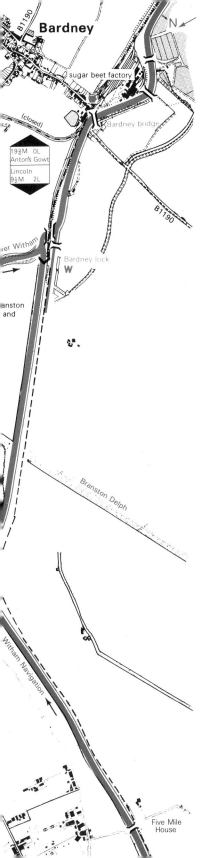

Branston Island

Leaving Five Mile House, where,
paradoxically, no house stands, the river
continues eastwards for nearly 2 miles through
the unchanging flat and empty landscape. Then
it turns south east and maintains this general
course right through to Boston. There is a small
pumping station at the point where the old
course of the river branches off round a loop to
the north, forming a large island known as
Branston Island. Meanwhile the navigation
runs in a straight line to Bardney Lock, the
only lock between Lincoln and Boston. Below
the lock, the old course of the river flows in
again from the north, the railway crosses and a
river-sized drain enters from the north west.
(Boats heading *upstream* at this point should be
sure to pass under the railway bridge and turn
immediately left.) The village of Bardney is
near the next bridge; pubs and fish & chips are
close here, but access is poor with no form of
wharf or jetty at which to land. The big
industrial buildings here are the famous
sugar-beet factory works.

Bardney
Lincs. PO, tel, stores, garage, banks. A small
village to the east of the river, on a slight rise.
Bardney is attractive, with a mellow 15thC
church and a pleasant village green. The parish
almshouses by the green were built in 1712.
There are the remains of a Cistercian abbey to
the north of the village. Bardney has become
well known in recent years as the scene of music
festivals; in fact the site is to the south east of
the village, towards Southrey. Bardney station
is closed but the sugar-beet factory keeps the
line open for goods between here and Lincoln.
Downstream, the line is now closed.

PUBS
● **Railway** Bardney, by the old station.
Telephone outside, and *fish & chips* nearby.
● **Jolly Sailor** Bardney. Near the railway.
●✕ **Nags Head** Bardney. In the village centre.
Food.
● **Angel Hotel** Bardney.
● **Tyrwhitt Arms** Short Ferry, between
Bardney and Fiskerton. Snacks, caravan site.
Access for boats by sailing north from Bardney
Lock up the old course of the Witham.

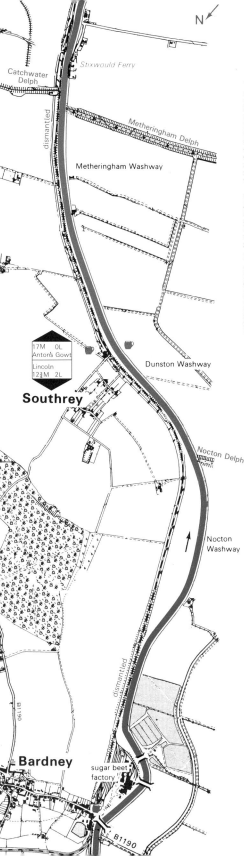

Southrey

Two bridges over the river connect the Bardney sugar-beet works with its associated settling ponds. The big ungainly buildings of the factory continue to dominate the flat landscape for several miles. The river flows between high banks to Southrey, passing the drain (or field dyke) called Nocton Delph. At Southrey there are two pubs facing each other across the water connected by a small ferry. There are occasional farms on the south bank; the closed railway continues to hug the other side of the navigation to Stixwould. There is an ancient wooden ferry there, now no longer used.

Southrey
Lincs. PO, tel, stores. A small village of little intrinsic interest, but with reasonable river access. The little wooden church, with its belfry, was built by the villagers in 1898. A mile to the north, in undulating countryside, are the ruins of Tupholme Abbey, founded in 1160.

PUBS
🍺 **Copper Hood** Southrey. On north (Lindsey) side of river.
🍺 **White Horse Inn** Dunston Fen, Metheringham. (Bardney 398341). This homely and welcoming pub offers bar meals *lunchtime and evenings*, and a variety of services for boaters, including: moorings, children's facilities, games room, showers, laundry, shop, Unigas butane, telephone.

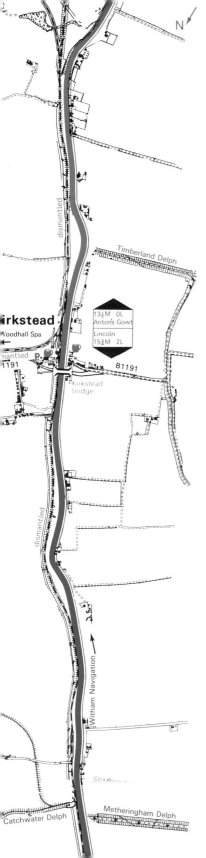

Kirkstead Bridge

The river continues on its straight course
through the quiet flat Lincolnshire countryside.
At Kirkstead there is a large new bridge –
virtually a viaduct – built in 1968 to replace an
older, low-level bridge. Unfortunately there is
no proper place to moor. South of Kirkstead,
the river is flanked on one side by the old
railway line and on the other by a minor road
linking many old farms and cottages along the
river bank.

Woodhall Spa
*Lincs. EC Wed. PO, tel, stores, garage, bank,
cinema.* A curious resort town in the woods a
mile north east of Kirkstead Bridge. The town
grew up in Victorian times after waters rich in
mineral salts were discovered in 1824. It has the
characteristic atmosphere of most English 'spa
towns'. There is a very popular 'Kinema'
tucked away in the woods; also the town boasts
Lincolnshire's only championship golf course.
Kirkstead Abbey ¾ mile east of Kirkstead
Bridge is a solitary finger of masonry about 30ft
high. This is all that remains of the enormous
Cistercian monastery known as Kirkstead
Abbey, founded in 1139. The trained eye can
recognise the former fishponds attached to the
monastery ground.
St Leonard's Church, Kirkstead Originally an
extramural chapel of the abbey, the church was
built in the mid 13thC, and survives largely
intact. It contains a 13thC wooden screen, one
of the oldest in the country, and an effigy of a
knight of the same period. The church is just a
few hundred yards north east of the bridge.

PUBS

🍺 **King's Arms** Kirkstead. On the west bank
of the river.
🍺 **Railway Hotel** Kirkstead. On east bank near
the station.

Dogdyke

The river continues southward on a winding course, providing a pleasant contrast to the former straight navigation. The old railway line runs in a straight line over to the east. Along the Kesteven bank are a number of farm cottages served by a minor road. The old junction with the Horncastle Canal can be seen as a slight dent in the east bank. At the three-arched Tattershall Bridge there is a pub and a grocer's shop, but no moorings. A mile from Tattershall Bridge is Dogdyke beyond the old steam pump, an attractive place where there is a boatyard, a restaurant and another riverside pub. Coningsby airfield is nearby: one end of the runway is near the river, so navigators may find aircraft screaming over them at a height of perhaps 100ft. This can be disconcerting on an otherwise quiet summer's afternoon. South of Dogdyke there is a small landing stage on the west bank; this marks a caravan site with facilities useful to those on boats (shop, shower gas, water etc). Beyond it are the houses of Chapel Hill, where the Kyme Eau or Sleaford Navigation joins (see below). Beyond Chapel Hill, the river becomes straight and wide once again, with piling to protect and strengthen the bank on one side and reeds on the other. Boston Stump, the tower of the church, can be seen from here. It is 9 miles away.

Chapel Hill
Lincs. PO, tel, stores, garage. A pleasantly compact tiny village at the entrance of Kyme Eau into the Witham.

Dogdyke
Lincs. Tel. A curious riverside settlement with a pub and boatyard on one side and a restaurant opposite. The ferry still works. Pleasure boats moor where the River Bain joins the navigation. The old railway station is now occupied by a residential caravan site. A nearby signpost indicates 2½ miles to New York and 12 miles to Boston. One is reminded that the names of two settlements in the New World originated here.

Dogdyke Pumping Station Between Tattershall Bridge and Dogdyke. An 1855 steam beam-engine and scoop-wheel. *Open 13.30–17.00 first Sun in each month May–Oct.* Admission charge.

Tattershall Castle 1 mile north east of Tattershall Bridge. Only the keep of this superb building remains. The castle was rebuilt in brick in the 15thC for Ralph Cromwell, Treasurer of England 1434–5. Stone was used only for some windows and door frames. Best approach is on foot along the derelict Horncastle Canal, which used, at one time, to feed the moat at Tattershall Castle. *Open daily.*

Horncastle Canal This navigation, 10 miles long, was built 1792–1802 to serve the small country town of Horncastle. It left the River Witham ½ mile upstream of Tattershall Bridge, but now an embankment has been built over the junction in the cause of flood prevention, so those travelling on the river must look carefully to discover any trace of the junction. The remains of the first lock are about 300yds from the river. Nearer Horncastle parts of the canal are still in water, and the town basin survives. It was abandoned in 1885.

Kyme Eau Sleaford Navigation Society, Red Gables Farm, Pointon Fen, Sleaford (240501). Now navigable through Kyme Lock (BWB key needed) for over 4 miles to Cobblers Locks. Full restoration to Sleaford is planned.

BOATYARDS
Ⓑ **Belle Isle Marina** Dogdyke (Coningsby 42124). Ⓦ Overnight mooring, long-term mooring, slipway, toilets, showers.

PUBS AND RESTAURANTS
🍺 **Crown** Chapel Hill.
🍺 **Packet Inn** Dogdyke. Riverside.
✕🍷 **Captain's Table** Dogdyke. (Coningsby 42434). Riverside restaurant. Mooring.
🍺 **Royal Oak** Tattershall Bridge. Shop nearby.

Round House Farm

The river continues south east in familiar straight, wide reaches with occasional bends of a few degrees that do little to break the monotony. The navigation is accompanied by the disused railway line on one side and high grassy banks on the other. Cattle graze on the banks. All around, but hidden from those in boats by the high bank, is a flat fenland landscape.

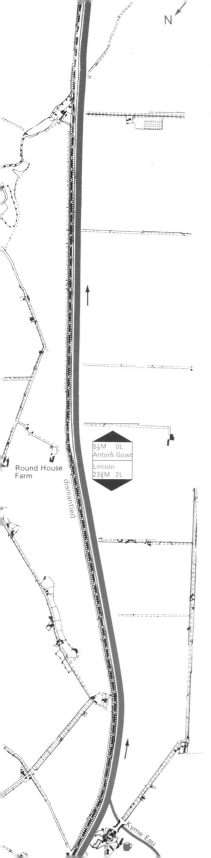

N

Round House
Farm

dismantled

5½M   0L
Anton's Gowt

Lincoln
23¾M   2L

Kyme Eau

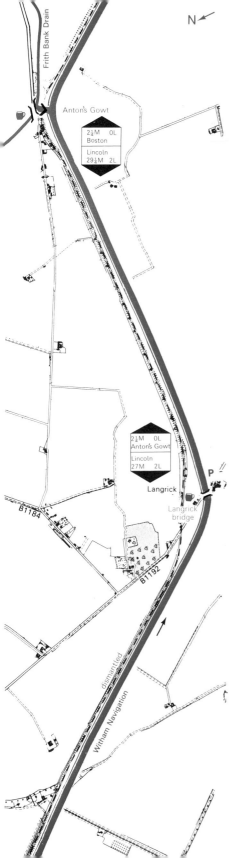

Langrick

At Langrick the river is crossed by a big iron girder bridge as it curves round to head due east for 2 miles. At the end of this reach is Anton's Gowt; there is a lock and its cottage here, for this is the entrance into the great network of waterways known as the Witham Navigable Drains, and navigators with time to spare can easily continue through to Boston by this alternative route and will, as a reward, find good moorings in the *centre* of Boston. At Anton's Gowt there is a sailing club near the lock. The river turns here on its final course to Boston and the sea.

Witham Navigable Drains
This remarkable network of waterways north of Boston exists to drain and irrigate the flat and highly vulnerable tract of fenland. The network is a vital part of the local economy and of the defence of the area against the encroachment of the North Sea. Castle Dyke Drain, Houghbridge Drain, Newham Drain, West Fen Drain, Medlam Drain, Stonebridge Drain and the Maud Foster Drain are usually navigable *early May–mid Sep*. Craft of 75ft × 18ft can pass through Anton's Gowt Lock, the limiting size at Cowbridge is 62ft × 11ft 5in. Information regarding water levels should be obtained by ringing the Witham Fourth Internal Drainage Board on Boston 65226 before you venture in. The key to Cowbridge Lock is held by Keightley & Sons, 156 Willoughby Road, Boston (63616). However, one should always remember that navigation is not the top priority of the drainage authority: sometimes a navigator is brought up sharply by a low bridge, often in a place where the channel is no wider than 30ft for several miles. Anton's Gowt Lock is the only entrance to these waterways. The best (widest) course is to head east from here, along Frith Bank Drain for 2 miles, to the great junction of waterways at Cowbridge Lock. From here one may go north towards the Lincolnshire Wolds, or south into Boston along the Maud Foster Drain. (But note that there is no longer a connection with the tidal Witham this way).

Langrick
Lincs. Stores, garage. This tiny settlement grew to serve the ferry crossing, replaced by an iron bridge in 1907. There is an old jetty facing Witham Lodge, an attractive house where the ferry used to be. The pub is nearby. The late Georgian brick church was built in 1828.

PUBS
● **Malcolm Arms** Anton's Gowt, on north side of Frith Bank Drain.
●✕ **Ferry Boat Inn** Langrick, on north side of river. Snacks, *L & D*.

Boston

The River Witham now completes its journey
to Boston, aiming straight for Boston Stump,
the tower of St Botolph's Church. A low black
iron railway bridge crosses at the Boston Grand
Sluice, which marks the end of the non-tidal
Witham. Boats should keep away from the
powerful 'draw' of the sluices on the south west
side of this structure (the lock is at the north
east end of it). The river here is a very attractive
scene, and a fitting end to the trip from
Torksey. On either side of the river is a line of
town houses; these are particularly elegant on
the north bank. There are two boat clubs:
Boston Sailing Club and Boston Motor Yacht
Club, also a rowing club, a boatyard and a
riverside pub. There are good moorings here.
The centre of Boston is a short walk away.

Navigational note
At Boston Grand Sluice the River Witham
becomes tidal, leading down through Boston
past the docks and into the Wash. It is most
inadvisable to venture down the tideway unless
you have a suitable, sea-going boat and are
familiar with the currents and shallows in the
Wash. The Grand Sluice is of course a sea lock,
with gates facing both ways, but what is
particularly interesting about it is that, unlike
most tidal locks, the sea gates (referred to
locally as 'doors') here are actually used at every
tide. In other words the North Sea at high
water is always above the level of the non-tidal
Witham, and the sea gates close automatically
twice a day to keep out the tide. This makes
locking through the Grand Sluice somewhat
complicated as far as times are concerned. It is
not possible to lock up into the tide, since there
is only one pair of outward facing gates, but on
the other hand the tidal river practically dries
out at low water. The best time to lock through
is in fact 2 to 3 hours either side of high water.
The lock will take boats up to 50ft long by 30ft
wide. A lock keeper is on duty in the nearby
office: his telephone number is Boston 64864
and you should give him at least 24 hrs notice if
you intend to pass through (answerphone).

Boston
Lincs. EC Thur. MD Wed. All services. An
immensely attractive town at the mouth of the
Witham, Boston has been an important seaport
for over 800 years. There are many splendid
buildings in the town, but of course the most
conspicuous among them is the famous Boston
Stump – the 272ft tower of the parish church.
There are two large market places, virtually
contiguous. This area is the scene of much
revelry in the spring, when the May Fair takes
place. Under a charter of Elizabeth I dated 1573
the fair is held from *3–10 May.*
St Botolph's Church beside the Witham. This
enormous building is a magnificent example of
late Decorated architecture, and reflects the
prosperity of Boston following the rise of its
wool trade in the 13thC. The thriving guilds
paid for the church, into which were built their
respective chapels. Inside, the church is
immensely spacious, the tall roof carried by
slender quatrefoil columns. There are plenty of
interesting things to look at here. The main
south door is a remarkable piece of dovetailing,
the pulpit is an elaborate Jacobean affair and
the choir stalls are an excellent example of
14thC carving. There are some good brasses
and other monuments. The 272ft tower may be
ascended, at a small charge; with hundreds of
steps up a claustrophobic narrow turret, this
can be heavy going, but one may walk right
around a balcony near the top and of course the
view over the fenland is unbeatable – on a clear
day Lincoln, 32 miles away, is visible. The
church is much loved by the inhabitants of
Boston, Massachusetts, who have largely
financed its structural repairs this century.
The Guildhall South Street. An ancient and
fascinating building, now a museum illustrating
Boston's history. It contains the cells that in
1607 held William Brewster and his friends
after their unsuccessful attempt to leave the
country. They were tried in the courtroom
above. On the ground floor of this dark but
historic building is the original kitchen. The
roasting spit is self-propelled; the heat rising
from the fire drives simple fans connected to a
chain that operates the turning gear. This

remarkably useful device is over 500 years old. *Open Mon–Sat (not Sat afternoon in winter).*
Fydell House next to the Guildhall. A superb town house built in 1726 by William Fydell, a successful wine merchant who was three times Mayor of Boston. The building was saved from demolition in 1935 by the pioneering Boston Preservation Trust, who have fully restored this and many other venerable buildings hereabouts. Fydell House is now partly financed and used by Nottingham University as a college for Americans (Pilgrim College). *Open daily until sunset.*
Blackfriars Spain Lane, next to the Guildhall. This was once part of a 13thC Dominican friary, and much of the old stone structure remains. But the building has now been skilfully converted by the Boston Preservation Trust into Boston's only theatre. It backs onto Spain Court, a charming little square.

BOATYARDS
Ⓑ **Boston Marina** Witham Bank, Boston (64420). Ⓡ Ⓦ Ⓓ Gas, chandlery, mooring, engine sales and repairs. *Closed in winter.*

PUBS
🍺 **Witham Tavern** Boston. Riverside, above the Grand Sluice.
🍺 **Barge** Boston, near the Grand Sluice. There are plenty more pubs and restaurants in the town.

The Grand Sluice at Boston, separating the tidal River Witham (foreground) from the non-tidal Witham.

LANCASTER

Maximum dimensions

Preston to Tewitfield
Length: 75'
Beam: 14'
Headroom: 7' 6"
Glasson Branch
Length: 70'
Beam: 14'
Headroom: 8'

Mileage

PRESTON to
Garstang: 16¼
Junction with Glasson Branch: 24
Lancaster: 29¼
Carnforth: 37¼
CANAL TERMINUS: 41¼

No locks

Glasson Branch: 2¾ miles, 6 locks

The city of Lancaster has always been slightly unfortunate in being situated a little too far up the Lune estuary to allow easy navigation. By the late 18thC industrial developments in north west England created a great demand for better access from Lancaster to Preston, Manchester and the busy manufacturing areas near the River Mersey. A link such as a canal would enable much needed coal to be brought up from the pits around Wigan, while farm produce from the fertile plains of north Lancashire could be sent back to feed the teeming town workers to the south.

After various proposals had been aired, including suggestions for a ship canal up the Lune estuary and a canal along the coast, a smaller canal was promoted to run from Kendal to Westhoughton (a few miles east of Wigan). This was authorised as the Lancaster Canal by Parliament, and construction began in 1792, after a survey by John Rennie, the company's engineer. He designed the new navigation as a 'broad' canal, with locks 72ft long by 14ft wide, to take barges with a 50-ton carrying capacity. The water supply for the canal was – and still is – drawn from a reservoir at Killington (between Sedburgh and Kendal).

The route chosen included only 8 locks (at Tewitfield), but several aqueducts, the most important being across the River Lune at Lancaster. It was intended that the Ribble should be crossed at Preston by locking down to the river and up the other side, but this plan was constantly shelved because of lack of capital. By 1799 the canal was open from Tewitfield to Preston (including the great Lune Aqueduct), and from Clayton to Chorley. There remained a 5-mile gap between the two sections, which became known as the North and South Ends respectively. The gap was closed in 1803 by a horse tramway from Walton Summit to Preston, which was carried over the River Ribble by a wooden trestle bridge. This tramway was intended only as a cheap, temporary solution to the gap, but it was never replaced by a proper canal line, so the North End was doomed to be separated for ever from the rest of the country's inland waterways. (The tramway was closed in 1857.)

On the South End, the Lancaster Canal Company agreed with the Leeds & Liverpool Canal Company to extend the former's line past Chorley to Wigan (they never continued it to Westhoughton). The L & L then shared the Lancaster Canal for 10 miles – for a substantial consideration. Meanwhile the North End was extended from Tewitfield to Kendal and opened in 1819. The branch down to Glasson Dock, near Lancaster, was opened in 1826 as the canal's only direct outlet to the sea.

There are several unusual aspects about the Lancaster Canal and its history. One is that the 75-mile-long main line was constructed with only eight locks, at Tewitfield. (There are of course also six locks on the Glasson branch.) This was naturally a great benefit to traders and helped to counteract the disadvantage imposed by the tramway at Preston. One may also notice that the towpath is on the same side all the way along the canal, except for a short stretch in Lancaster. This fostered the growth in the 1820s of an express passenger service along the canal. Using special 'fly-boats', a constant change of horses at special staging posts, and precedence over all other craft, this service lived up to its name, averaging up to 10mph along the run from Preston to Kendal.

Another interesting aspect of the Lancaster Canal was the extraordinary but canny interest the company took in the new railway companies, alternately leasing whole lines and then being leased by the railways. Eventually, in 1885, the Canal Company sold out altogether to the London & North Western Railway – except for the South End, which was already leased in perpetuity to the Leeds & Liverpool Canal Company.

Since the 1930s the canal has been progressively shortened from the Kendal end; and in 1968, after Tewitfield locks had been disused for several years, the canal north of Tewitfield was closed so that the M6 motorway could be driven across the canal. In Preston the canal has been shortened by over half a mile.

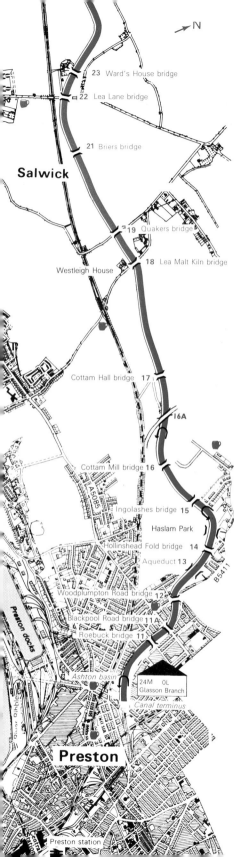

Preston

The canal in Preston, shortened many years ago
by over ½ mile, now starts in the middle of
nowhere, on an embankment by the old Ashton
Basin where there is a boatyard. (There is not
much left of the original line, although pubs in
Preston like the Lamb & Packet recall the days
when passenger 'fly boats' or 'packet boats'
used to leave Preston to do the trip to Kendal in
8 hours – a remarkable speed.) From Ashton
Basin, the canal runs through dull urban areas
for a short while. However, the attractive
Haslam Park appears at bridge 12 and while
housing estates line the offside bank for a mile,
the towpath side of the canal is effectively
already in the countryside. Soon Preston is left
behind and the canal runs through flat and
featureless but always green, open, agricultural
countryside; the first of many sheep and cows
are seen grazing along here. Passing Westleigh
House and several farms, one begins to see the
large industrial works at Salwick where fuel
elements are made for atomic power stations.
Farm eggs may be bought at bridge 18.

Navigational note
Overnight mooring in Preston is not
recommended.

Salwick
Lancs. PO, tel, stores, station. A village scattered
over a large area. The school, post office,
telephone and pub are just ¼ mile south of
bridge 22: the station is ¼ mile south west of
bridge 25.
Preston
Lancs. MD Mon, Wed, Sat. All services. A large
industrial town which prospered as a cotton
manufacturing centre. The teetotal movement
was founded in Preston in 1834, and Joseph
Livesey's Temperance Hotel (the world's first)
used to stand at the corner of Church Street and
North Road. The Market Place is dominated by
the huge classical building of the Harris Public
Library and Museum. There are many
churches whose tall spires are a distinctive
feature of the town. Attempts to redevelop the
centre of the town have resulted in a good new
shopping precinct and a large modern bus
station housed in a remarkably long multi-
storey car park. With the end of commercial
use, the huge basin of Preston Dock has been
developed as a marina complex, with the
turbine steamer 'Manxman' as the centrepiece.
Harris Museum & Art Gallery Market
Square, Preston (53191). The museum has a
specialised collection of the Devis family of
painters in addition to exhibits illustrating
18thC and 19thC art, including ceramics,
porcelain, glass, toys, stamps and costume.
Closed Sun.
Tourist Information Centre Town Hall,
Harris Street, Preston (54881).

PUBS
● **Smith's Arms** Lea Lane, Lea Town. South
of bridge 22. Thwaites real ale in a village pub
next door to British Nuclear Fuels works.
Lunchtime food.
● **Cotty Brook** South of bridge 18. McEwans
and Youngers real ale and *lunchtime* food.
● **John O'Gaunt** Cottam Avenue. North of
bridge 16. Boddingtons real ale in a large estate
pub.
● **Lane Ends Hotel** 442 Blackpool Road.
South of bridge 12 (no access from bridge 11A)
Large popular Boddingtons real ale pub.
Lunchtime snacks.
● **Wheatsheaf** Water Lane. ¼ mile south west
of Ashton Basin. A basic pub serving Tetley's
and Jennings real ales.
● **Maudland** 1 Pedder Street. ⅓ mile south
east of Ashton Basin via Fylde Road and
Ashton Street. In the shadow of the third tallest
spire in the country, this popular local offers
Matthew Brown real ale. Pedder Street is
named after one of the sponsors of the
Lancaster Canal.

Park Head bridge **41**

Hankinson bridge **40**

Hepgreave Lane bridge **39**

Hollowforth aqueduct **38**

Hollowforth swing bridge **37**

Moons bridge **36** Ⓑ

Bell Fold bridge **35**

B5269

Whinneyfield bridge **34**

Woodplumpton aqueduct **33**

Catforth

Swillbrook bridge **32** Ⓑ

| 17M | 0L |
| Glasson Branch |
| Preston |
| 7M | 0L |

31 Stone Chimneys bridge

30 Roots bridge

M55 motorway

29 Kellet's bridge

28 New bridge

27 Six Mile bridge

26 Salwick bridge

Salwick Hall

24 ⇌

25 Wilsons bridge ↓ to Salwick station

Catforth

The canal now reaches Salwick Wharf, where the moorings are administered by the Duchy of Lancaster. On one side of the wharf is the moated Salwick Hall, screened by trees; on the other side is Salwick station, on the Preston–Blackpool line, and a disused windmill beyond. Here the canal turns north into a wooded cutting, passing a canalside pub – unfortunately a rare sight on this canal. At Kellet's Bridge the navigation turns sharply east to Catforth (*PO, tel, stores*). All along this section the countryside is soft, open pastureland dotted with dairy farms; entirely peaceful and untouched by busy roads. At Swillbrook Bridge there is one of the few boatyards on this canal: the proprietor's house was formerly the old canal cottage with stables for the towing horses.

The Fylde

A large flat area of north west Lancashire (west of the canal) which is the 'market garden' of the many industrial towns in the area. There used to be a wonderful array of windmills covering the land, but nearly all of these are gone now.

BOATYARDS

Ⓑ **Preston Hire Cruisers** Moons Bridge Wharf, Hollowforth Lane, Woodplumpton, Preston (690627). RWD Gas, hire craft, overnight mooring, long-term mooring, winter storage, crane, chandlery, boat and engine repairs.
Ⓑ **Adventure Cruisers** The Jolly Roger, Catforth (690232). WD Pump-out, gas, hire craft, day hire boats, overnight mooring, long-term mooring, winter storage, slipway, books and maps, boat and engine sales and repairs, gift shop, tea shop, off licence, toilet. *Closed Thur Sep–June.*

PUBS

🍺 **Plough** Woodplumpton, east of bridge 35. Matthew Brown real ale and food at *lunchtime, also evenings Wed–Sat, with a buffet Sun.* Garden with children's play area.
🍺 **Bay Horse Hotel** Catforth. North of bridge 32. Matthew Brown real ale and bar meals *lunchtime and evenings Mon–Fri.*
🍺 **Running Pump** Catforth. North of bridge 31. A popular pub serving snacks at *lunchtime* every day, and full lunches *Sun & Tue–Fri.* Robinson's real ale.
🍺 **Hand & Dagger** Canalside at bridge 26. Once the Clifton Arms, this pub was nick-named the Hand & Dagger because of its signs. It was renamed when modernised. Greenall Whitley real ale and *lunchtime* food.

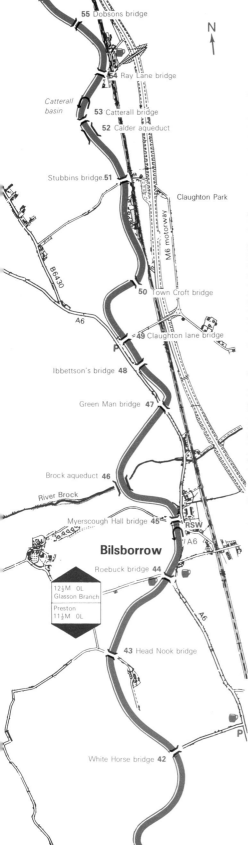

55 Dobsons bridge

54 Ray Lane bridge

Catterall basin

53 Catterall bridge

52 Calder aqueduct

Stubbins bridge 51

Claughton Park

M6 motorway

50 Town Croft bridge

B6430

A6

49 Claughton lane bridge

P

Ibbettson's bridge 48

Green Man bridge 47

Brock aqueduct 46

River Brock

Myerscough Hall bridge 45

RSW

A6

Bilsborrow

Roebuck bridge 44

12½M 0L
Glasson Branch

Preston
11½M 0L

A6

43 Head Nook bridge

P

White Horse bridge 42

Bilsborrow

Starting at White Horse Bridge (¼ mile to the
east of which is a pub, garage, post office and
telephone kiosk), the canal sweeps round to
enter the village of Bilsborrow on a minor
embankment: the A6 joins the canal here and
continues to dog it for many miles, as does the
main railway line to Scotland, and the M6.
When these rival transport routes keep their
distance the canal is again delightfully quiet,
still passing through peaceful green farmland,
while the foothills of the Pennines begin to
converge from the east. Just south of Stubbins
Bridge can be seen the canal cottage and stable
which was one of the places where towing
horses were exchanged for fresh teams to pull
the express passenger boats between Preston
and Kendal. Near the former Garstang and
Catterall station is Catterall Basin; both are now
disused.

Claughton Hall ¼ mile east of the canal. This
hall was originally an Elizabethan mansion built
next to the village church for the Croft family,
but in 1932–5 the whole house, except for one
wing, was dismantled and reassembled on top
of the moor north of the village. It was quite a
remarkable undertaking and still stands there
in defiant isolation.

Bilsborrow
Lancs. PO, tel, stores, garage. A village
straggling along the A6, which must have been
very noisy before the M6 was built. The church
is set apart, up on a hill: there are three pubs
very close to the canal.

PUBS

Kenlis Arms Garstang, 100yds east of
bridge 54. Boddingtons real ale and food
lunchtime and Fri, Sat & Sun evenings. Children
welcome.

Roebuck Garstang Road, 30yds east of
bridge 44. *Lunchtime* food and Matthew Brown
real ale in a large modernised pub with a
children's room and bowling green.

White Bull Canalside at bridge 44. Friendly
village local dispensing Matthew Brown real
ale, and *lunchtime* snacks.

Owd Nell's Canalside at bridge 44. (Brock
40010). Newly built farmhouse-style thatched
pub and restaurant. Snacks *lunchtime and
evenings,* meals *L & D until 20.00.*
Boddingtons, Tetley's and Whitbread real ales.

White Horse ¼ mile east of bridge 42.
Small, comfortable pub serving home-made
food *lunchtime and evenings* and Matthew
Brown real ale.

Garstang

The canal moves away from the hills and the remains of Greenhalgh Castle, crossing the River Wyre on a fine stone aqueduct and passing the attractive town of Garstang; Garstang Basin is a popular mooring for pleasure boats. There is a restaurant and museum in the restored wharf buildings here. The canal then winds through countryside that is as green and pleasant as ever but which is now overlooked by the steep slopes of the Pennines. Those who walk up the hills will be rewarded with splendid views over Cockerham Sands and the Fylde.

Winmarleigh Hall ½ mile west of bridges 68 and 70. A red brick hall built in 1871 for Lord Winmarleigh. It was largely rebuilt after a fire in 1927. It is now an agricultural college.

Garstang
Lancs. PO, tel, stores, bank, garage. A friendly place, touching the canal, which retains the feeling of a small market town. Just near the canal is the 18thC church of St Thomas surrounded by a tidy churchyard. Opposite the cobbled market place is an interesting little town hall with its diminutive bell-tower. The Town Hall, built in 1680 to acknowledge its promotion by the king to borough status, was rebuilt in 1939. There used to be a dozen ale houses in the town; but the present six seem quite enough.

Greenhalgh Castle Just north of the canal on a grassy knoll are the modest ruins of Greenhalgh Castle. It was built in 1490 by the Earl of Derby, who placed Richard III's crown on Henry Tudor's head after the victory at Bosworth Field. In the 17thC it was destroyed by the Roundheads during the Civil War when the Royalists made a final stand there. Ask at the adjacent farm to visit the ruins.

St Helen's Church 1½ miles south west of the canal at Churchtown, west of the A6. A magnificent parish church known as the 'Cathedral of the Fylde', in an attractive setting of a shady churchyard near the River Wyre. Parts of the building date from c1300 and inside are 15thC arches on Norman pillars with the Creed written on them. The massive beams in the roof are from the four oaks that Henry IV granted to Churchtown when forests were the property of the monarch.

BOATYARDS

Ⓑ **Bridge House Marina** Nateby, Garstang (3207). Between bridges 64 & 65. Ⓡ Ⓢ Ⓦ Ⓓ Gas, long-term mooring, winter storage, slipway, chandlery, boat sales, repairs, toilets, showers, grocery shop.

PUBS

Patten Arms Winmarleigh, north of bridge 71. Whitbread real ale and bar food *lunchtime and Sat & Sun evenings.*

Chequered Flag Nateby, 200yds south of bridge 64. (Garstang 2126). Bass and Stones real ales and bar meals *lunchtime and evenings.*

Eagle & Child High Street, Garstang. *Lunchtime* bar meals.

Farmer's Arms Church Street, Garstang. Tetley's and Jennings real ales, meals *lunchtime and evenings* and a children's room.

Royal Oak Hotel Market Place, Garstang (3318). Robinson's real ale, bar meals *lunchtime and evenings.*

Crown Garstang, east of bridge 62. Thwaites real ale, bar meals *lunchtime and evenings.*

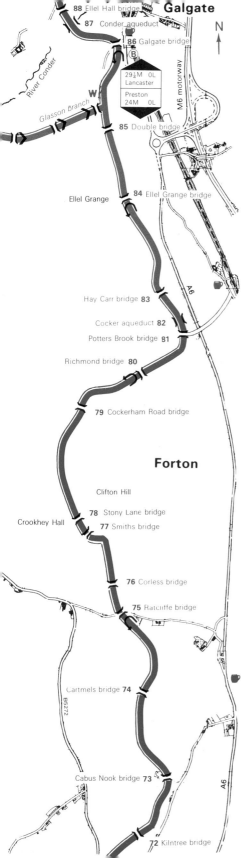

88 Ellel Hall bridge

Galgate

87 Conder aqueduct

86 Galgate bridge

Ⓑ

N

29¼M 0L
Lancaster
Preston
24M 0L

M6 motorway

River Conder

Glasson Branch

W

85 Double bridge

84 Ellel Grange bridge

Ellel Grange

A6

Hay Carr bridge 83

Cocker aqueduct 82

Potters Brook bridge 81

Richmond bridge 80

79 Cockerham Road bridge

Forton

Clifton Hill

78 Stony Lane bridge

Crookhey Hall

77 Smiths bridge

76 Corless bridge

75 Ratcliffe bridge

Cartmels bridge 74

B5272

A6

Cabus Nook bridge 73

72 Kilntree bridge

Galgate

Continuing northwards through quiet, modest and unspoilt pastureland, the canal passes countryside that is empty of villages but full of farms and houses dotted about the landscape. The absence of any locks certainly makes this an ideal waterway for restful cruising, while the wildlife and the generously proportioned stone-arched bridges always supply interest along the way. Near Forton, a sharp S-bend carries the canal between Clifton Hill and Crookhey Hall, while from Potters Brook Bridge a lane across the A6 leads to a post office, telephone and hotel beside what used to be Bay Horse Station. Just north of Potters Brook is the Ellel Grange estate with its remarkable spired church, ornamental canal bridge and the Grange itself, shrouded by tall trees; unfortunately the estate is private. Double Bridge is worth a closer look; beyond the rocky cutting that it spans is the junction with the Glasson Branch, and round the corner is Galgate and a large boatyard and mooring site.

Galgate
Lancs. PO, tel, stores, garage. An unassuming village on the A6 but dominated by the main railway to Scotland, which strides through the place on a high embankment and an impressive viaduct. The back of the village up the hill is quiet; by the church of St John are the buildings of what is apparently the oldest surviving silk spinning mill in England (built in 1792).
Ellel Grange On the banks of the canal. A very fine Italianate villa built for a merchant in 1857–9. It is a large mansion with two broad towers that compete in vain with the graceful spire of the charming little church of St Mary that stands in the grounds of the house. Both are private.

BOATYARDS

Ⓑ **Marina Park** Canal Wharf, Galgate, Lancaster (751368). Ⓡ Ⓦ Gas, winter storage, slipway, chandlery, provisions, boat and engine sales and repairs, toilet, showers, launderette.

PUBS

🍺 **Plough Inn** Galgate, near bridge 86. *Lunchtime* bar food and Boddingtons real ale.
🍺 **Green Dragon** Galgate. Thwaites real ale in a village pub. Food *lunchtime and evenings*.
🍺 **New Inn** Galgate, in the village. Mitchell's real ale and food at *lunchtime*.
🍺 **Bay Horse** North east of bridge 81, across the A6. Mitchell's real ale and bar meals *lunchtime (not Mon) and Sat & Sun evenings* in a cosy pub which has its own rugby team. Family room, open fire, garden.
🍺✕ **Hamilton Arms** North east of bridge 73. (Lancaster 791257). Matthew Brown real ale, bar and restaurant meals.

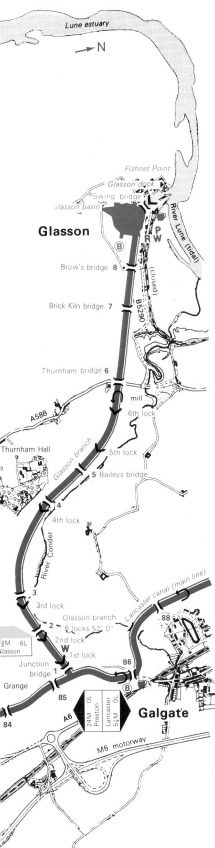

Glasson

Between Ellel Grange and Galgate the Glasson Branch leads off down to the west to connect the Lancaster Canal with the Lune estuary via Glasson Dock. The branch was finished only in 1826, long after the main line of the canal was completed, and provided the canal with its only direct link with the sea. There are six wide locks whose bottom gates feature the same excellent type of sliding paddles as one sees on the Leeds & Liverpool Canal. The top gates are all kept padlocked for security reasons: boatmen should ensure that they have the requisite key on board (available from British Waterways staff) and are asked to lock the gates after use, and also to leave the locks *empty* after use, even when going up the locks. The arm falls through the Conder valley, a pleasant, quiet stretch of countryside whose proximity to the sea is betrayed by the many seagulls cruising around. The spire in the trees on the south bank belongs to Thurnham church; Thurnham Mill is beside the bottom lock, and its mill race shows that it still takes water from the canal. After the bottom lock, the canal runs in a straight line through saltings and marshland to Glasson Basin, where there is a large boatyard, mainly for seagoing yachts, and British Waterways moorings.

Navigational notes
1. The entrance lock from Glasson Dock up into Glasson Basin will take boats up to 95ft long, 24ft wide and 12ft draught. Anyone wishing to use the lock (for which 24hrs notice is required) or take up a mooring in the basin should contact the lock keeper on Galgate 751566.
2. The locks on the Glasson Branch will take boats up to 72ft long, 14ft wide and 4ft draught.
3. Crew or owners wishing to leave via the entrance lock should give the lock keeper 24hrs notice. The lock is in operation 2hrs before high water.
4. In case of emergency, when the Glasson lock keeper is not available, telephone Lancaster 32712.

Glasson
Lancs. PO, tel, stores, garage. A fascinating tiny port that is still busy with trade from coastal and continental vessels. The canal no longer contributes to this trade and the huge basin is only occupied by an assortment of pleasure boats using its excellent sheltered mooring. In the tidal dock, however, there are usually plenty of coasters that discharge into lorries, since the old railway line from Lancaster has now been dismantled.
Thurnham Hall On the south west bank of the canal. This ancient family home of the Daltons is a battlemented 16thC mansion that was given a new façade and beautiful chapel in the 19thC.

BOATYARDS
Ⓑ **Marina Park** See page 74.
Ⓑ **Glasson Basin Yacht Co** Glasson Dock, nr Lancaster (Galgate 751491). ⓌⒹⒺ Pump-out, gas, overnight mooring, long-term mooring, winter storage, slipway, 55-ton crane, chandlery, provisions, books and maps, boat building and sales, boat and engine repairs, toilet, showers, telephone. Charter for sea.

PUBS
🍺 **Caribou Hotel** Glasson Dock. Dating from 1781, this large pub has an open fire and plenty of cosy corners. Bar food *lunchtime and evenings*, and Thwaites real ale. Children welcome.
🍺 **Dalton Arms** Glasson Dock. Thwaites real ale and food *lunchtime and evenings*.
🍷 **Victoria** Glasson Dock. Mitchell's real ale and bar meals *lunchtime and evenings*.
🍺 **Plough Inn** Galgate, near bridge 86. *Lunchtime* bar food and Boddingtons real ale.
🍺 **Green Dragon** Galgate. Thwaites real ale in a village pub. Food *lunchtime and evenings*.
🍺 **New Inn** Galgate, in the village. Mitchell's real ale and food at *lunchtime*.

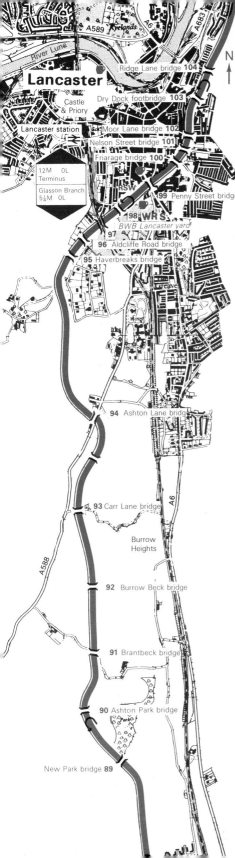

Lancaster

The canal continues northwards through
beautiful undulating green countryside, then
passes through an unusually long wooded
cutting which ends in the outskirts of
Lancaster. Going underneath the main line
railway, one can see the two-storey building
where the old packet boats used to be refitted,
being hauled out of the water from pulleys on
the beams of the upper floor. The British
Waterways maintenance yard is nearby, at the
bridge where the towpath changes sides. Past
the bridge are the Aldcliffe basins and wharves
which were once the headquarters of the canal
company. Opposite are some canal stables
which have been tastefully converted into a
place for punting, eating and drinking. At
bridge 101 the towpath returns to the left side
of the canal, where it stays for the rest of the
journey northwards. The navigation now leaves
Lancaster, on the side of the hill that overlooks
the Lune estuary.

Lancaster
Lancs. EC Wed. MD Sat. All services. The
name Lancaster is derived from a combination
of Lune (after the river) and Latin 'castrum'
meaning camp, which refers to the Roman
fortress that once stood on this site. Today the
quay, once a great shipping port handling more
cargo than Liverpool, is only a quiet backwater,
with a pleasant walk provided by the tree-lined
quayside promenade. A large new university
was opened at Bailrigg, south of the town, in
1964. The Boat Regatta takes place annually in
May and the Agricultural show in *Aug*.
Lancaster Castle A handsome but forbidding
building on the site of Roman fortifications;
mainly 13thC and 14thC construction, except
for the Norman keep, which is surmounted by
a beacon tower known as John of Gaunt's
Chair. The Shire Hall contains an impressive
display of over 600 heraldic shields. Most of the
castle has reverted to its earlier function as a
prison. *Various escorted tours (Lancaster 64637).
Closed during the winter, and while Assizes,
Quarter Sessions or County Courts are sitting.*
Priory Church of St Mary Vicarage Lane, by
the castle. Attractive 15thC church in late
Perpendicular style though the original Saxon
western doorway still remains and the belfry
was added in 1754. Elaborately carved choir
stall c1340 and fine Jacobean pulpit.
Town Hall Dalton Square. A very impressive
building of classical design, with a grand
marble staircase and domed council chamber.
It was the generous gift of Lord Ashton to the
city of Lancaster in 1909. It is open to visitors,
who are shown the magnificent entrance hall,
the council chamber and concert hall, as well as
the historic charters. To arrange a visit contact
the Town Clerk (Lancaster 65272).
Lancaster Museum Old Town Hall, Market
Square, Lancaster (64637). Prehistoric, Roman
and medieval exhibits; pottery and porcelain,
firearms and topographical paintings. *Open
weekdays.*
Ashton Memorial Williamson Park,
Quernmore Road. The 'Taj Mahal' of the
north. Yet another generous gift from Lord
Ashton to the city as a memorial to his family.
In the centre of a beautiful park, containing a
palm-house and ornamental lake, the memorial
is a vast structure consisting of two domed
chambers, one on top of the other. It was
designed in neo-classical style by J. Belcher and
constructed of Portland stone in 1907–9.
Maritime Museum Old Customs House, St
George's Quay, Lancaster (64637). Walk
towards the river from bridge 99, turn left into
Damside. Lancaster once handled a greater
tonnage of shipping than Liverpool; the display
in the 18thC Customs House reflects this
maritime heritage. *Open daily 10.00–
17.00.*
Tourist Information Centre Nelson Street,
Lancaster (32878).

BOATYARDS

Canal Cruises Penny Street Bridge Wharf, Lancaster. (0836 633189). R W D Pump-out, trip boat. Between bridges 99 and 100.
British Waterways Lancaster Yard At bridge 98. (Lancaster 32712). R S W

BOAT TRIPS

'Lady Fiona' is a canal motor barge converted and licensed to carry 100 passengers. *Trips Easter–Nov, lasting 3½hrs* leave from near bridge 98. Licensed bar on board. Only party bookings accepted, will run any day of the week. Enquiries to Lancaster 39279.
Duke of Lancaster Public trips *Easter–Sep*, youth weekends in *winter*, private hire *all year*. Up to 12 passengers. Licensed bar on board. Enquiries to Canal Cruises (0836 633189).

PUBS

There are plenty of pubs in Lancaster.
Waterwitch Canalside between bridges 98 and 99. A choice of real ales and food *lunchtime and evenings*.
White Cross Canalside after bridge 99. (Lancaster 841048). Bass and Stones real ales, bar and restaurant meals *lunchtime and evenings*.
Farmer's Arms Lancaster. North west of bridge 99. Thwaites real ale and food *lunchtime and evenings*.
Waggon & Horses 27 St George's Quay, Lancaster. Well worth a look in if you are visiting the Maritime Museum. Good mixed clientele and Hartley's real ale to enjoy. *Lunchtime food*, open fire.

A typical stone bridge on the Lancaster Canal. *Derek Pratt.*

Bolton Cinder Ovens bridge **125**

Salt marsh

N

Chorleys bridge **124**

A6

Bolton Turnpike bridge **123**

Bolton Church bridge **122**

Bolton-le-Sands

6¼M 0L
Terminus

Lancaster
5¾M 0L

A5105

121 Town End bridge

120 Hatley Swing bridge

119 Hatlex bridge

Hest Bank

118 Hest Bank bridge

117

116 Rakes Head bridge

115 Blind Lane bridge

114 Belmount bridge

113 Williamlands bridge

112 Folly bridge

A6

Halton Road bridge **108**

River Lune
aqueduct

107

Beaumont Hall **109**
bridge

Hammerton Hall
bridge **111**

Bulk Road aqueduct **106**

110 Beaumont Turnpike bridge

Dolphin Lea bridge **105**

A683

Lancaster

River Lune

Ridge Lane bridge **104**

Dry Dock footbridge **103**

Hest Bank

This is a very interesting and varied section.
After crossing a new aqueduct (built in 1961)
over the A683, one launches out along the
superb aqueduct that carries the canal over the
broad River Lune – definitely a high spot on his
journey. At the far end of the aqueduct the
canal rejoins the side of the valley, turning west
then north again through quiet countryside.
Gradually one begins to approach the sea: there
are good views over the expanse of Morecombe
Bay. Past Hest Bank, the navigation winds
along to the pretty village of Bolton-le-Sands.

Bolton-le-Sands
Lancs. PO, tel, stores. A village that obviously
values its canal. There are some pretty houses,
several of them with gardens landscaped down
to the water's edge. Ducks, too, are often seen
on the canal hereabouts. The village used to be
a stop on the Preston–Kendal 'fly-boat' run:
the pub survives to remind one of the service.
Hest Bank
Lancs. PO, tel, stores, bank. Until the Glasson
Branch was cut, Hest Bank used to be the scene
of much transhipment between canal boats and
coasters, as Hest Bank was the canal's nearest
point to the sea. Now, the village is
nondescript, a seaside suburb of Lancaster; but
the seashore is only a couple of hundred yards
from the navigation, and at low water miles of
sandy beach are uncovered. The west coast
main railway runs along the shore.
Lune Aqueduct
This splendid edifice, probably the greatest feat
of engineering on the Lancaster Canal, carries
the navigation for some 600ft across the River
Lune, which is 60ft below. A handsome stone
aqueduct with an elegant balustrade, it was
designed by John Rennie and completed in
1797. The smooth modern lines of the M6
motorway bridge can be seen ¾ mile upstream.

PUBS
 Blue Anchor Main Street, Bolton-le-Sands.
Mitchell's real ale and bar meals *lunchtime and
evenings (not Mon)*.
 Packet Boat Hotel Main Street,
Bolton-le-Sands. Once a staging post on the
canal 'fly-boat' service, it now serves Thwaites
real ale and food *lunchtime and evenings*.
 Hest Bank Canalside at bridge 118. You can
still see the window for the guiding light, which
showed the way across the sands. Now this old
coaching inn with an open fire is justly popular,
offering Boddingtons real ale and *lunchtime* bar
food. Canalside garden, children welcome.

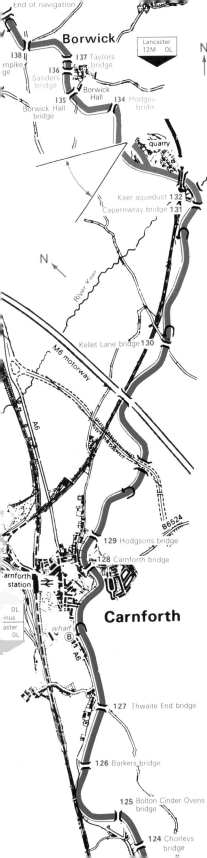

Carnforth

The A6 now runs beside and below the canal into Carnforth. One may catch occasional glimpses westward of the distant shores around Morecambe Bay, then the canal passes Carnforth, mostly in a cutting. A few small abandoned quarries are scattered between the canal and the M6. After passing under the motorway spur road, the canal finds itself diverted along a new channel for several hundred yards before going under the main line of the M6: this diversion was presumably cheaper to build than a long, finely angled skew bridge over the navigation. Beyond the motorway lies peaceful green countryside backed, unmistakably, by the foothills of the Lake District. At Capernwray the canal crosses the River Keer on a minor aqueduct; the nearby railway, which goes to Leeds, crosses the Keer on an impressive viaduct, framing a tiny old derelict watermill. Past the railway bridge is a short branch to a worked-out quarry, then the canal winds round the hillside to end abruptly just beyond Borwick. The abandoned Tewitfield locks are just beyond the terminus. It is possible to walk from Tewitfield to the original terminus at Kendal (and get a bus back). Boats can safely be left at the terminus moorings (facilities available, and a winding hole).

Borwick
Lancs. Tel. A small, old and attractive village, spread around a green. Overlooking the canal is Borwick Hall, a large and sombre Elizabethan manor house, built around a high 15thC tower. Extensive gardens.

Warton
Lancs. PO, tel, stores. About 2 miles west of Borwick. Ancestors of George Washington lived in this village and their family crest containing the famed Stars and Stripes is to be seen on the 15thC tower of the church of St Oswald.

Carnforth
Lancs. PO, tel, stores, garage, bank, station. Not particularly attractive but of interest as an important railway junction. One may catch trains not only north–south but east over the beautiful green hills to Skipton and Leeds, west to Barrow and right round the coast to Carlisle. Carnforth was the last town in the country to lose its regular British Rail steam locomotive service in 1968. Since then a company of steam engine enthusiasts and volunteers have privately set up the 'Steamtown' museum – a depot with 5 miles of track along which preserved engines steam on certain weekends. The collection of motive power includes the 'Flying Scotsman'. At Carnforth Wharf are some useful facilities: moorings, slipway and sanitary station. A petrol station is nearby.

BOATYARDS
ⓑ **Nu-Way Acorn** Lundsfield, Carnforth (734457). Ⓡ Ⓢ Ⓦ Ⓟ Ⓓ Pump-out, gas, overnight mooring, long-term mooring, winter storage, slipway, boat and engine sales and repairs, toilet.

PUBS
🍺 **Longlands Hotel** Tewitfield. 100yds north east of the canal terminus. Boddingtons real ale and *evening bar meals (not Mon)*.
🍺 **Shovel** Carnforth. West of bridge 128. Boddingtons real ale and snacks.
🍺✕ **Royal Station Hotel** Carnforth (732033). Mitchell's real ale, bar meals *lunchtime and evenings*, and restaurant meals *evenings*.
🍺 **Cross Keys** Carnforth. Mitchell's real ale and snacks.

The Leeds & Liverpool Canal in Wigan. The hump in the towpath to the right is Wigan Pier; Trencherfield Mill stands in the background with the new Orwell pub on the left. *David Perrott*.

LEEDS & LIVERPOOL

Maximum dimensions

Liverpool to Wigan, and Leigh Branch
Length: 72'
Beam: 14' 3"
Headroom: 8' 6"
Wigan to Leeds
Length: 60'
Beam: 14' 3"
Headroom: 8'
Rufford Branch
Length: 62'
Beam: 14'
Headroom: 8'

Mileage

LIVERPOOL. Canal terminus to Burscough, junction with Rufford Branch: 24½
Wigan, junction with Leigh Branch: 35
Johnson's Hill Locks: 47¼
Blackburn, Top Lock: 56
Burnley: 72½
Skipton: 98
Bingley Five Rise: 110¾
Apperley Bridge: 118
LEEDS, River Lock: 127

Locks: 91

Leigh Branch: 7¼ miles, 2 locks
Rufford Branch: 7¼ miles, 8 locks

With a length of 127 miles excluding branches, the Leeds & Liverpool Canal is easily the longest single canal in Britain built by a single company. It is hardly surprising that its construction costs amounted to £1.2 million, and that it took well over 40 years before the main line was completed.

The canal has its beginnings in the River Douglas, a little river made navigable by 1740 – well before the canal age – all the way from Wigan to Parbold, Tarleton and the Ribble estuary. The navigation provided a useful outlet for coal from the Wigan area.

After a few years the idea of purely artificial canals as traffic routes became popular among businessmen, and several ambitious trans-Pennine schemes were mooted; one of these was for a canal from Liverpool to Leeds, where it would connect with the head of the Aire & Calder Navigation.

After much predictable argument between the promoters in Yorkshire and those in Lancashire about the actual route of the proposed canal, the Leeds & Liverpool Canal was authorised in 1770, and construction began at once, with John Longbotham as engineer. The first lock-free section from Bingley to Skipton was opened within 3 years; by 1777 two long sections were open from the Aire & Calder at Leeds to Gargrave (incorporating many of the dramatic new staircase locks) and from Wigan to Liverpool. The River Douglas navigation had been embarrassingly close to the new canal's line, so the L & L had bought it out at an early stage to gain control of its valuable water supply. It was replaced by a proper canal branch to Rufford and Tarleton, where it joined the (tidal) River Douglas.

Construction was halted at this stage while trade flowed on to the separate lengths of navigation and the company summoned the resources to continue work on the canal. In 1790 a new money-raising Act of Parliament gave fresh impetus to the scheme for completing the difficult middle section of the canal. Work began again, with Robert Whitworth as the company's engineer; but after 1792 and the outbreak of war with France, the nation's purse strings grew steadily tighter and, after the boom year of 1794, investment in canals declined steadily. The canal company did not do badly to finish the whole of the main line from Leeds to Liverpool by 1816 (under a convenient arrangement with the Lancaster Canal Company, the finished L & L line actually *shared* the channel of the Lancaster Canal for 10 miles). This stretch is from Wigan Top Lock to Johnson's Hill Bottom Lock. The Lancaster used then to branch off up what later became the Walton Summit Branch.

In 1820 a branch was opened to join the Bridgewater Canal at Leigh. A short branch (the Springs Branch) was also made to rock quarries at Skipton and an important 3-mile-long canal from Shipley to Bradford. The cut down into the Liverpool Docks was made in 1846.

The prosperity of the company after 1820 was not, at first, greatly affected by the early advent of railways in that part of the country. The scale of the navigation (the locks were built – and remain – as barge locks 62ft by 14ft, allowing big payloads to be carried in each barge along the canal) no doubt contributed to the high dividends paid to shareholders for several years. Water supply was, however, a thorny problem from the very beginning, and in spite of the building of many reservoirs along the summit level, the canal had to be closed for months on end during many dry summers. Although through traffic has never been a very significant proportion of the trade on the canal, this lack of reliability tended, not surprisingly, to drive carriers' custom away to the railways. Use of the navigation for freight has declined throughout this century; the hard winter of 1962/63 finished off many traders. Today there is no large scale commercial traffic at all, although the occasional independent carrier may be seen at the eastern end.

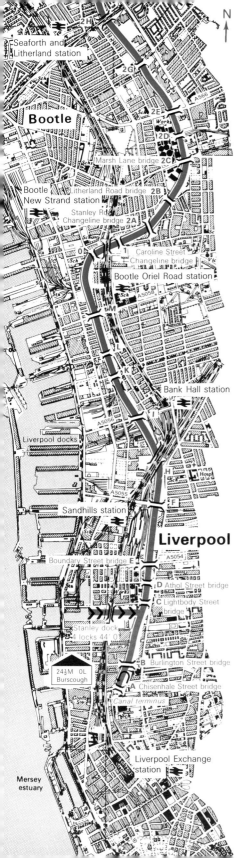

Liverpool

The first ¼ mile of this canal has been filled in,
so the navigation begins now at bridge 'A'. It
runs north from the city centre for about 6
miles, parallel and close to Liverpool Docks,
before turning east to Aintree, Wigan and the
Pennines. Liverpool is not an attractive place
from the canal, which is completely shut off
from the town by rows and rows of factories
with their backs turned to the canal. For much
of the way, substantial electricity pylons span
the navigation. Access at the bridges to or from
the canal is very difficult, because the towpath
is officially closed to walkers, but naturally it is
often alive with small boys fishing, playing and
dropping or throwing things into the canal. The
water, however, is surprisingly clear.

Navigational notes
1. Just north of the terminus is the Stanley
Dock Branch. This useful connection from the
canal down into Liverpool Docks and the River
Mersey is nowadays the main *raison d'etre* of the
west end of the Leeds & Liverpool Canal.
There are four locks on the branch: they can be
opened only by the resident lock keeper *in
working hours Mon–Fri*. Any person wishing to
use these locks should give *24hrs notice* to the
Liverpool Section Inspector on Burscough
893160. Below the locks, one enters
immediately the Stanley Dock: this belongs to
the Mersey Docks & Harbour Company, whose
permission should be sought before one enters
the dock. (Telephone 051-200 2177). The MD
& HC is unlikely to refuse such a request, but
does not like pleasure boats to tie up in the
dock. Navigators are encouraged to move
straight on to the big lock down into the tidal
River Mersey. (The lock is operated *24hrs a
day*.)
2. Those navigating the Leeds & Liverpool will
need, as well as a windlass, a British Waterways
anti-vandal key and a sanitary station key.
3. Mooring at unrecognised sites in city centre
is not recommended.

Liverpool
Merseyside. All services. EC Wed. In the first
century AD it was 'lifrugpool', a settlement
next to a muddy creek; now it is one of Britain's
largest ports with a population of over ½
million. Famous worldwide as the place where
the Beatles began their march to fame, (in the
'Cavern' club, now demolished), and equally
well known for the exploits of Liverpool
Football Club, attracting a fanatical and
generally good-natured following. There is
much to be seen in this ancient port – for
example the Anglican Cathedral, begun in 1904
and finished in 1978, is the largest in the world;
the Roman Catholic Cathedral is a striking
conical structure topped with a lantern tower
and illuminated with stained glass by John
Piper and Patrick Reyntiens. The Walker Art
Gallery has a collection of paintings second only
to those in London, and includes the original of
Yeames popular work 'And when did you last
see your father' among works by Reubens,
Holbein, Stubbs (born in Ormond Street),
Turner and Reynolds. Gladstone, Prime
Minister during the reign of Queen Victoria,
was born in Rodney Street in one of a row of
superb Georgian houses. Down by the Mersey
is the Royal Liver Building and Cunard offices,
a reminder of the days when the great
transatlantic liners used to berth here. Beneath
the river are the Queensway Tunnel (opened in
1934, and at 2 miles then the world's longest
underwater tunnel) and the Kingsway Tunnel
(opened in 1971). On the pierhead is a
memorial to the engineers lost on the 'Titanic'
which sank in 1912.
Tourist Information Centre Near Lime Street
station (051-709 3631).

PUBS
There are many to be found here.

Litherland

North of Litherland the conurbation thins out and wastelands and suburbs appear, while the canal turns east to Aintree. Soon the first of many swing bridges is encountered; for the first few miles these bridges have to be padlocked to combat vandalism, so progress through them is necessarily slow. All navigators should ensure that they have the requisite key before reaching these bridges. (Keys obtainable from the British Waterways section offices at Burscough, Wigan, Burnley and Apperley Bridge.)

PUBS

🍺 **Tailor's Arms** Canalside, at bridge 4A.

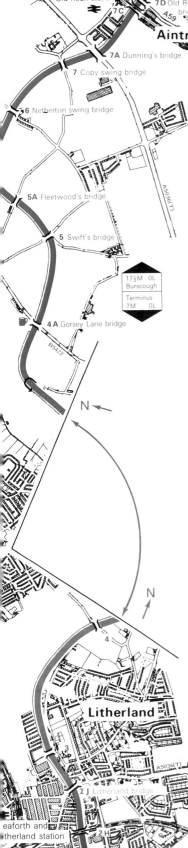

Old Roan station

7D Old Roan bridge

A59

7C

Aintree

7A Dunning's bridge

7 Copy swing bridge

6 Netherton swing bridge

A5036(T)

5A Fleetwood's bridge

5 Swift's bridge

17½M 0L
Burscough

Terminus
7M 0L

4A Gorsey Lane bridge

B5422

N ←

N ↑

4

Litherland

A5036(T)

2J Litherland bridge

eaforth and
therland station

2H

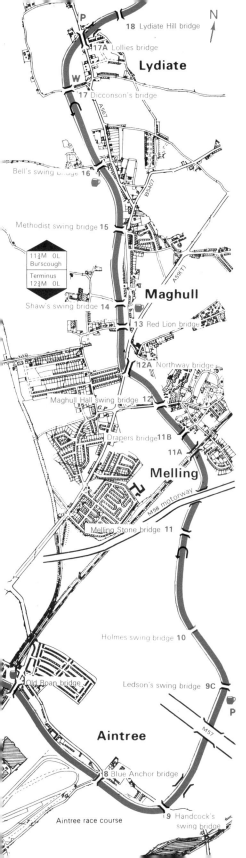

Maghull

Aintree marks the limit of Liverpool's outskirts. The great feature here is of course the Aintree Race Course: the famous Grand National steeplechase is run every year on a spring Saturday. Much of the course lies right beside the canal, but would-be spectators from the canal will have to stand upon their boat's cabin top to see over the fence surrounding the course. At the east end of the racecourse is another swing bridge; this carries a busy main road and traffic lights are installed, but boat crews operate the bridge themselves. Here the canal turns north again, and as the little church tower at Melling comes into view the navigation emerges at long last into open countryside, although Maghull soon looms up to interrupt this with a series of swing bridges.

Navigational note
Those heading towards Liverpool should remember that all the usual city problems with vandals will become apparent beyond bridge 11. There is a winding hole here for those who wish to turn around.

Maghull
Merseyside. EC Wed. All services. A small town astride the canal, convenient for supplies. Since the last war it has greatly expanded, but still maintains its former village atmosphere.
St Andrew's Church Damfield Lane. Just north of bridge 12A. Though separated from the rest of the town by a dual carriageway, it is well worth a visit: it has a cosy setting among trees that seem to compete with the tower for height. It was built in the late 19thC but its style is in imitation of that of the 13thC to accord with the tiny 700-year-old chapel known as Old St Andrew's in its grounds. The chapel is a charming little building, said to be the oldest church in the Merseyside area.
Melling
Merseyside. PO, tel. The sight of this little village is like a breath of fresh air to anyone coming along the canal from Liverpool, although southbound travellers probably find it unremarkable. The village stands on an isolated hillock at a safe distance from the big city. The church is a landmark in the area; it was built in the 15thC with rock from an adjacent quarry.

PUBS
Running Horses Maghull. Canalside, at bridge 16. Ind Coope and Walkers real ales.
Hare & Hounds Maghull. Near bridge 14.
Bootle Arms Melling. Burtonwood real ale.
Horse & Jockey Near bridge 9C.
Old Roan Aintree. Near Old Roan Bridge 7D.

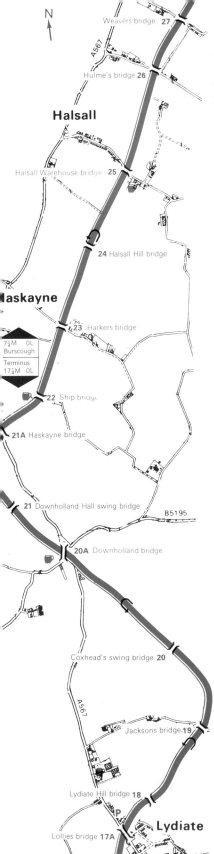

Halsall

The canal now enters continuous open
countryside, which soon establishes itself as
extremely flat and intensively cultivated
lowlands: indeed it is more akin to
Cambridgeshire or Lincolnshire than to the rest
of Lancashire. However it is pleasant enough
and the canal forms one of its more important
features – a view which is borne out by the large
number of people usually to be seen walking
and boating upon it, as well as the hundreds of
anglers enjoying their sport in this well-stocked
length of canal. As if in compensation for the
unexciting landscape, the traveller is offered a
truly astonishing number of pubs on or near the
canal all the way from Lydiate to Wigan.

Halsall
Lancs. PO, tel, garage. There is a handsome tall
14th–15thC church here (St Cuthbert's), with a
fine spire. The choir vestry, erected in 1592,
was formerly a grammar school. There is an
interesting pair of pulpits/lecterns. One of them
is generously illuminated by a solitary overhead
window; the other, more sheltered, gives the
occupant the unfortunate air of being behind
bars . . .

Haskayne
Lancs. PO, tel, stores. There are just two pretty
houses here: the post office and the old
thatched cottage opposite. No sign of a church.

PUBS
🍺 **Saracen's Head** Halsall. Canalside, at
Halsall Warehouse Bridge.
🍺 **Ship** Haskayne. Canalside, at Ship Bridge.
A well-known canal pub with a garden serving
Tetley's real ale.
🍺 **King's Arms** Haskayne. 100yds north of
bridge 21A.
🍺 **Scarisbrick Arms** Canalside, at
Downholland Bridge. Greenall Whitley real
ale.
🍺 **Scotch Piper** About 400yds north of bridge
17A. A beautifully preserved award-winning
pub with no bar, serving Burtonwood real ale
straight from the barrel.

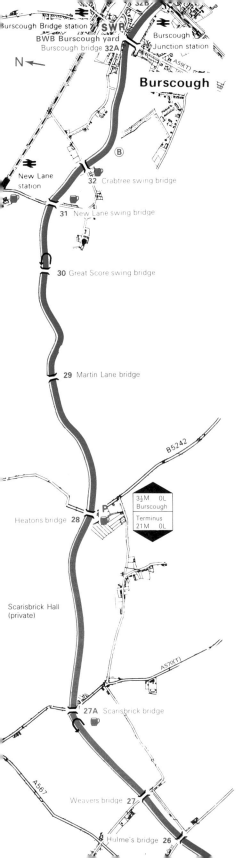

Burscough

One moves now past a massive caravan site on one side and attractive woods containing the private Scarisbrick Hall on the other; then out again into the open flatlands. The Southport–Manchester line converges from the north west; it runs near the canal all the way into Wigan, and has some wonderfully remote stations. A flurry of swing bridges brings the canal into Burscough: just beyond is the junction with the Rufford Branch.

Navigational note
You will need your British Waterways key, and a windlass, to open bridge 32.

Burscough
Lancs. PO, tel, stores, garage, bank, station.
Formerly a canal village and a staging post on the one-time Wigan–Liverpool 'packet boat' run, this place attaches more significance nowadays to the benefits of road and rail transport. It still boasts two stations (one is on the Preston–Liverpool line) and suffers from heavy through traffic. A very convenient place for taking on victuals.

BOATYARDS

Ⓑ **Latham Marina** The Workshop, Crabtree Lane, Burscough (894782). Pump-out, slipway, boat and engine repairs, salvage works, toilets.
British Waterways Burscough Yard (Burscough 893160). Ⓡ Ⓢ Ⓦ Dry dock.

PUBS

🍺 **Royal Coaching House** Liverpool Road, Burscough. Boddingtons and Higsons real ales in a pub 2 minutes' walk from the canal. *Lunchtime* food, children's room, garden.
🍺 **Railway** At New Lane station.
🍺 **Latham Slipway** Canalside at bridge 32. Thwaites real ale and an extensive range of food *lunchtime and evenings*. Children allowed in *until 20.30*, garden with play area, good moorings.
🍺 **Farmers Arms** Canalside, by bridge 31. A pub of great character with an open fire and a choice of Jennings, Walkers and Tetley's real ales. Children are allowed in *until 20.00*, and snacks are served. Good moorings.
🍺 **Heatons Bridge** Friendly unspoilt canalside pub, at bridge 28. Tetley's and Walkers real ales, garden.
🍺✕ **Red Lion** Near Scarisbrick Bridge.

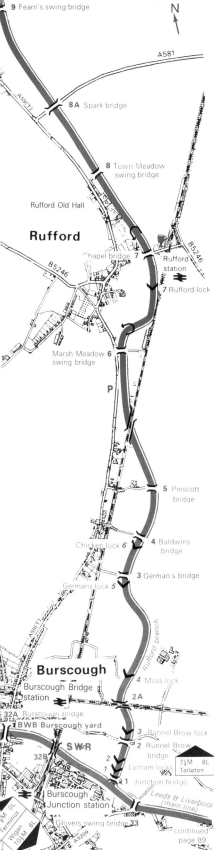

Rufford

The Rufford Branch leaves the Leeds &
Liverpool main line just east of Burscough,
through an imposing arched bridge dated 1816.
A little canal settlement surrounds the top lock
and the roomy dry dock for barges here. The
locks come thick and fast to begin with, as the
canal falls through the very fertile and gently
sloping farmland towards the distant Ribble
estuary. The country is generally quiet, flat and
unspectacular but agreeable. A line of trees and
the spire of Rufford church are followed by the
beautiful Rufford Old Hall, on the west bank.

Navigational notes
1. If you wish to make the diversion off the
main line to visit Tarleton, please note that
craft over 60ft will have difficulty turning at
James Mayor's boatyard.
2. You will need your British Waterways key to
open bridge 33.

Rufford
Lancs. PO, tel, stores, garage, station. Main road
village noted for its Hall. The church is a small
Italianate Victorian building containing many
monuments to the Heskeths who owned
Rufford Hall for many centuries; obviously a
prolific family judging by one large sculpture
depicting a brood of 11 children, dated c1458.
The family now resides in Northamptonshire.
Rufford Old Hall *NT property*. (Rufford
821254). On the west bank of the canal. A
medieval timber-framed mansion with
Jacobean extensions given to the National
Trust in 1936. The interior is magnificently
decorated and furnished in period style,
especially the great hall with its hammerbeam
roof and 15thC intricately carved movable
screen – one of the few still intact in England.
The Hall also houses a folk museum. *Open
afternoons Apr–Oct (closed Fri)*. Admission
charge.
Note: although the Hall is beside the canal, one
may **not** enter the grounds direct from the
canal. Navigators should therefore tie up near
bridge 7, then walk up to the village and turn
right at the main road. The entrance is a few
hundred yards along the wall on the right.

PUBS
🍺 **Hesketh** Rufford. Greenall Whitley real ale
served via fake handpumps in a cocktail bar
atmosphere.
🍺 **New Fermor Arms** East of bridge 7. An
unremarkable modern pub replacing an earlier
building famous for its tilt which was finally
demolished in 1974. Youngers real ale and bar
food. Garden.
🍺 **Ship** Burscough. Near second lock down.
An old canal pub formerly known as the 'Blood
Tub' – black puddings were once made here,
and a bucket of pig's blood could be exchanged
for a pint of beer.

continued
page 89

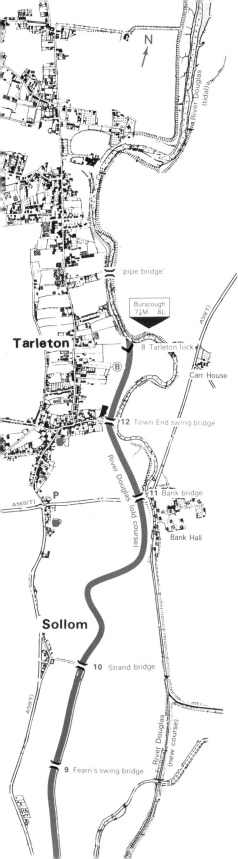

Tarleton

At Sollom there used to be a lock, but now it is
no more. This is where the canal turns into the
old course of the River Douglas, and it twists
and turns as though to prove it. The towpath
has been ploughed up from here onwards. The
'new' course of the Douglas (which was once
navigable from the sea right up to Wigan)
comes alongside the canal at the busy road
bridge near Bank Hall, a house hidden by trees.
From here it is only a short distance to the final
swing bridge and Tarleton Lock, where the
canal connects with the tidal River Douglas –
which in turn flows into the River Ribble near
Preston.

Navigational notes
1. Vessels wishing to enter or leave the Rufford
Branch via Tarleton Lock can only do so at
high water. The Douglas is then a relatively
easy navigation, and since the removal of the
old railway swing bridge a mile downstream,
there has remained only one limitation on
headroom from Tarleton to the open sea. This
is a pipe bridge not far north of Tarleton Lock:
the clearance at normal high water is about
20ft. The boatyard at the lock may help callers
with advice regarding tide times, etc.
2. Navigators entering the Rufford Branch
canal from the sea should remember that they
will need a padlock key – as well as a windlass –
to open the locks up the branch. Arrangements
can be made with the British Waterways
Burscough Yard (Burscough 893160) to have
such a key left with James Mayor's boatyard.

Tarleton
Lancs. PO, tel, stores, garage, bank. A large
village luckily avoided by the A59 road. There
are some useful shops and a good take-away
food shop.

BOATYARDS
Ⓑ **James Mayor** The Boatyard, Tarleton,
Preston. (Hesketh Bank 2250). Ⓡ Ⓦ Ⓓ Caters
for canal craft and sea-going boats. Gas,
chandlery, five slipways up to 90ft, 3-ton crane,
moorings. Boat and motor sales, motor repairs.
Steel and wood boats built and fitted out.
Telephone, showers, toilets. Extremely helpful
people.

PUBS
🍺 **Cock & Bottle** Church Lane, Tarleton.
Thriving village-centre pub dispensing
Thwaites real ale. *Lunchtime* snacks, garden,
children allowed in side rooms *until 21.00.*
🍺 **Ram's Head** West of bridge 11. Large
young persons' pub serving Greenall Whitley
real ale and food *at all times.* Garden, children
allowed in until *20.00.*

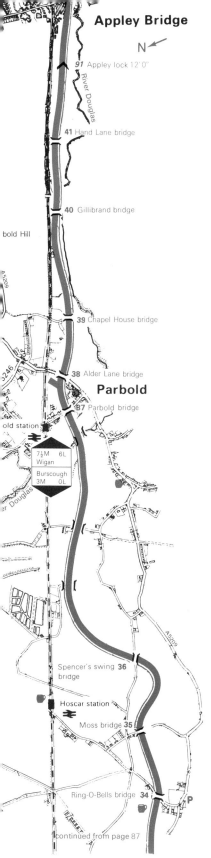

Appley Bridge

91 Appley lock 12'0"

River Douglas

41 Hand Lane bridge

40 Gillibrand bridge

bold Hill

39 Chapel House bridge

38 Alder Lane bridge

Parbold

37 Parbold bridge

old station

7½M 6L
Wigan

Burscough
3M 0L

er Douglas

Spencer's swing **36**
bridge

Hoscar station

Moss bridge **35**

Ring-O-Bells bridge **34**

P

continued from page 87

Parbold

East of the junction with the Rufford Branch, the canal meanders through the flat countryside to the village of Parbold with its ancient sail-less windmill. Here the scenery changes completely as the canal crosses the River Douglas and then joins the Douglas Valley. This is a very pretty, narrow wooded valley which the canal shares with the railway: there are several convenient stations along the line. Appley Lock is reached: there are two locks alongside, now restored, and you can choose either to use these or the very deep main lock. The shallower locks were once used as a navigable sidepond for boats passing in opposite directions.
As with all subsequent locks, the gates should be closed and the paddles lowered and padlocked after use to combat vandalism and wastage of water.

Navigational note
You will need your British Waterways key to open bridge 36.

Parbold
Lancs. PO, tel, stores, garage, station. A large village climbing up from the west end of the Douglas Valley. Parbold is prettiest near the canal bridge, where the big brick tower of the old windmill is complemented by an equally attractive pub. Unfortunately the rest of the village is being engulfed by acres of new housing. Local landmarks are the tall spires of Parbold's two churches, and Ashurst's Beacon high on a hill to the south. The latter was built in 1798 by Sir William Ashurst in anticipation of an invasion by the French. (The beacon was intended as a local warning sign.)
Douglas Navigation
The little River Douglas, or Asland, was made navigable in the first half of the 17thC, well before the great spate of canal construction. It provided the Wigan coalfield with a useful outlet to the tidal River Ribble, from which the cargoes could be shipped over to Preston or along the coast. When the Leeds & Liverpool Canal was built to share the Douglas Valley, the old river navigation became superfluous. It was bought up by the new company, who constructed their own branch to the Ribble estuary (the Rufford Branch). Between Parbold and Gathurst it is possible to find many traces of the old navigation, including several locks.

PUBS

Stocks Tavern Alder Lane, Parbold, south of bridge 37. Very fine traditional country pub serving excellent bar meals *lunchtime and evenings*. Tetley's real ale. Children allowed in *until 20.00.*
Railway Parbold, north of bridge 37. Typical village local. Burtonwood real ale and meals *lunchtime and evening*. Children allowed in *until 20.00.*
Windmill Parbold. By bridge 37. Old village local dispensing Greenall Whitley real ale, and meals *lunchtime and evening*. Children allowed in *until 20.00.*
Ring O'Bells Canalside at bridge 34. (Burscough 893157). Tastefully modernised country pub serving bar and restaurant meals (*L & D, not Mon*) along with Higsons and Boddingtons real ales. Canalside tables, children welcome.
Railway Tavern Hoscar Station, north east of bridge 35. Small country pub serving Tetley's and Jennings real ales and snacks. Children allowed into side rooms.

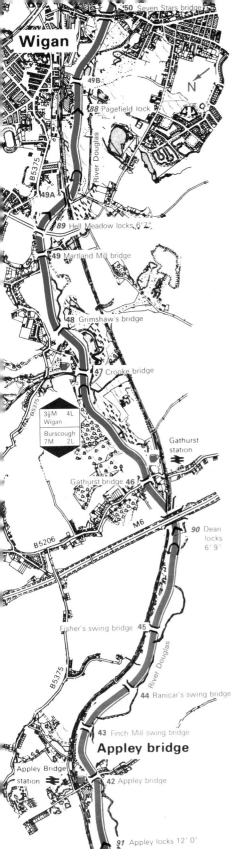

Douglas Valley

The canal now goes through Appley Bridge and
runs up the beautifully rural Douglas Valley,
with the river on one side and the
Wigan–Southport railway on the other. Passing
three consecutive swing bridges, one soon
reaches Dean Locks, a pleasant spot in spite of
the high motorway viaduct nearby. This used
to be a very busy place, for in addition to the
now restored duplicated canal locks, there used
to be a lock down into the River Douglas
Navigation, when this was navigable before the
Rufford Branch was built. Just east of the locks
is a pleasant canalside pub, then the valley
widens out to reveal the chimneys and factories
of Wigan. Hell Meadow (sometimes mistaken
for 'Ell Meadow') and Pagefield Locks lead the
canal up towards the centre of Wigan.

Navigational note
You will need your British Waterways key to
open bridge 43.

Appley Bridge
Lancs. PO, tel, stores, station. A canalside
hamlet dominated by large mills and works, the
place is nevertheless attractively situated in the
wooded Douglas Valley.

PUBS
Crooke Hall Inn Crooke. Near bridge 47.
Garden, mooring. Greenall Whitley real ale.
Navigation Gathurst. Canalside, at bridge
46. Tetley's real ale.
Railway Appley Bridge by the canal.
Tetley's real ale.

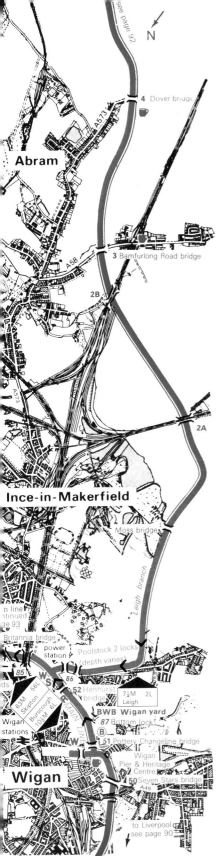

Abram

The Leigh Branch leaves the main line of the
Leeds & Liverpool Canal in Wigan, between
the big power station and the 22nd lock. The
famous 'Wigan Pier', a coal staithe, is by bridge
51 and has been rebuilt. It was made fun of by
George Formby snr, and written about by
George Orwell in 'The Road to Wigan Pier', in
1937. Descending through two locks, the canal
enters the lock-free level that extends all the
way along the Bridgewater Canal to Preston
Brook and Runcorn, over 40 miles away
passing through a landscape once spoiled by
mining but now painstakingly restored as
parkland – a wildlife haven. Most of the way,
the canal is on an embankment, well above the
level of the surrounding landscape; this is a
relatively new situation and is due to severe
mining subsidence in the area. (The canal has
had to be built up – appropriately with pit
waste – while the land on either side has sunk.)

Wigan Pier & Heritage Centre
A wonderful complex of restored and new
canalside buildings housing a wide range of
superb exhibits and entertainments. Enquiries
to: The Piermaster's Office, Wigan Pier, Wigan
(323666).
Waterways Gardens By Seven Stars Bridge.
Boats, stonemason's blocks and a lock-keeper's
garden.
The Way We Were Opposite Wigan Pier, this
is a stunning exhibition/museum/theatre
illustrating how the local people worked and
played, laughed and suffered around the turn of
the century.
Orwell Pub and restaurant, see below.
Trencherfield Mill Probably the largest
working mill engine in Britain, installed when
the mill was built in 1907. Manufactured by
J & E Wood of Bolton it is a horizontal
four-cylinder triple expansion engine with a
26½ft diameter flywheel. A magnificent sight.
Also textile machinery.
Mill at the Pier Concerts, exhibitions,
conferences.
Waterbus Operates daily to transport visitors
from The Waterways Garden at one end to the
Mill at the other.
Café, shops, walks, information centre. *All
open daily 10.00–17.00*. Charge. A remarkable
initiative.

BOATYARDS
British Waterways Wigan Yard at Wigan
Bottom Lock. (Wigan 42239). R S W and
toilet opposite at lock 86.
Ⓑ **Wayfarer Narrow Boats** Mayors Boatyard,
Swan Meadow Road, Wigan (41890). R S
W D Pump-out, gas, narrowboat hire, repairs,
chandlery, short-term mooring. Slipway and
dry dock close by.

PUBS AND RESTAURANTS
🍺 **Red Lion** Canalside at Dover Bridge on the
Leigh Branch. Greenall Whitley real ale, food
lunchtime and evenings and children's play area.
There used to be two locks nearby: they were
removed years ago, becoming unnecessary as
the level of the land changed.
🍺✕ **Orwell** Wigan (323034). Large pub and
restaurant in a warehouse opposite bridge 51.
This is a very handsome building, and the
conversion has been well done – the pub is
spacious, comfortable and restrained. Tetley's
and Jennings real ales; bar meals (*lunchtime and
evenings*) are available. Outside drinking on
canalside verandah. Plenty of moorings close
by.
🍺 **Royal Oak** Standish Lower Ground, Wigan.
Burtonwood real ale and a wide variety of food
at all times.
🍺 **Swan & Railway** Wallgate, Wigan. A
5-minute walk from the Orwell towards the
town centre. Bass and John Smith real ales;
food *lunchtime and evening (not Sun)*. Children's
room.
🍺 **Seven Stars Hotel** Wallgate, canalside.
Thwaites real ale and food *lunchtime and evening*
in a friendly and interesting pub.
🍺 **Bamfurlong Hotel** Lily Lane. 200yds south
West of bridge 3 on the Leigh Branch. Walkers
real ale.

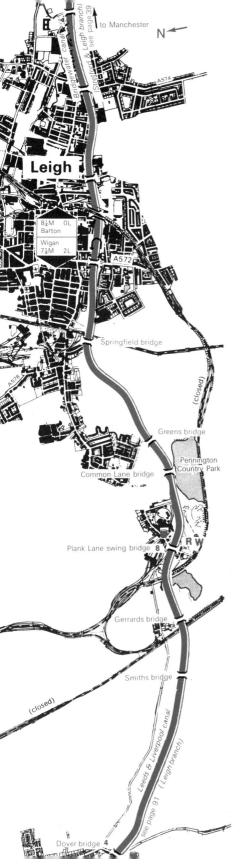

to Manchester

N ←

Leigh

8¼M	0L
Barton	
Wigan	
7¼M	2L

A572

Springfield bridge

(closed)

Greens bridge

Pennington
Country Park

Common Lane bridge

Plank Lane swing bridge **8** **R W**

Gerrards bridge

Smiths bridge

(closed)

Leeds & Liverpool canal (Leigh branch)

see page 91

Dover bridge **4**

Leigh

The Leigh Branch continues eastwards through what was once a wasteland – now reclaimed and landscaped – towards Plank Lane swing bridge (actually a lift bridge) which is mechanically operated. Navigators should knock at the adjacent house in *daytime only (08.00–20.00 summer, 17.00 winter)* to ask the resident bridge keeper to operate the bridge, which carries a busy road. Past the bridge, in Leigh, the canal suddenly becomes the Bridgewater Canal (without the customary stop lock), giving access to Manchester and the Trent & Mersey via Preston Brook. This navigation is owned by the Manchester Ship Canal Company: boats licensed by British Waterways may use the Bridgewater without further charge for up to 7 days.

Leigh
Gt Manchester. EC Wed. All services. Once the archetypal mill town, most of the tall buildings and chimneys have now been demolished. In the market place you can see the fine Edwardian baroque Town Hall, built 1904–7, facing the battlemented church of St Mary.

PUBS
🍺 **Eagle & Hawk** Chapel Street, Leigh. Walkers real ale and food.
🍺 **Railway Hotel** Twist Lane, Leigh. A beer enthusiast's pub offering Tetley's, Walkers, Jennings and Ind Coope Burton real ales. *Opens 12.00 and 19.00 (sometimes later).*
🍺 **Nevison** Plank Lane. A comfortable miners' pub serving Tetley's and Walkers real ales 400yds from the swing bridge. Snacks at *lunchtime*.

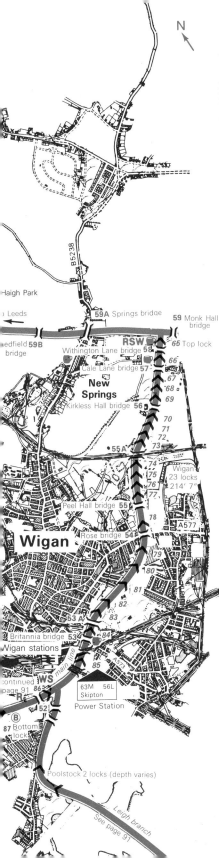

Wigan Locks

Leaving the junction with the Leigh Branch, the main line reaches the Wigan flight of 21 locks. It is a long and arduous climb to the top by boat, for these wide, deep locks raise the canal level by over 200ft. For the faint-hearted, there are shops and pubs near bridges 53 and 54. Up at the top lock, however, are two canal pubs – a comforting sight. Here is a T-junction as the canal meets what used to be the southern end of the Lancaster Canal (see the history section) on its disjointed way to Johnson's Hill Locks, Walton Summit and Preston. In the middle of the housing estate behind the Kirkless Hall is a fish & chip shop, *open for lunch and supper most days except Sun.* Turning left, the traveller is soon aware of the great height he has climbed as the navigation winds along a hill. It soon enters the woods that precede Haigh Hall and Park.

Navigational notes
1. The locks between Wigan and Leeds are 60ft long, and therefore cannot accommodate a full length narrowboat.
2. The locks are heavy to work and the paddle gear varies from great levers on the ground paddles to ratchet gear worked from precarious platforms on the gates. The top gate paddles are *very fierce* – always open the ground paddles first when filling a lock, and wait until the water level reaches the bottom of the gates before slowly opening the gate paddles. Great care is needed.
3. You will require a British Waterways anti-vandal key.

Wigan
Gt Manchester. EC Wed. MD Fri. All services. A large, heavily industrialised town whose skyline is now a mixture of industrial chimneys and towering concrete blocks of offices and flats. There is a good and extensive covered market. The old market place in the centre of the town has some attractive black-and-white half-timbered houses above the shops. It has long been the butt of many jokes referring to Wigan Pier – not a Victorian structure devoted to amusement at sea, but a coal staithe! George Formby snr started the confusion, which lasted for years. *See page 91 for details of the Heritage Centre.*
All Saints Church A very large and impressive parish church surrounded by beautiful rose gardens. Parts of the original medieval structure remain but it was largely rebuilt in 1845–50, still following the rather ornate design of the former church. There are several very fine stained glass windows and numerous monuments and effigies.
Powell Museum Station Road. Exhibits include geology, coins and the history of local industrial development. *Open weekdays.*

BOATYARDS
British Waterways Wigan Yard At Wigan Bottom Lock. (Wigan 42239). [R][S][W] and toilet opposite at lock 86.
Ⓑ **Wayfarer Narrow Boats** Mayors Boatyard, Swan Meadow Road, Wigan (41890). [R][S][W][D] Pump-out, gas, narrowboat hire, repairs, chandlery, short-term mooring. Slipway and dry dock close by.

PUBS
🍺 **Crown Hotel** West of bridge 59A. Burtonwood real ale, meals *lunchtime and evenings (except Tue eve),* garden and children's room.
🍺 **Colliers Arms** Near bridge 59A. Burtonwood real ale in a charming old pub overlooking the canal.
🍺 **Kirkless Hall** Canalside, near Wigan Top Lock. Distinctive black and white building housing spacious and comfortable bars. Burtonwood real ale and good bar meals *lunchtime and evenings.*
🍺 **Commercial Inn** Canalside, at bridge 57. A sturdy pub dispensing Tetley's and Walkers real ales and bar snacks *lunchtime and evenings.* Payphone here.
🍺 **Shepherds Arms** Tetley's real ale pub at bridge 53. Good cafe 100yds north west of this bridge.

Adlington

The canal continues to run as a 9-mile lock-free pound – known as the 'Lancaster Pool' – along the side of the valley from which the industries surrounding Wigan can be viewed in the distance. It enjoys a pleasant and quiet isolation in this lightly wooded area. Already the navigation is well over 300ft above the sea, and the bleak hills up to the east give a hint of the Pennines that are soon to be crossed. The conspicuous tower east of Adlington stands on a hill that is over 1500ft high. Points of interest on this stretch include Arley Hall, a large and elegant moated house that is now the club house of the local golf club, and the nearby skewed aqueduct over a closed railway track.

Adlington
Gt Manchester. PO, tel, stores, garage, station. A small industrialised town very useful for pubs and supplies – the local licensed store east of bridge 69 is open late most evenings.
Haigh Hall (Wigan 832895). On east bank of the canal. The pre-Tudor mansion was rebuilt by its owner, the 23rd Earl of Crawford, between 1830 and 1849. The reconstruction was designed and directed by the Earl, and all the stone, timber and iron used on the job came from the estate. The Hall is now owned by Wigan Corporation, who allow the citizens to use it for private wedding receptions, etc. There is little to see in the house and it is not normally open to the public. The park and grounds around the hall are *open daily all year*, and contain much that caters for the family: there are children's amusements, glasshouses, a nature trail, a miniature railway, a mini zoo and a golf course.

BOATYARDS
Ⓑ **L & L Cruisers** Rawlinson Lane, Heath Charnock, nr Chorley. (Adlington 480825). ⓇⓈⓌⒹ Pump-out, gas, hire craft, overnight mooring, narrowboat slipway, chandlery, boat building and repairs, toilets, gift shop, day hire boats.
Ⓑ **White Bear Marina** Park Road, Adlington (481054). ⓇⓈⓌⒹ Pump-out, slipway, gas, overnight mooring, long-term mooring, winter storage, boat and engine sales and repairs, showers, toilets, chandlery, gifts. Resident night watchman.

PUBS
🍺 **Cardwell Arms** East of bridge 71. Vaux and Ward's real ales in a boisterous pub.
🍺 **White Bear** East of bridge 69. An old roadside pub serving Theakstons and Matthew Brown real ales. *Lunchtime* food.
🍺 **Bridge Inn** By bridge 69. Greenall Whitley real ale.
🍺 **Waggon & Horses** East of bridge 68. Dark rustic pub offering Whitbread and Hartley's real ales and *lunchtime* food.
🍺 **Crawford Arms** Canalside by Red Rock Bridge (63). Comfortable split-level pub with a garden. Greenall Whitley real ale and meals *lunchtime and evenings*.

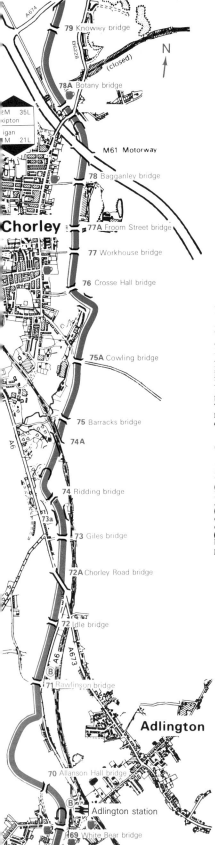

79 Knowley bridge

(closed)

78A Botany bridge

2M 35L
kipton
igan
M 21L

M61 Motorway

78 Bagganley bridge

Chorley

77A Froom Street bridge

77 Workhouse bridge

76 Crosse Hall bridge

75A Cowling bridge

75 Barracks bridge

74A

74 Ridding bridge

73a

73 Giles bridge

72A Chorley Road bridge

72 Idle bridge

B 71 Rawlinson bridge

Adlington

70 Allanson Hall bridge

B Adlington station

69 White Bear bridge

Chorley

This is an initially attractive section as the canal wanders northwards from Adlington. Hemmed in for much of the way by woodland, the canal is undisturbed by the railway and main roads that for a while follow it closely. Soon the greenery gives way to views of Chorley's rows of rooftops across the valley. The canal crosses this valley, but shuns the town: it passes instead some large and resplendent outlying textile mills. The M61 motorway zooms up from Manchester around the mills and over the navigation before disappearing in the direction of Preston in a flurry of flyovers, feeder roads and roundabouts.

Chorley
Lancs. EC Wed. MD Tue, Fri, Sat. All services.
On the west bank of the canal, a busy town based on the manufacture of textiles and spare parts for commercial and public service vehicles. (Leyland, where the vehicles are built, is just a few miles away to the north west.) Chorley has avoided too much industrial grimness by maintaining its market-town traditions and by extensive new housing development. Sir Henry Tate, the founder of the Tate Gallery in London, was born in Chorley in 1819 and began his career here as a grocer's assistant.
St Laurence's Church Church Brow. Surrounded by trees in the centre of the town, parts of the church date back to the 14thC. The bones that are enshrined in a recess in the chancel are believed to have belonged to St Laurence.
Astley Hall At the north west end of the town just over a mile from Botany Bridge. Set in a large park beside a lake, the appearance of this Elizabethan mansion is very striking, for in the 17thC the existing timberframing was replaced by a new façade that is lacking in symmetry. The interior is very fine with splendid ceilings, furnishings, tapestries and pottery. *Open afternoons.*

PUBS
🍺✕ **Railway** Canalside at bridge 78A. (Chorley 75864). Modernised pub and restaurant (*L & D*) serving Whitbread real ale. The railway line has long disappeared – the viaduct was blown up to make room for the motorway.
🍺 **Bretherton** West of bridge 78. Matthew Brown real ale in a comfortable lounge bar. *Lunchtime* food.
🍺 **Seven Stars** 84 Eaves Lane, Chorley. West of bridges 76 and 77. Basic town local dispensing Matthew Brown real ale.
🍺 **Hop Pocket** Carr Lane, Chorley, West of bridge 75. Thwaites real ale in a modern estate pub decorated with hop sacks. Snacks.

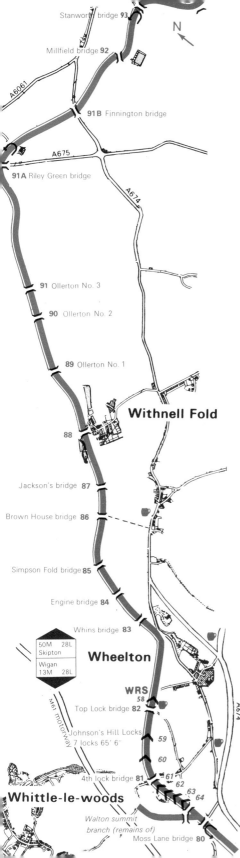

Withnell Fold

This is a most delightful stretch of waterway.
The junction with the old Walton Summit
Branch features a canal cottage and the bottom
lock in the Johnson's Hill flight. A short but
energetic spell of windlass-wielding is required
here, for the seven locks are very close together.
It is rewarding work, for the steep countryside
yields good views, and the locks are tidily
maintained and painted. Near the middle lock
is an old toll house, a post office, telephone and
store; at the top lock is a pub and, usually, a
medley of boats (there is a boat club here). The
canal now changes course to north east and
flows along a beautifully secluded and often
wooded valley at a height of over 350ft above
sea level. Even the old mills at Withnell Fold,
which once brought a glimpse of industry, are
now gone.

Withnell Fold
Lancs. A remarkable village well worth a short
visit. It is a small estate village, built to house
workers at the canalside paper mills which are
now demolished. They used to export banknote
paper all over the world until 'rationalisation'
transferred their work elsewhere.
Symmetrically grouped around three sides of a
spacious square, the terraced cottages present
an intimately united front which is almost
unnerving to the casual visitor – especially as on
the fourth side of the square is an old set of
wooden stocks.

Wheelton
Lancs. PO, tel, stores, garage. There are steep
terraces and cobbled streets in this village
which has been recently bypassed and has thus
rid itself of much road traffic.

Walton Summit Branch
The short branch leading off to the north from
Johnson's Hill Locks used to be part of the
Lancaster Canal, which was originally
projected to run south from Preston past Wigan
to the Bridgewater Canal. But the Lancaster
Canal Company was very short of money and,
after arranging with the Leeds & Liverpool
Company to share a common course between
Johnson's Hill Locks and Wigan Top Lock,
was daunted by the prospect of constructing a
large and necessarily expensive aqueduct over
the River Ribble in Preston. A 'temporary'
tramroad was therefore built to connect the two
lengths of canal between Preston and Walton
Summit about 3 miles north of Johnson's Hill.
The tramway, which opened in 1803, featured a
short tunnel and a light trestle bridge over the
Ribble. Through traffic now began to use the
canal, and one may imagine the busy scenes at
either end of the tramway as cargoes were
transhipped from boats into wagons and back
into boats at the far end. The tramroad,
although designed only as a short-term
measure, was never replaced by a canal; indeed
the whole line was closed by 1880. Most of the
canal branch has recently been severed by the
building of a motorway, although plenty of it
still remains in an unnavigable state.

PUBS AND RESTAURANTS

🍺 **Royal Oak** Preston Old Road, Hoghton.
North of bridge 91A. Busy, rambling old pub
serving Thwaites real ale, and meals *lunchtimes
and Wed–Sun evenings.*
🍺 **Golden Lion** Blackburn Road, Higher
Wheelton. South of bridge 86. Thwaites real ale
in a small, pleasant main road pub.
🍺✕ **Dressers Arms** Briers Brow, Wheelton
(830041). East of bridge 82. An excellent pub
with a Cantonese restaurant upstairs (*L & D*)
and a fine choice of real ales and food in the bar.
🍺 **Top Lock** Canalside at Johnson's Hill Top
Lock. Good bar food and Matthew Brown real
ale in a comfortable pub. Moor below the top
lock – there is no room above.
✕🍺 **Red Cat** Blackburn Road, Heapey.
(Chorley 63966). East of bridge 80. Pizzeria
with a small bar area overlooking the cellar.
Matthew Brown real ale.

Blackburn

The canal now curls round a steep and thickly wooded valley, crossing it on a high embankment before entering the outskirts of Blackburn. Close to bridge 94 there is a useful shop. It seems to take a long time to get through this large town, as there is a flight of six locks here, raising the canal's level to a height of over 400ft above sea level. However one can get an excellent view of local bowls matches from the embankment between bridges 97 and 98. The best place to moor (although space is limited) in Blackburn is just above lock 56: shops and pubs are close at hand, and the lock keeper lives here. He keeps a tidy flight – indeed most of the passage through the city is now pleasant – there is little rubbish or graffiti, and the views are excellent. A good towpath exists throughout. Of particular interest to those on the canal are the fine old canopied wharves of the defunct BWB Blackburn depot – although clearly its days are numbered. The aroma of the Thwaites brewery is refreshing.

Blackburn
Lancs. EC Thur. All services. Few of the Pennine towns which sprang up with the Industrial Revolution can be described as beautiful, as aesthetic feelings were rarely consulted in the rush to raise mills and cram houses round them. In an attempt to rectify this, Blackburn has taken drastic steps in recent years to construct a new city centre, which includes multistorey blocks of flats, a large shopping precinct and a vast covered market. Nevertheless the most impressive features of the town are still the old cotton mills.
Blackburn Cathedral Dating from 1820–6, the parish church was raised to cathedral status in 1926. Extensive renovations have been made inside. Very striking 13ft sculpture of 'Christ the Worker' in aluminium and black iron by John Hayward. Large churchyard.
Lewis Textile Museum Exchange Street, Blackburn (667130). A series of period rooms demonstrating the development of the textile industry from the 18thC onwards by means of full-size working models, including Hargreaves' 'Spinning Jenny'. *Closed Sun.*
Museum & Art Gallery Library Street, Blackburn (667130). Exhibits include natural history, pottery, early manuscripts and a large collection of English, Greek and Roman coins. In the art gallery are over 1200 beautiful Japanese prints, as well as English watercolours of the 18thC–20thC. *Closed Sun.*
Witton Park At the western end of the town, north of Cherry Tree station. Nearly 500 acres of magnificent parkland, including the beautiful landmark, Billinge Hill. Splendid abundance of rhododendrons and azaleas. *Open daily to the public.*
Tourist Information Centre Town Hall, Blackburn (53277).

PUBS
🍺 **Packet House Inn** Near bridge 103A. Bass real ale.
🍺 **Infirmary** Blackburn. By lock 56. Thwaites real ale, good bar food, children welcome in this down to earth pub.
🍺 **Navigation** Blackburn. Canalside, at bridge 96A. Thwaites real ale.
🍺 **Barge Inn** Blackburn. By bridge 102A. New pub with canal theme serving Thwaites real ale.
🍺 **Atlantic** 100 yds south of bridge 100. Matthew Brown real ale.
🍺 **Royal Oak** 100 yds south of bridge 100. Whitbread real ale.

Rishton

Clayton-le-Moors

114B Whalley Road bridge

114A Enfield Changeline bridge
114AA Enfield Green bridge

Rileys
114 swing bridge

Church

35M	22L
Skipton	
Wigan	
28M	34L

113A Peel Bank bridge
Church swing bridge **113**

Dunkenhalgh Park

urban development
Simpson's bridge **111D**

Church Kirk Changeline bridge **112**

Burys bridge No 2 **111B**
Burys bridge No 1 **111A**
Fox Hill Bank bridge **111**

New Barn bridge **109**
aqueduct

Tottleworth bridge
108

108 A Rishton bridge

P

Aspen bridge **110**

Rishton

107A Norden bridge

Rishton station

107 Cut bridge

106 Side Beet bridge

power station

P

Whitebirk bridge **104 B**

Greenbank Bridge **104A**

104 Sour Milk Hall bridge

Blackburn

Paradise bridge **103B**

Blackburn station

Enam bridge **103A**

The canal leaves Blackburn and embarks upon a course of twists and turns that emphasise the hilliness of the countryside. The scenery varies all the time between heavy industrial development (and its effects) and – just around a corner – green fields, farms and distant views of wild moorlands. The contrast repeats itself time and again, but the moorlands always seem to remain tantalisingly out of reach. However, anyone prepared to take a short but energetic walk away from the canal will find remote and beautiful countryside remarkably close. The Calder Valley motorway (M65) follows the line of the canal to Burnley, making many crossing and requiring re-routing of the navigation in two places. It is pleasing to see the care taken with such items as stone walling, which makes the new aqueduct by bridge 109 a positive asset to the canal. Of less recent vintage, but of equal interest, is the fine wharf building with a large central arch at Simpson's Bridge. Beyond Church, the first of four swing bridges appears; they are the only ones between Wigan and Gargrave.

Church
Lancs. EC Wed. PO, tel, stores, garage, bank. An industrial community which was originally based on calico printing, established on the canal bank by the family of the famous statesman Sir Robert Peel. The rows of terrace houses are characteristic of so many of the towns in this industrial area. The parish church of St James is right on the banks of the canal; only the tower and font remain from the original 15thC building.

Dunkenhalgh Hall
Clayton-le-Moors. Standing in 16 acres of gardens and woodland, it is a beautiful Elizabethan mansion, extensively altered in the 19thC. Its name is said to be derived from a Scottish raider named Duncan, who chose to settle there. The Hall is now used as an hotel.

Rishton
Lancs. EC Wed. PO, tel, stores, garage, bank, station. A small grey town that grew up around the cotton mills in the 19thC by courtesy of the Petre family of the Dunkenhalgh Estate, who used to be lords of the manor and are still local landowners.

PUBS
🍺 **Hare & Hounds** 250 yds east of bridge 114A. Thwaites real ale. *Shops and fish & chips nearby.*
🍺 **Old England Forever** Church Street, Clayton-le-Moors. Matthew Brown real ale.
🍺 **Wellington** Barnes Square, Clayton-le-Moors. Thwaites real ale. *Both the above are about 250yds west of bridge 114B.*
🍺 **Roebuck** Rishton, near bridge 108A. Matthew Brown and Theakstons real ales, and food.

126A
Rose Grove station
ugdale A671
bridge

126 Liverpool Road bridge

A671

125 Old Rose Grove bridge

124C

Halstead bridge
124B

Molly Wood bridge
124A   124A

123 Knott's bridge

A679

29¼M | 22L
Skipton

Wigan
33¾M | 34L

Ⓑ 121 Hapton bridge

Hapton station

Hapton

worth bridge
119A   120 Higher Shuttleworth bridge
        119 Shuttleworth Hall bridge

M65 motorway

n bridge 118

Huncoat station

Clough Bank bridge 117

116 Smith's swing bridge

115A

115 Foster's swing bridge

A678

114C Pilkington bridge

Clayton-le-Moors

A680

Enfield
Changeline bridge
Whalley Road bridge 114B   114A

Hapton

The navigation continues to wind eastwards
along the side of what turns out to be the Calder
Valley with the new motorway to the south.
High ground rises on each side of the valley,
and in the distance the summit of Pendle Hill
(1831ft high) can be clearly seen when it is not
obscured by cloud. This is an attractive length
of canal, unspoilt by industry and greatly
enhanced by the ever-changing views from the
side of the hill along which the canal is cut,
although the motorway is uncomfortably close
throughout, and power station cooling towers
are ever present. Soon the distant mass of
dwellings is recognisable as the suburbs of
Burnley.

Navigational note
You will require a British Waterways key to
operate Foster's swing bridge 115.

Hapton
Lancs. PO, tel, stores, station. A small and
unmistakably northern town, with its regular
streets of terraced houses.

BOATYARDS

Ⓑ **Hapton Boatyard** Hapton. (Padiham
73178). Ⓦ Ⓓ Gas, long-term mooring, repairs,
slipway, chandlery, 8-ton crane. National boat
transporters.

PUBS

◪ **Bridge House** Hapton, by bridge 121.
Thwaites real ale, *lunchtime* bar snacks.
◪ **Railway** Hapton. Along the road from the
Bridge House. Thwaites real ale.

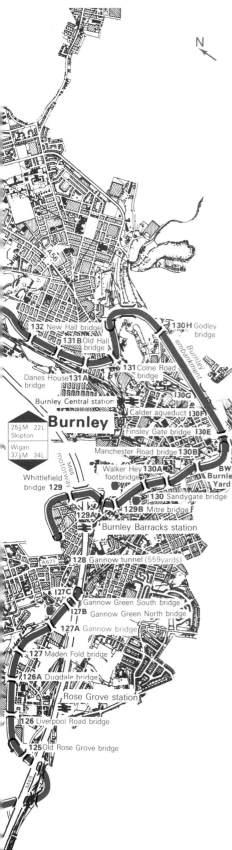

N

Burnley

The canal now wanders through the suburbs
into Gannow Tunnel (559yds long), then round
the hillside into Burnley. This is an industrial
stretch where the canal was once a main artery
for the town and its industries. The area around
bridge 130 known as the Weavers' Triangle has
been recognised to be of great interest – fine
warehouses, tall chimneys and loading bays
flank the canal here. There is a museum in the
Toll House, and a steam mill engine has been
restored. The huge Burnley Embankment
carries the navigation across part of the town –
called 'the straight mile' it is ¾ mile long, but
no less dramatic for that fact; 60ft high, it
incorporates an aqueduct over a main road. The
whole area of the embankment has been tidied
up and the towpath opened and improved:
access is now good and this, together with the
British Waterways yard, makes a good mooring
site. Shops are within easy reach.

Burnley
Lancs. All services. A large industrial northern
town, which has worked hard to improve its
appearance. It was once the world centre for
cotton weaving. The excellent shopping centre
is only 10 minutes' walk from Finsley Gate
Bridge, and if you feel like a swim, a sauna or a
solarium, the Thompson Recreation Centre is
even closer. Fish & chips are two minutes' walk
south west of the bridge.
Queen Street Mill Museum Harle Syke,
Burnley (412555). North east of Burnley
Embankment, along Eastern Avenue and
Briercliffe Road from the football ground. This
is Britain's only working 19thC weaving mill,
powered by the 500hp steam engine 'Peace'.
Virtually unchanged until it closed in 1982, the
mill has now found a new lease of life, with
some of the former employees back again to
work the looms. Mill shop and café. *Open
10.30–16.30 Thur–Sun Easter–Sep.* Charge.
The Weavers' Triangle The area between
bridges 129B and 130B is one of the
best-preserved 19thC industrial districts in the
country – there are weaving sheds with 'north
light' roofs, engine houses, spinning mills and
well-preserved terraces of 19thC houses. An
explanatory leaflet and town trail guide are
available from: the Tourist Information Centre
or the Toll House Museum of local history and
the cotton industry, which is also the
information centre for the Weavers' Triangle.
*Open 14.00–16.00 Tue, Wed, Sat, Sun & B.
Hols Easter–Sep. Free.*
Townley Hall (Burnley 24213). On the
southern outskirts of Burnley, 1¼ miles south
east of the BWB yard. Set in extensive parkland
with a golf course and play area, the grandiose,
battlemented house dating from the 14thC was
the home of the Townley family until 1902. It is
now an art gallery and museum with the rooms
lavishly furnished in period style. *Closed Sat &
Sun morning.*
Tourist Information Centre Burnley
Mechanics, Manchester Road, Burnley
(30055).

BOATYARDS

British Waterways Burnley Yard Finsley Gate,
Burnley (28680). R W S Toilet, slipway,
moorings. Telephone kiosk outside.

PUBS

There are plenty of pubs in Burnley.
🍺 **Stork** North of bridge 129B. Tetley's ales.
🍺 **Mitre Hotel** By bridge 129B. Bass.
🍺 **Sparrowhawk** Church Street, Burnley.
Moorhouse real ale, brewed in the town.
🍺 **Grey Mare** 110 Gannow Lane, Burnley.
Typical cosy local serving Bass real ale.
🍺 **Gannow Wharf** Canalside at bridge 127A.
Bass and bar snacks.

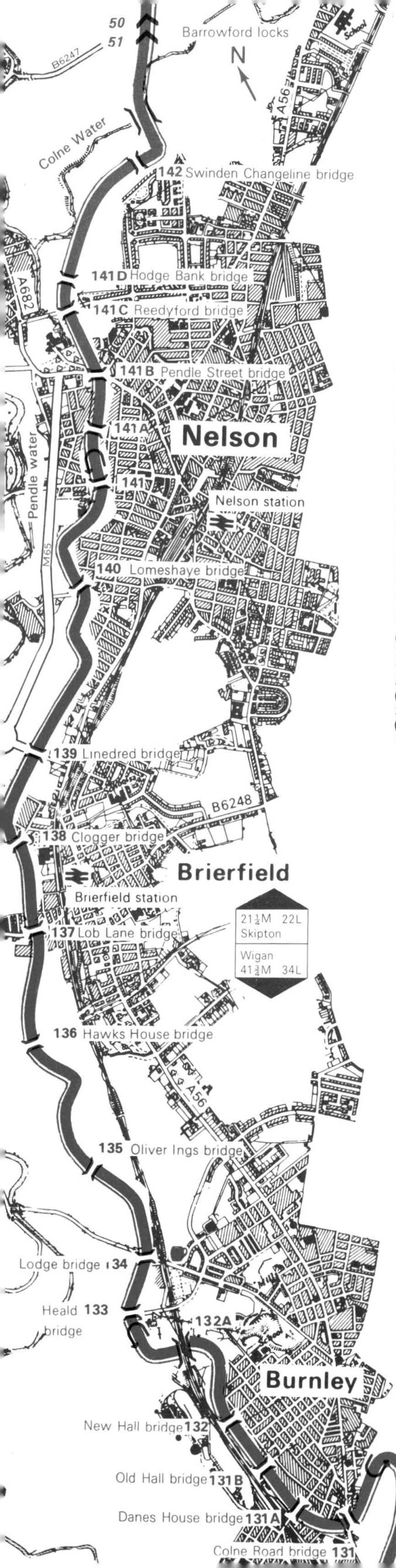

Brierfield

Here again the canal negotiates a landscape which alternates between open country, towns and semi-towns, with the massive distant bulk of Pendle Hill in the background. Cobbled streets of terraced houses run down to the canal, and old wharves lie disused and overgrown. The navigation winds as it follows the hillside; but this ceases at Nelson, where it crosses the valley on a minor aqueduct and begins to climb the pretty Barrowford Locks having finally seen off the new motorway.

Nelson
Lancs. EC Tue. MD Wed, Fri, Sat. All services.
Nelson is a conglomerate of a number of small villages that combined in the 19thC to form one industrial town. The centre has been redeveloped with a large covered shopping precinct. One of Nelson's more valuable assets is the easy access to the beautiful moors and Forest of Pendle, behind which looms Pendle Hill.

Brierfield
Lancs. PO, tel, stores, garage, bank, station, cinema. A small industrial town merging into Burnley at one end and into Nelson at the other. The parish church of St Luke in Colne Road is a Victorian building with an unusually designed clock tower culminating in a steep pyramid roof.

PUBS

🍺 **Waggon & Horses** Brierfield, up the road from bridge 139. A beautifully restored pub with an open fire, offering Thwaites real ale, and food *lunchtime and evenings*. Garden.
🍺 **Leeds & Liverpool** Brierfield. Up the hill from bridge 137.
🍺 **Reedley Hallows Hotel** 50yds east of bridge 134. Castle Eden real ale.

Map labels:

- 50
- 51
- B6247
- Barrowford locks
- N
- A56
- Colne Water
- 142 Swinden Changeline bridge
- B6283
- 141 D Hodge Bank bridge
- 141 C Reedyford bridge
- 141 B Pendle Street bridge
- 141 A
- **Nelson**
- 141
- Nelson station
- Pendle water
- M65
- 140 Lomeshaye bridge
- 139 Linedred bridge
- B6248
- 138 Clogger bridge
- **Brierfield**
- Brierfield station
- 137 Lob Lane bridge
- 21¼M 22L Skipton
- Wigan 41¾M 34L
- 136 Hawks House bridge
- 135 Oliver Ings bridge
- Lodge bridge 134
- Heald 133 bridge
- 132A
- **Burnley**
- A56
- New Hall bridge 132
- Old Hall bridge 131B
- Danes House bridge 131A
- Colne Road bridge 131

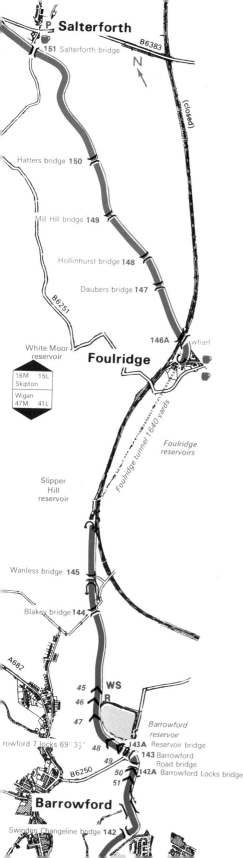

Foulridge

This is a refreshing stretch, in which the canal
leaves the succession of industrial towns. It
rises through the seven Barrowford Locks,
passing Barrowford reservoir (in which the
summit level's surplus water is stored), and at
the beautifully kept top lock reaches the
summit level of the whole canal. Soon one
begins to notice the various feeder streams
continuously pouring vital water supplies into
the navigation. Meanwhile, distant
mountainous country frames beautiful old
stone farms nearer at hand. Soon everything is
blotted out as one enters Foulridge Tunnel; at
the other end, by the railway bridge, is an old
wharf where one can tie up to visit the village.
Meanwhile the navigation continues northward
through this very fine countryside to
Salterforth, crossing over the little 'Country
Brook' between bridges 149 (milk and eggs for
sale) and 150.

Salterforth
Lancs. PO, tel, stores. A small village of narrow
streets and terraced houses in an upland
setting.
Foulridge
Lancs. PO, tel, stores. Attractive around the
green, where alleys festooned with washing
lines give the place a homely air. In the
surrounding countryside are scattered the
reservoirs that feed the summit level of the
canal.
Foulridge Tunnel
1640yds long, with no towpath, this tunnel is,
not surprisingly, barred to unapproved boats.
The hole in the hill sprang to fame in 1912
when a cow fell into the canal near the tunnel
mouth and for some reason decided to struggle
through to the other end of the tunnel. The
gallant but weary swimmer was revived with
alcohol at the Foulridge end. Photographs in
the Hole in the Wall pub recall the incident.
The tunnel roof drips liberally.
Barrowford
Lancs. PO, tel, stores. There are still some
attractive terraces of stone cottages in this
village, which lies a short walk to the west of
the locks. The Toll House, the last intact
survivor from the old Marsden (Nelson) to
Long Preston turnpike road, together with the
17thC Park Hill (the birthplace of Roger
Bannister, the first 'four minute miler') now
houses The Pendle Heritage Centre (Nelson
695366). *Open afternoons; closed Mon & Fri*,
charge). John Wesley preached from the
packhorse bridge in the 1770's; there is a fine
park by the river containing traces of a mill
dating from 1311.

PUBS

🍺 **Anchor** Salterforth. Canalside, at bridge
151. A traditional pub serving Bass
Charrington real ale, where a second building
was built on top of the first – hence where you
now drink was once the bedrooms. The cellar
has stalactites. Good moorings, children's
room.
🍺 **Hole in the Wall** Foulridge. 250yds east of
tunnel, north end. Here is recorded the famous
cow in the canal incident. Stones real ale is
served, and there is a room where children can
sit. Steeles stores close by gives genial service
and stocks splendid pies – savoury or sweet.
🍺 **New Inn** Foulridge. Carry on past the Hole
in the Wall and cross the main road. Thwaites
real ale, bar food (*not Sun or Mon Oct–Mar*).
Children may eat here. Spotlessly clean.
🍺 **George & Dragon** Gisburn Road,
Barrowford. Large Victorian bar counter and
18thC fireplace in the public bar of this lively
village pub opposite the Toll House. John
Smith real ale.

Barnoldswick

This is one of the most remote sections of the whole canal and probably the most beautiful. There is also much canal interest, for just south of bridge 153 was the junction, now disappeared, of the Rain Hall Rock Branch, essentially a linear quarry where the limestone was loaded directly from the rock face onto the boats. Walk up the road from the bridge (east) and turn right at the top where it will come into view, straddled by a tall three-arched viaduct. A mile further along one rounds a corner and is confronted by Greenberfield Top Lock, which introduces the beginning of the long descent towards Leeds. (The feeder from the distant Winterburn reservoir enters the canal at the top lock.) The three locks here were built in 1820 to replace the original flight (the old dry bed of the earlier route can be seen on the towpath side) and are set in beautiful uplands – for the next few miles the canal winds through scenery that is composed of countless individual hillocks, some topped by clumps of trees. Beyond are distant mountains. Around East Marton, after skirting the isolated church, the surroundings change briefly: the navigation enters a cutting, passes under a double-arched main road bridge and enters a sheltered fold housing a farm, a pub and some moorings. But a steep wooded cutting leads the canal out of this pastoral interlude and back into the rugged moorlands. There is a useful shop and café at Wilkinsons Farm by bridge 162.

Pennine Way The Pennine Way is a walking route covering over 250 miles of Pennine highland from Edale in the south to Kirk Yetholm in the north. Because of the nature of the route much of the Way is rough, hard walking, but it gives a superb view from the mountains. At East Marton the Pennine Way shares the canal towpath for a short distance – you will notice that the stones here abound with fossils.

Barnoldswick
Lancs. EC Tue. PO, tel, stores, garage, bank. Set back from the canal, the mainstay of this town's existence is the Rolls Royce factory, where experimental work is done on aero engines. The centre of the town is compact and dominated by the modern Holy Trinity Church completed in 1960.

BOATYARDS

Ⓑ **Doug Moore (Boatbuilders)** Lower Park Marina, Kelbrook Road, Barnoldswick (815883). Ⓓ Pump-out, gas, day hire craft, overnight mooring, long-term mooring, winter storage, chandlery, boat building, repairs, gift shop, fresh milk, telephone.

PUBS

Cross Keys East Marton. (Earby 843485). By bridge 161. Large and handsome pub with a comfortable polished wood interior. Theakstons, Thwaites and Websters real ales, bar snacks and more substantial meals in the candlelit dining room. Next door is the Cottage Stores – it does not look like a shop and can be easily missed. Telephone kiosk close by. There are plenty of pubs in Barnoldswick.

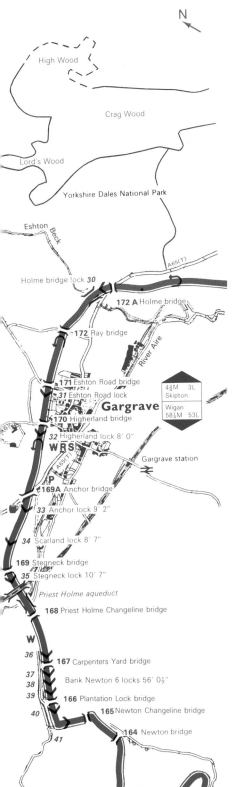

Gargrave

This is another outstanding stretch, in which the navigation continues to snake extravagantly around the splendid green and humpy hills that fill the landscape. The six Bank Newton Locks in their wooded setting lower the canal into Upper Airedale, yielding excellent views across the valley to the hills and moors beyond. The River Aire flows in from the north, accompanied by the railway line to Skipton and Leeds from Morecambe, Settle and distant Carlisle. The canal crosses the river by a substantial stone aqueduct. Meanwhile, yet more locks take the canal round Gargrave, between the village and the hills; the beauty of the area may be judged by the fact that the Yorkshire Dales National Park borders the navigation along here. There is a launching slipway at Higherland Lock.

Gargrave
N. Yorks. PO, tel, stores, garage, bank, station.
A very attractive and much-visited village. Holding an enviable position near the head of Airedale between the canal and the river, this place is the ideal centre for boat crews to explore the surrounding countryside. The River Aire cuts Gargrave in two, and the bridge over it forms the centre of the village. There is a charming station, and some pretty stone cottages along the green. The church is mostly Victorian, except for the tower, which was built in 1521. Excellent home bakery.
Yorkshire Dales National Park Some of England's finest walking country is contained in this area of fine views, deep valleys, open moorland and rugged hills. Designated as a National Park in 1954 the Dales, covering 680 sq miles, are hardly scarred by habitation.

PUBS

 Mason's Arms Gargrave. An old attractive local opposite the church. Whitbread real ale and snacks.
 Old Swan Main Street, Gargrave. Imposing village centre hotel serving Whitbread real ale and meals *lunchtime and evenings*. Accommodation.
 Anchor Inn By Anchor Lock, Gargrave (749666). A large smart pub/hotel/restaurant with comfortable low-ceilinged bars where you can enjoy Theakstons and Youngers real ales. Meals (*L & D*) and a large garden with a superb children's play park.

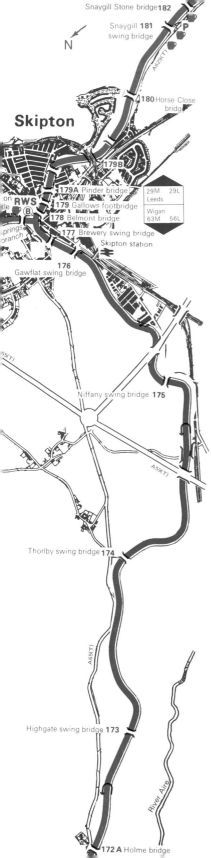

Skipton

The canal now turns south east and proceeds down Airedale, a valley which contains it from here right through to Leeds. Upper Airedale is a flat, wide valley defined by tall steep hills. The countryside is open, unploughed and very inviting to walkers, especially with the moorlands stretching away over the top of the hills. In this robust landscape the navigation hugs the hillsides just above the valley floor, enjoying a lock-free pound that is 17 miles long – although the navigator's relief at the absence of locks may be tempered by the abundance of swing bridges (173, 174, 175, 176 and 177 require an anti-vandal key). Entering Skipton, which is usually bristling with pleasure boats, the navigator will see the Springs Branch, a little arm that leads off past the town centre and soon finds itself in what is virtually a ravine, overlooked by the castle more than 100ft above. Boats longer than 35ft will have difficulty in turning round along the branch. At the junction is a boatyard: next door is a restored canal warehouse.

Skipton
N. Yorks. EC Tue. MD Wed, Sat. All services (including cinema) and excellent shops. Skipton is probably the most handsome town along the whole Leeds & Liverpool Canal. It is an excellent place for visiting from the canal, for one can moor snugly and safely away about 1 minute's walk away from the centre. It still maintains its importance as a market town, which is referred to in its name: Saxon 'Scip-tun' means sheep-town. The wide High Street is very attractive, lined with mostly Georgian houses, and headed at the northern end by the splendid castle and the well-kept graveyard of the parish church. There is an interesting watermill beside the Springs Branch.
Church of the Holy Trinity Standing opposite the castle, it is a long battlemented church, encircled by large lawns and flourishing gardens. It is in Perpendicular style dating from the 14thC, though it was greatly renovated after suffering serious damage during the Civil War. It has a fine oak roof and a beautifully carved Jacobean font cover.
Skipton Castle Skipton (2442). A magnificent Norman castle, with 17thC additions, that dominates Skipton High Street. After a three-year siege during the Civil War, Cromwell's men allowed the restoration of the castle, but ensured that the building could never again be used as a stronghold. The six massive round towers have survived from the 14thC and other notable features are the 50ft-long banqueting hall, a kitchen with roasting and baking hearths, a dungeon and the 'Shell Room', the walls of which are decorated with sea shells. *Open daily (closed Sun morning). Admission charge.*
Tourist Information Centre High Street Car Park Approach, Skipton (2809).
Springs Branch
A short (770yds) but very unusual branch that leaves the Leeds & Liverpool Canal, passes the centre of Skipton and soon finds itself in what is virtually a ravine, overlooked by the castle that towers 100ft above. The branch is navigable, and makes an interesting diversion by boat or foot. (The towpath continues past the arm, into Skipton Woods.) It was built by the Earl of Thanet, the owner of Skipton Castle, to carry limestone away from his nearby quarry. It was extended by 240yds in 1797 from the watermill bridge through the deep rock cutting, and chutes were constructed at the new terminus to drop the rock into the boats from the horse tramway that was laid from the quarry to the castle. The quarry still flourishes, but the canal and tramway have not been used since 1946. Trains and lorries have replaced them. The Springs Branch acted for many years as a feeder to the Leeds & Liverpool Canal, taking water from Eller Beck, which runs beside it. It is now a picturesque backwater and an excellent place

to moor if your boat is less than 35ft long or you
are confident that you can reverse out, as
turning is restricted.
Skipton Woods Fine woods leading up the
little narrow valley from the Springs Branch.
For access, just keep on walking up the
towpath of the branch.
Yorkshire Dales Railway Embsay Station
(Skipton 4727). 1 mile north of Skipton off the
A59/65 bypass. Bus service from Skipton. A
4-mile round-trip either steam or diesel hauled.
Museum, mining centre, picnic area, shop,
café. Real ale buffet car. *Services every hour
11.00–16.15. Sun, Apr–Dec; Tue & Sat, Jul &
Aug; plus various 'specials'.*

BOATYARDS

ⓑ **Pennine Cruisers** The Boat Shop, 19 Coach
Street, Skipton (5478). At junction with
Springs Branch. Ⓦ Ⓓ Pump-out, narrowboat
hire, gas, chandlery. Dry dock, boat building
and repairs, extensive boat sales, 24hr
emergency service, day hire boats.

TRIP BOAT

Pennine Boat Trips Skipton (60829). Trips
and party hire in 'Cobbydale'.

PUBS AND RESTAURANTS

🍺 **Bay Horse** Canalside at bridge 182. A
'Family Inn' serving meals *lunchtime and
evenings*. Tetley's real ale, garden and
children's room.
✕🍺 **Copper Beech** Close to bridge 181.
(Skipton 2970). Youngers real ale and meals
lunchtime and evenings in this large modern
hotel/restaurant. Garden with pond, children's
room.
✕🍺 **Inn Between** Not far from bridge 181.
(Skipton 5711). Modern restaurant (*L & D*)
serving Tetley's real ale.
🍺 **Rose & Crown** Coach Street, Skipton. By
the junction with the Springs Branch. Tetley's
real ale served in this town centre pub.
🍺 **Royal Shepherd** Canal Street, Skipton.
Whitbread, Castle Eden and Chester real ales
available in this lively pub overlooking the
Springs Branch.
✕🍷 **Waterfront** Skipton (60121). Restaurant
and disco at junction of Springs Branch.
🍺 **Hole in the Wall** High Street, Skipton.
🍺 **New Ship** Canalside, up the Springs
Branch.
There are at least 25 other pubs and hotels in
the town.

The Springs Branch, Skipton. *David Perrott.*

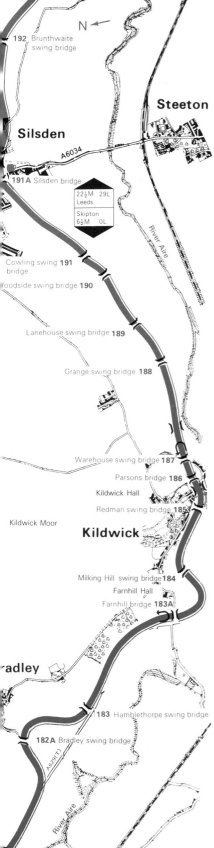

Kildwick

The canal continues along the hillside down the valley of the River Aire, with the main road just beside and below the navigation. Excellent views are offered up and down this splendid valley and the surrounding countryside. The village of Bradley has an attractive waterfront – the *PO stores* are situated beyond the imposing mill building. There is a fine wooded stretch north of Kildwick; then one curves sharply round the outcrop on which crouches Farnhill Hall, a mellow stone building. The intriguing village of Kildwick has some well restored canalside buildings now used as private residences. There are good moorings here prior to quieter country: the main road and the railway cut the valley corner while the canal takes the longer route round to Silsden and beyond. This stretch of the navigation is liberally punctuated with swing bridges many, thankfully, not requiring an anti-vandal key.

Silsden
W. Yorks. EC Tue. PO, tel, stores, garage, bank. A well-contained, stone-built industrial town spreading uphill from the canal. In addition to its proximity to the Yorkshire Dales National Park, it offers plenty of shops near the canal. The canalside warehouses are attractive; there is also an old corn mill dated 1677.

Kildwick
W. Yorks. PO, tel, stores. An interesting and unusual village spilling down the hillside. The streets are extremely steep; one of them goes under the canal through a narrow skewed aqueduct.

BOATYARDS

Ⓑ **Black Prince Holidays, Silsden Boats** The Wharf, Silsden, near Keighley. (Steeton 53675). Ⓡ Ⓦ Ⓓ Pump-out, narrowboat hire, canal shop, slipway, gas, toilets, winter storage. *Closed Sun.*

Ⓑ **Snaygill Boats** Skipton Road, Bradley, nr Keighley. (Skipton 5150). At bridge 182. Ⓡ Ⓢ Ⓦ Ⓓ Pump-out, boat hire, gas, dry dock, boat and engine repairs, canal shop, long-term mooring, some overnight mooring, toilets, showers.

PUBS

🍺 **Bridge Inn** Main Street, Silsden. Cosy canalside local serving John Smith real ale.
🍺 **Grouse Inn** Main Street, Silsden. Tetley's real ale in a popular pub close to the canal.
🍺 **King's Arms** Bolton Road, Silsden. Young persons' pub offering Tetley's real ale.
🍺 **White Lion** Priestbank Road, Kildwick. 17thC coaching inn near the canal. Tetley's real ale, *lunchtime* food, garden.

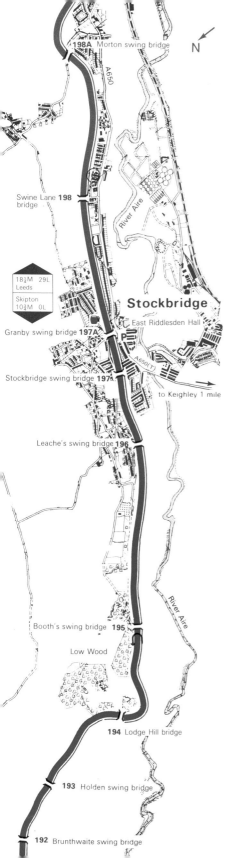

Keighley

Here the canal continues south east along the side of the green hills that overlook Airedale. The hills are very steep and beautifully wooded in places. The distant rows of chimneys, factories and terraced houses across the valley comprise Keighley; most of its industrial and suburban tentacles are quickly passed by the canal, although the constant succession of little swing bridges intermittently impedes a boat's progress. Some of these bridges can be rather stiff to operate.

East Riddlesden Hall (Keighley 607075). *NT property*. Just south of swing bridge 197A. A 17thC stone manor house complete with tithe barn. Fine collection of furniture, paintings and armour. Fishing is permitted in the ponds in the grounds. *Open Jun–Aug 11.00–18.00 Wed–Sun; Apr & May, Sep & Oct 14.00–18.00 Wed–Sun. Closed Nov–Mar.* Charge.
Keighley
W. Yorks. EC Tue. MD Wed, Fri, Sat. All services. Compared with some other industrial centres in the area, Keighley is a clean and pleasant town. It boasts a large new shopping centre, much modern housing and some handsome older stone terraces. The oldest part is around the parish church of St Andrew, a large perpendicular building whose main attraction is its shady churchyard.
Cliffe Castle Spring Gardens Lane, Keighley (64184). Once the home of the Butterfield family, it has been completely restored and now houses the museum and art gallery. Local exhibits illustrate the archaeology, natural history and industrial history of the area. There are reconstructed craft workshops and a textile room. Picturesque grounds where band concerts are held. *Open afternoons, closed Mon.* Free.
Keighley & Worth Valley Railway (Haworth 42329). Privately preserved by volunteers of the Keighley & Worth Valley Railway Preservation Society, the line runs for 5 miles from the British Rail station at Keighley up to Haworth, the home of the Brontë family, and Oxenhope. British Railways closed the line in 1961, but the Society eventually succeeded in reopening it in 1968 with a regular service of steam trains. In the mornings, the service is operated by diesel railbuses but in the afternoons magnificent steam engines puff their way along the track. In the goods yard at Haworth the Society has a splendid collection of steam engines and carriages, mostly ancient. The line was made famous by the film 'The Railway Children'.

PUBS

🍺 **Marquis of Granby** At swing bridge 197A. *PO and stores* the other side of the bridge.
🍺 **Worth Valley Inn** 1 Wesley Place, Ingrow. Useful for visitors to the railway. A cosy little pub serving Whitbread real ale. *Lunchtime* food, and children allowed in then as well. There are plenty of pubs in Keighley.

Bingley and Shipley

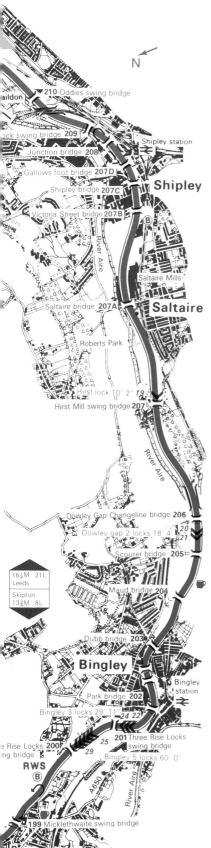

The impressive Bingley Five-Rise staircase
locks (see below) mark the end of the long level
pound from Gargrave, and from here to Leeds
there are no more views of a sweeping,
uncluttered river valley. Just a few hundred
yards south of the five locks are the three-rise
staircase locks, which bring one steeply down
into Bingley. The canal bisects this town but
one can see little of the place from the water.
Leaving Bingley, trees lead to Dowley Gap and
the two staircase locks. At the foot of the locks
the towpath changes sides and the navigation
crosses the River Aire via a stone aqueduct.
Woods escort the canal along the single Hirst
Lock; from here one moves past the big mills at
Saltaire and right through Shipley.

Baildon
W. Yorks. EC Tue. All services. 1½ miles north
of Shipley. A very old industrial town huddled
on a hilltop on the edge of Baildon Moor.
Stretching from Baildon to Bingley is The
Glen, a wooded valley that curves below the
heights of the moor. A splendid scenic tramway
carrying two tramcars connects the coach road
to the higher parts of Baildon Moor. (In
summer a frequent service operates, but in
winter it is arranged only to suit the needs of
residents at the upper level.)

Shipley
W. Yorks. EC Wed. MD Fri, Sat. All services. A
dark stone town built on a generous scale and
based on textile and engineering industries.
There are powerful-looking mills to be seen, as
well as the town hall and a suitably
battlemented Salvation Army citadel. Shipley is
lucky enough to be on the edge of Baildon
Moor and Shipley Glen. The 3-mile-long
Bradford Canal used to join the Leeds &
Liverpool in Shipley, by bridge 208, but this
has all been filled in for years.

Saltaire
W. Yorks. An estate village that owes its
existence to the Utopian dream of Sir Titus
Salt, a wealthy Victorian mill owner. He was so
appalled by the working and living conditions
of his workers in Bradford that he decided to
build the ideal industrial settlement. This he
did in 1850 on the banks of the canal and the
River Aire – hence the name Saltaire. He
provided every amenity including high
standard housing, but no pub – for he was a
great opponent of strong drink. The village has
changed little since those days; everything is
carefully laid out and the terraced houses are
attractive in an orderly sort of way. (And there
is still no pub!) There is an Italianate church
near the canal, and a large park beside the river.
(Rowing boats can be hired here in the summer.)

Bingley
W. Yorks. EC Tue. MD Fri. All services. An
industrial town now known nationally as a
centre for thermal underwear. Standing at the
south east end of it amidst several old cottages
is the large parish church of Holy Trinity, with
its massive spire conspicuous from the canal.

Bingley Five-Rise Locks A very famous and
impressive feature of the canal system built in
1774 in 'staircase' formation, ie they are all
joined together rather than being separated by
pounds of 'neutral' water. The top gates of the
lowest lock are the bottom gates of the lock
above, and so on. This means it is not possible
to empty a lock unless the one below is itself
empty. The rapid elevation thus resulting is
quite daunting. The locks are *open 08.00–18.30*
and may be used only under the supervision of
the lock keeper, who lives in the interesting
house at the top of the flight. The BWB
Sanitary Station is housed in a handsome old
stable, where towing horses were once rested.

BOATYARDS

ⓑ **Apollo Canal Carriers** Wharf Street,
Shipley. (Bradford 595914). Ⓡ Ⓦ (emergency
Ⓓ) Pump-out. 46-seater passenger boat and
50-seater cruising restaurant. Temporary
mooring by arrangement.

ⓑ **Hainsworths Boatyard** Bingley. (Bradford
565925). 200yds above the five-rise. Ⓦ Ⓓ
Pump-out, gas, overnight mooring, long-term
mooring, winter storage, slipway, chandlery,
boat building, boat sales, repairs, emergency
call out.

PUBS

There are plenty of pubs in Bingley and
Shipley.

🍺 **Shoulder of Mutton** Otley Road,
Charlestown. ¼ mile east of bridge 210.
Tetley's real ale.

🍺 **Sun** Market Place, Shipley. 250yds south of
bridge 207C. Tetley's real ale.

🍺 **Fisherman** Canalside, above Dowley Gap
locks.

🍺 **Brown Cow** Ireland Bridge, Bingley. ¼ mile
west of bridge 202. Timothy Taylor real ale.

🍺 **Ferrands Arms** Queen Street, Bingley.
250yds south of bridge 202. Timothy Taylor
real ale.

🍺 **Royal** 200yds down the hill from
Micklethwaite swing bridge. Tetley's real ale.

Ascending the Five-Rise, Bingley. *David Perrott.*

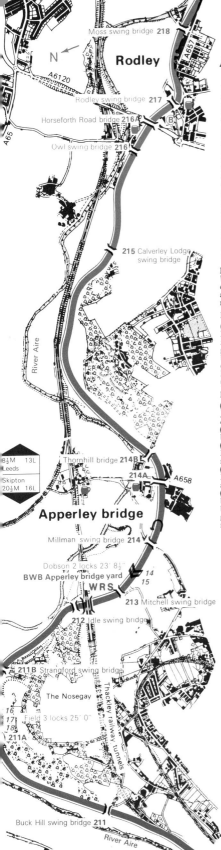

Apperley Bridge

This section sees the end of the wide open moorlands that frame the scenery further upstream: from now on, industry and housing begin to feature more as one approaches the outskirts of Leeds. The navigation, however, is thankfully sequestered from these intrusions into the landscape. Leaving Shipley, the adjacent railway cuts through a 500-ft high hill in two mile-long tunnels. The canal goes all the way round this delightfully wooded hill, tenaciously following the Aire Valley. Halfway round the long curve are Field Locks: there is an extensive but inconspicuous sewage works nearby, which boasts its own railway system. Beyond the main railway bridge is a British Waterways maintenance yard at the head of Dobson's Locks. Here the British Waterways facilities for boats are housed in former canal stables. Temporarily traversing a built-up area, the navigation emerges yet again onto a wooded hillside overlooking the still rural and charming valley that contains the River Aire.

Rodley
W. Yorks. PO, tel, stores. A useful village on the canal bank. There are two pubs, several shops and a launderette, as well as good temporary moorings.

BOATYARDS

Ⓑ **Rodley Boat Centre** Canal Wharf, Canal Road, Rodley, Leeds (576132). By bridge 216A. Ⓡ Ⓢ ⓌⒹ Pump-out, boat hire, slipway, gas, mooring, chandlery, winter storage, trip boat for charter. Marine engineering and outboard repairs.
BWB Apperley Bridge Dobson Locks. (Bradford 611303). Ⓡ Ⓢ Ⓦ.

PUBS AND RESTAURANTS

🍺 **Owl** Rodley. Pleasant and friendly pub. John Smith real ale. Meals *lunchtime and evening (not Sun eve).*
🍺 **Rodley Barge** Unpretentious canalside pub by bridge 217.
🍺 **Railway** Near the canal at bridge 216A. Pleasant young persons' pub serving Tetley's real ale. Garden with swings, *lunchtime* food.
🍺 **Crown & Anchor** Town Street, Rodley. Large lounge and small public bar. Tetley's real ale.
🍺✕ **George & Dragon** 200yds north east of bridge 214A. A Cavalier restaurant with two bars, built around an old oak tree which still grows through the ceiling. Tetley's real ale and meals *(L & D).*

Leeds

This is a section full of contrasts; and it
probably represents the most pleasant way of
entering the city of Leeds. Although the area
becomes more and more built up as one travels
eastward, the canal remains unaffected by it,
maintaining its privileged position on the
wooded south side of the narrowing Aire
Valley. Leaving the ruined Kirkstall Abbey on
the other side of the river, the navigation passes
the Mackeson brewery and borders for a while
the steeply sloping edges of an extensive park.
Kirkstall Power Station is reached, with its own
private canal 'lay-by': until the mid 1960s,
scores of barges used to come up to fuel this
establishment every week; now both dock and
power station are unused. Beyond, by bridge
225, is the Leeds Industrial Museum. There are
six locks in the last mile down to Leeds and the
junction with the Aire and Calder navigations at
River Lock which, along with the preceding
two locks, looks spruce and smart, due to
recent landscaping and refurbishment. A good
place to moor a boat in Leeds is just above
Office Lock or above River Lock; an arm leaves
this short pound to disappear into the dark
under City station – it once served the river
wharves, but is now closed off. The route of the
Aire and Calder to Castleford and Wakefield is
continued on page 16.

Leeds
*W. Yorks. EC Wed. MD Tue, Fri, Sat. All
services.* A vast industrial city whose mass of
factory chimneys is the price it has paid for
prosperity. Its major industry is the clothing
and textile trade. Large areas of the city centre
have now been redeveloped. Headingly, the
home of Yorkshire cricket, is a famous test
match venue.
See also page 16.
Leeds Industrial Museum Armley Mills, by
bridge 225. (Leeds 637861). There have been
corn and fulling mills on this site since at least
1559, with the present building dating from
1805. When built it was the most advanced in
the country and it now houses a superb range of
real-life exhibits demonstrating the local textile,
heavy engineering, tanning and printing trades.
There are working cranes, locomotives and
waterwheels, and a cinema of the 1920s. The
little stone bridge over the canal here dates
from around 1770. *Open Tue–Sat, & Sun
afternoons. Charge.*
Kirkstall Abbey The large elegant ruins of a
Cistercian abbey founded in the 12thC. The
remaining walls narrowly escaped demolition in
the late 19thC, but are now carefully preserved
surrounded by a small, attractive park.
Abbey House Museum (Leeds 755821). Just
near the abbey is the splendid folk museum
illustrating the life and work of the people of
Yorkshire during the last 300 years. As well as
exhibiting toys, costumes and pottery, it houses
three streets of fully furnished 19thC shops,
cottages and workshops, including those of a
saddler, chemist, tanner and blacksmith. *Open
Mon–Sat, & Sun afternoons.*

BOATYARDS

Ⓑ **Yorkshire Hire Cruisers** 26 Canal Wharf,
Leeds (456195). Ⓢ Ⓦ Pump-out, gas, hire
craft, mooring, toilets, restaurant trip boat.
Basin café *open daily.*

PUBS

See also page 17
🍺 **Ancestor** Just south of bridge 223. Tetley's
real ale.
🍺 **Bridge** 100yds east of bridge 222. Whitbread
and Castle Eden real ales.
🍺 **Abbey** 50yds downhill from bridge 221.
Whitbread real ale.

MACCLESFIELD

Maximum dimensions

Length: 70'
Beam: 7'
Headroom: 7'

Mileage

HARDINGS WOOD JUNCTION (Trent & Mersey Canal) to
Congleton Wharf: 5¾
Bosley Top Lock: 11½
Macclesfield: 17
Bollington: 20
MARPLE JUNCTION (Peak Forest Canal): 27¾

Locks: 13

Ever since the Trent & Mersey Canal had been completed in 1777, there had existed a demand for an alternative canal link between the Midlands and Manchester, and a more direct line through the manufacturing town of Macclesfield was an obvious choice of route.

However, it was not until 1825 that Thomas Telford was asked by promoters of the canal to survey a line linking the Peak Forest Canal and the Trent & Mersey Canal. The 28-mile line he suggested was the canal that was built, from Marple to just north of Kidsgrove, but Telford did not supervise the construction. (He left to go and build the Birmingham & Liverpool Junction Canal.) William Crosley was the canal's engineer. It is interesting to note that the Macclesfield Canal (which opened in 1831) was built so long after the peak period of canal construction that it was actually envisaged by some of its promoters as the route for a possible railway track and was consequently quite shallow.

The canal, which runs along the side of a tall ridge of hills west of the Pennines, bears the distinctive mark of Telford's engineering. Like his Birmingham & Liverpool Junction Canal (ie the Shropshire Union from Autherley to Nantwich), the Macclesfield is a 'cut and fill' canal, following as straight a course as possible, and featuring many tremendous cuttings and embankments. Apart from the stop lock at Hall Green whose 1ft rise was insisted upon as a

water preservation measure by the Trent & Mersey Canal Company – to whose Hall Green Branch the Macclesfield Canal connected at the stop lock – all the locks are grouped into the flight of 12 at Bosley. The canal is fed from nearby reservoirs, at Bosley and Sutton.

In spite of intense competition from neighbouring railways and the Trent & Mersey Canal, the Macclesfield carried a good trade for many years. Much of this was coal, and cotton from the big mills established along its northern reaches.

This was not greatly affected by the surrender in 1846 to what was to become the Great Central Railway Company. (The Peak Forest and Ashton canals were also bought by that railway.) The railway company ran the three canals efficiently, but as narrow canals they were all bound to decline sooner rather than later.

The Macclesfield Canal today is an extremely interesting cruising waterway, and forms part of the popular 100-mile 'Cheshire Ring' canal circuit. Look out for the original, and very large, stone milestones showing distances from Hall Green stop lock (the original end of the canal) and Marple. These were removed during the Second World War in fear of helping invading forces. They have been lovingly restored to their former glory by the Macclesfield Canal Society.

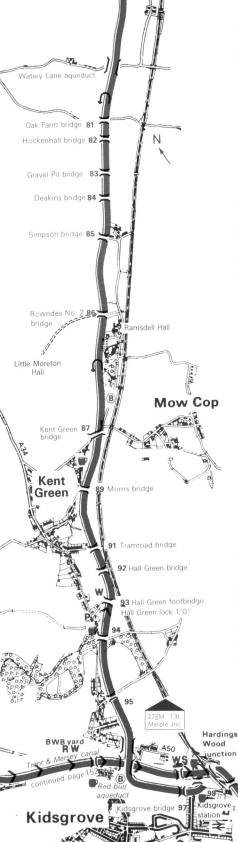

Watery Lane aqueduct

Oak Farm bridge **81**

Hockenhall bridge **82**

N

Gravel Pit bridge **83**

Deakins bridge **84**

Simpson bridge **85**

Rowndes No. 2 **86**
bridge

Ramsdell Hall

Little Moreton
Hall

Mow Cop

Kent Green **87**
bridge

**Kent
Green**

89 Morris bridge

91 Tramroad bridge

92 Hall Green bridge

W

93 Hall Green footbridge
Hall Green lock 1′0″

P

94

95

27¾M 13L
Marple Jnc

**Hardings
Wood
junction**

BWB yard
R W

A50

W S

Trent & Mersey canal

continued page 152

Red bull
aqueduct

98

Kidsgrove bridge **97**

Kidsgrove
station

Kidsgrove

Kent Green

The junction of the Macclesfield with the Trent & Mersey Canal is a curious one, for the former leaves the Trent & Mersey on the south side, then crosses it on Red Bull Aqueduct after the T & M has fallen through two locks. After passing through the stop lock in the cutting at Hall Green, one comes out into the open countryside at Kent Green. To the east, Mow Cop crowns the tall ridge of hills that stretches parallel to the navigation for miles to come. The canal wanders past the front lawn of the mansion that is Ramsdell Hall. Beyond this point, the canal loses itself in the countryside for several miles. A telephone box is situated near bridge 85.

Navigational note
The Macclesfield Canal is quite shallow, and mooring is usually only possible at recognised sites.

Little Moreton Hall
NT property. (Congleton 272018). ¾ mile west of canal. (Walk north west from bridge 86, along the footpath on the left side of the hedge.) This fabulous moated house is an outstanding example of black-and-white-timbered architecture. It was built between 1559 and 1580, with carved gables and ornate windows and has scarcely changed since. It contains a fine collection of oak furniture and pewter. *Open afternoons (except Tue) Mar–Oct.*
Mow Cop
NT property. A hill nearly 1100ft above sea level, which gives a magnificent view across the Cheshire Plain, beyond Stoke and into Wales. (This looks particularly good at night.) On top of the hill is Mow Cop Castle, an imitation ruin built in 1750. It was on this spot that the Primitive Methodists held their first meeting in 1807 which lasted 14 hours.
Kent Green
Ches. PO, tel, stores. The main interest of this place is in its pubs, especially the little one on the canal by swing bridge 88.

BOATYARDS
Ⓑ **Heritage Narrow Boats** Kent Green, Scholar Green, Kidsgrove (5700). Ⓦ Ⓓ Ⓔ Pump-out (*not Sat*), hire craft, slipway, mooring, chandlery, shop. *Open daily Mar–Oct.*
Ⓑ **David Piper** Red Bull Basin, Church Lawton, Kidsgrove (4754). By Red Bull Aqueduct. Ⓓ Pump-out, gas, slipway up to 60ft, winter storage, chandlery, shop. Boat and engine sales and service. Steel boats built and fitted out.

PUBS
🍺 **Bird in Hand** Canalside at Kent Green. A superbly old-fashioned pub. Emmy, the landlady, fetches beer up from the cellar in a jug. Canal talk is the usual entertainment.
🍺 **Rising Sun** Kent Green. Near the canal.
🍺 **Three Horseshoes** Kent Green. Near canal.
🍺 **Bleeding Wolf** Hall Green. Near bridge 94. Food, except at weekends. *PO, tel, stores* nearby.
🍺 **Canal Tavern** Canalside, at Hardings Wood.
🍺 **Blue Bell** Canalside, at Hardings Wood Junction. Real ale.
🍺 **Red Bull** By lock 43 on the T & M. Bar meals, snacks, children welcome.

River Dane
Stringers bridge **60**
Stanier 1st **62**
bridge
61 Congleton bridge
63 Stanier 2nd bridge
64 Pearson
bridge
A54
The Cloud
65 Stanleys bridge
66 Town Field bridge
67 Foden bridge
P **68** Buxton Road bridge
69 Wallworths bridge
A54
71
Galleys bridge **70**
Porters Farm bridge **72**
(closed)

Congleton

Galley bridge **73**
Congleton station
A527
Park Lane bridge **75** **74**
Morris bridge **76**
Congleton wharf
Lamberts Lane **77**
bridge

21¾M 12L
Marple Jnc

Hardings Wood
6M   1L

Peel Lane bridge **79**

stbury

Henshalls bridge **80**

Watery Lane aqueduct

Congleton

The canal continues north east. On one side,
the land falls away gradually; to the east, the
ever-present range of substantial hills reminds
one that the Pennine Chain lies just beyond.
Passing a golf course, one arrives at the
embanked wharf that overlooks Congleton:
there is an aqueduct over the road that runs
down into the town and then a beautifully
symmetrical 'roving' bridge (76). These are
known locally as 'snake bridges'. There is a
useful grocers/off-licence a short distance south
of Congleton Wharf. Past Congleton railway
station, the canal is carried by a high
embankment – a common feature of the
Macclesfield – across a narrow valley, affording
a good view westward of the tall and elegant
railway viaduct crossing the same valley.
Meanwhile the looming fell known as The
Cloud (over 1000ft high and with remains of
ancient earthworks) is given a wide berth as the
navigation continues on its lonely lock-free
course through this very fine landscape.

Congleton
Ches. EC Wed. MD Tue, Sat. All services. A
compact, busy market town hemmed in by
hills. The Victorian Town Hall in the High
Street, looks like a cross between a 17thC
Dutch guildhall and St Mark's, Venice.
Astbury
Ches. PO, tel, stores. About 1 mile north west of
bridges 79 and 80. A pretty village set back
from the A34. Tudor and 18thC houses are set
around the green. The church is amazing: its
roomy interior and wide aisles are
complemented externally by generous
battlements along the roof and a spired tower
standing quite separate from the body of the
church.

PUBS
● ✕ **Bull's Head Hotel** Congleton (273388).
● **Robin Hood** South west of bridge 61.
Marstons real ale.
● **Railway** Near Congleton station. Food.
● **Queen's Head** Canalside at bridge 75. Food
lunchtime and evenings, garden with swings,
children welcome *before 20.00*. Shops close by.
● **Wharf** Near Congleton Wharf. Greenall
Whitley real ale in a very pleasant pub. Snacks,
children welcome *lunchtime and early evening*.
● ✕ **Lion & Swan** Congleton (273115).
● **Egerton Arms** Astbury.

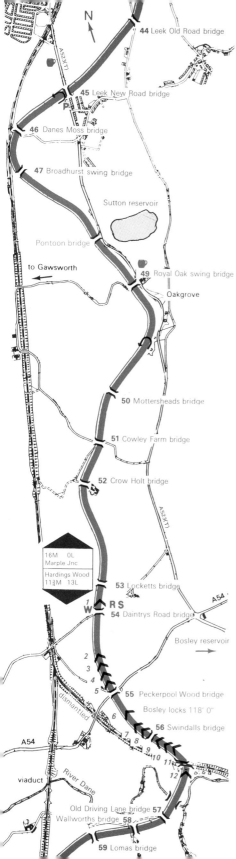

Bosley Locks

Scenically, this is another impressive stretch.
The massive hills to the right still dominate as
the canal crosses the River Dane on an
embankment and arrives at the foot of Bosley
Locks (good moorings here). These are in a
really delightful setting which is semi-wooded
and semi-pastoral, all the time overlooked by
The Cloud from the south. Beyond the locks,
the hills/mountains (some are over 1200ft high)
spill right down to the canal near Oakgrove.
The navigation follows the contour of the land
as it begins to swing round the hills containing
Macclesfield, which is now clearly visible to the
north.

Navigational note
The old and notorious Royal Oak Swing Bridge
has now been replaced with a new hydraulic
bridge. You will need a British Waterways key
to operate it; just follow the instructions on the
control box.

Sutton Reservoir
Close to the canal north of bridge 49, this
reservoir holds up to 94 million gallons of
water. There is a private sailing club: and the
public are welcome to ramble and picnic here.
Oakgrove A delightful spot with a nearby pub
and a superb backcloth of tall, green hills which
are ideal for energetic walks. The lane west of
the bridge leads to Gawsworth. Sutton reservoir
is just north.

Gawsworth
Ches. 2 miles west of Oakgrove. A refreshingly
unspoilt village with several small lakes and a
lovely 13thC church, approached by a long
avenue of elm trees. Facing the church is the
old rectory, a half-timbered house built by
Rector Baguley in 1470. Close to the church is
Gawsworth Hall, a beautiful 16thC black-and-
white manor house. The park encloses a
medieval jousting ground. *Open Wed, Sat, Sun
& G. Fri afternoons, Mar–Oct.*
Maggoty's Wood In this pleasant wood just
outside the village is the grave of the eccentric
fiddler and playwright, Maggoty Johnson.
After being totally rejected by London critics
he returned to Gawsworth where he died in
1773, having ordered that he should be buried
far from the vulgar gentry who did not
appreciate his genius.

Bosley Locks
Effectively the only locks on all the 27 miles of
the Macclesfield Canal, these 12 splendid stone
locks are relatively deep, raising the canal level
by fully 118ft to well over 500ft above the sea.
Each lock has a pair of mitre top gates instead
of only a single one – indeed Bosley Locks are
very rare among narrow locks in this respect.
They are a good example of Telford's practice
of grouping locks together in flights; here are 12
in 1 mile.

Bosley Reservoir
1 mile east of Bosley Locks, along the A54. A
canal reservoir with a wide variety of land and
water birds, which holds 402 million gallons of
water. An excellent rambling and picnic area.
The fishing rights are exercised by an angling
club.

PUBS
Star North of bridge 45. Marstons real ale,
in a quiet, popular local. Snacks, garden.
Fools Nook Oakgrove. Horse brasses, meals
and Higsons real ale in a rural pub.

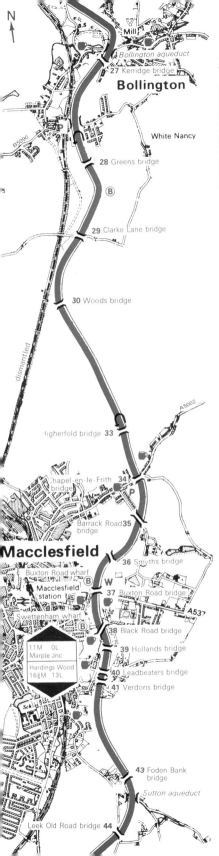

Macclesfield

Leaving the green and hilly countryside, the navigation enters the outskirts of Macclesfield, passing a coal yard at bridge 41. A very wide stretch is overshadowed by a vast and beautifully restored flour mill which marks the site of the original Macclesfield Canal Company. The town itself is down the hill; the best place to moor is south of bridge 37, which is also handy for the shops (including bottled gas supplies). Meanwhile the canal continues northwards near a closed railway line to Bollington, passing the Adelphi Mill, once a silk mill and now converted into offices, the Peaks & Plains Discovery Centre and a trip boat run by the Bollington Packet Boat Co. A 6oft-high embankment and two aqueducts then carry the navigation across the valley towards the huge Clarence Mill, a textile mill now converted into small manufacturing units.

Bollington
Ches. EC Wed. PO, tel, stores, garage, bank.
One gets a good view of this stone-built town from the huge canal embankment that cuts across it. Hills crowd round the town, which is only a mile from the boundary of the Peak District National Park. The white tower on the ridge south of the town is called White Nancy. One popular story is that it was built to commemorate the battle of Waterloo by a member of the Gaskell family and took its name from one of the ladies of the family called Nancy.

Macclesfield
Ches. EC Wed. MD Tue, Fri, Sat. All services.
An interesting combination of a thriving silk manufacturing town and an old market town with its cobbled streets and picturesque medieval Market Place. There are several interesting classical buildings, making the most of the local stone. In the 18thC it was one of the leading silk producing centres and is still important for its textile and pharmaceutical industries. An interesting feature of the town is the Unitarian Chapel in King Edward Street, approached through a narrow passage and guarded by a lovely wrought-iron gate: it is dated 1689 and is 'for William and Mary's subjects dissenting from the Church of England'.

St Michael's Church Market Place. Very little remains of the original structure founded in 1278 by Queen Eleanor but it still contains many fine monuments.

Paradise Mill Park Lane, Macclesfield (618228). Built between 1820–60, this hand-loom silk-weaving mill finally closed down in 1981. Here you can see Jacquard handlooms in action, authentic room settings and an exhibition of a whole wealth of material connected with one of Macclesfield's major industries. *Open 14.00–17.00 Tue–Sun. Charge (joint ticket for this and the museum results in a saving).*

Silk Museum Roe Street, Macclesfield (613210). The first museum in the country devoted entirely to the study of the silk industry: audio visuals, costume, textiles, room settings and even parachutes. Visit also The Heritage Centre in the old 1813 Sunday School building. Tea room, shop. *Open 11.00–17.00 Tue–Sat, 14.00–17.00 Sun. Charge (see above).*

West Park Museum Prestbury Road, Macclesfield (24067). Located on the edge of a park which has the largest bowling green in the country. Founded in 1898 by the Brocklehurst family, the museum contains fine and decorative art material, local history, Egyptian antiquities and, notably, some paintings by Charles Tunnicliffe, the bird artist who trained in Macclesfield. *Open 14.00–17.00 Tue–Sun. Free.*

Tourist Information Centre Town Hall, Market Place, Macclesfield (21955).

BOATYARDS

Ⓑ **Kerridge Dry Dock** Between bridges 28 and 29. (Bollington 74287).
Ⓑ **Peak Forest Cruisers** The Wharf, Buxton Road, Macclesfield (24172). Hire craft, moorings, winter storage, boat repairs. Day trip boat.

Ⓑ **Macclesfield Marina** Swettenham Wharf, Brook Street, Macclesfield (20042). ℝ 𝕊 𝕎 (£1 charge for this, 1988) 𝔻 Slipway, gas, boat building and repairs, mooring (charge for this), chandlery, provisions, winter storage. *Closed Wed.*

PUBS

Macclesfield and Bollington have been described as one of the seven wonders of the real ale drinkers' waterways, with 86 such pubs within striking distance of the canal.
🍺 **Waggon & Horses** 200yds beyond Adelphi Mill. Boddingtons real ale.
🍺 **Dog & Partridge** West of Bollington Aqueduct. A sociable village pub with an open fire offering Robinson's real ale and *lunchtime* snacks.

🍺 **Lord Clyde** West of Clarke Lane Bridge. Small country pub in a listed building. Greenall Whitley real ale.
🍺 **Three Crowns** East of bridge 34. Victorian stone terrace pub with a garden. Robinson's real ale.
🍺 **Britannia** West of bridge 34. Unspoilt terraced pub serving Greenall Whitley real ale.
🍺 **Puss in Boots** Canalside at bridge 37. Boddingtons real ale, open fire, garden.
🍺 **Navigation** South of bridge 38. Victorian local built for the original canal navvies. Tetley's real ale, *closed lunchtime Mon–Fri.*
🍺 **Dolphin Inn** West of bridge 40. Robinson's real ale in a friendly local with an open fire. Food at *lunchtime.*
🍺 **Bee Hive** South west of bridge 41. Cosy Boddingtons real ale local.

One of the beautifully situated Bosley Locks. Macclesfield Canal. *David Perrott.*

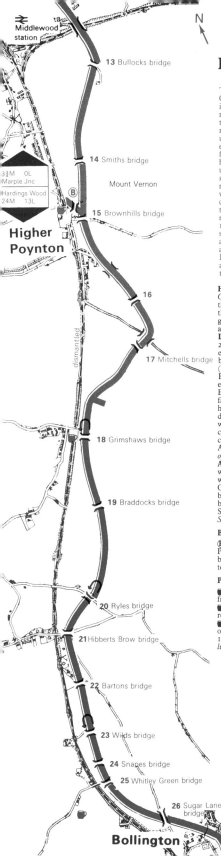

Higher Poynton

This lonely stretch is typical of the Macclesfield Canal and in its beautifully quiet, rural isolation it is representative of much of the charm that most canals possess. Winding northwards along the summit level at over 500ft above the sea, the navigation generally follows the contours of this upland country, but crosses several valleys on embankments and fine aqueducts. There are few centres of population, only the odd pub here or there, and the countryside is entirely unspoilt. Around Higher Poynton (*PO, tel, stores, garage*) the canal becomes wider, the result of ancient subsidence from a coalmine, which necessitated the continual raising of the canal banks and bridges (to hold the water in the sinking canal). Be sure to adhere to the main channel here. An old branch near bridge 15 used to lead to the mine; now it is a mooring site. A mile north of here, one crosses yet another massive embankment and a tall aqueduct (over a railway) on the way into High Lane. The towpath is in excellent condition, and the Middlewood Way follows the course of the old railway.

Higher Poynton
Ches. PO, tel, stores. Considered by some to be the most pleasant moorings on the canal, where the wide water supports large families of ducks, geese and swans. There is a recreation field adjacent, and a handy pub.
Lyme Park *NT property* (Stockport 62023). 2 miles east of Higher Poynton. Pedestrian entrance at West Parkgate, ¼ mile south east of bridge 17 or footpath from bridge 15. (Vehicular access from Disley, on the Peak Forest Canal, *see page 122*.) In the centre of an extensive park containing deer, is a magnificent Elizabethan house that belonged to the Legh family from the 14thC until 1947 when it was handed over to the nation in payment of death duties. It has a fine interior containing many works of art and four Chippendale chairs claimed to be covered with material from a cloak worn by King Charles I at his execution. Adventure playground for the children. *House open afternoons, except Mon, gardens open daily.*
Adlington Hall (Prestbury 827595). 2 miles west of bridge 21. An attractive manor house with a mixture of architectural styles: a Georgian south front and an Elizabethan black-and-white-timbered wing. The banqueting hall contains a 17thC Bernard Smith organ. Pleasant gardens. *Open summer Sun & B. Hols, also Sat in Jul & Aug.*

BOATYARDS
Ⓑ **Constellation Cruises** Lyme Road, Higher Poynton, Stockport. (Poynton 873471). Near bridge 15. Ⓦ (charge) Ⓓ Gas, 25ft slipway, temporary mooring.

PUBS
🍺 **Boar's Head** Higher Poynton. Down the hill from bridge 15. Boddingtons real ale.
🍺 **Miners Arms** Near bridge 18. Boddingtons real ale.
🍺 **Windmill** 250yds west of bridge 25. Large open-plan pub in a former cotton mill, built in 1675. Marstons and Boddingtons real ale, food *lunchtime and evenings*, garden, open fire.

Marple Junction

The canal proceeds northwards in a cutting
through High Lane, passing the junction with
the short High Lane Arm – now used as a club
mooring site – and a children's playpark. There
are moorings between the arm and bridge 11,
with shops close by. Beyond the town is a
restored mill; then open country intervenes,
offering views westward of Stockport and the
southern outskirts of Manchester. On the
offside, between bridges 8 and 7 is a deer farm.
The deer can often be seen feeding by the
(electrified) fence. There is a useful shop, the
Doodfield Stores, down the hill from bridge 6.
At bridge 3 Goyt Mill appears, heralding the
start of Marple, a busy boating centre much
enjoyed by the citizens of Manchester. Goyt
Mill is yet another mill which has been
thankfully restored, and now houses
workshops. There are shops, a café and a
launderette nearby. The area of the junction
with the Peak Forest Canal is delightful: an old
turnover bridge, mellow wharf buildings and
the nearby flight of Marple Locks are framed
by the distant mountainous country across the
Goyt Valley. The canal here is 500ft above sea
level – the highest useable pound on the
English canal system.

Marple
Gt Manchester. All services. A typical residential
town, serving as a dormitory base for Stockport
and Manchester. Elements of the old village can
still be seen, buried amongst the suburbia, but
much the most attractive part is by the canal.
The rugged Ludworth Moor is not far away,
where 'Robin Hood's Picking Rods' still stand,
the supposed remains of a Celtic Druid's
temple.

Marple Locks
The flight of deep, narrow locks is superbly
sited, at the top flanked by terraced houses and
a play park; midway, fine gardens and restored
stone cottages back on, and towards the bottom
the passage is tree-lined. The friendly lock
keeper lives by lock 9 opposite a superb canal
warehouse which has now been carefully
restored. The top lock is the second deepest
narrow lock in the country.

High Lane
*Gt Manchester. PO, tel, stores, garage, station,
fish & chips.* More a spread than a village; good
moorings and useful for supplies. High Lane is
effectively at the south-east corner of the
Manchester conurbation, and is quite
indistinguishable from its neighbours. The very
long Disley railway tunnel passes deep
underneath the place.

BOATYARDS

British Waterways Marple Yard Marple
Junction. (061-427 1079). R S W Toilet.

BOAT TRIPS

Top Lock Marine 5 Lime Kiln Lane, Marple.
(061-427 5712). 12-seater restaurant boat for
private charter and day boat hire. Also private
mooring marina and emergency engine repairs.

PUBS

Ring O'Bells Marple. By bridge 2.
Robinson's real ale, good food and excellent
children's menu. Garden. Telephone kiosk
outside.
Bull's Head High Lane. Near bridge 11.
Dog & Partridge 200yds from bridge 11.
Food.

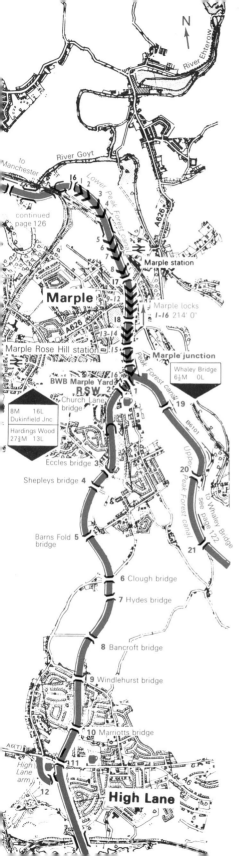

PEAK FOREST AND ASHTON

Maximum dimensions:

Length: 70'
Beam: 7'
Headroom: 6'

Mileages

ASHTON CANAL
Duckinfield Junction to
Ducie Street Junction: 6½

Locks: 18

PEAK FOREST CANAL
Whaley Bridge to
Marple Junction: 6½
Dukinfield Junction: 14½

Locks: 16

THE ASHTON CANAL

This navigation was authorised in 1792 and opened shortly afterwards, as an isolated narrow canal from the centre of Manchester to Ashton-under-Lyne. It is short, at only 6½ miles, but several substantial branches were built, with a total length twice that of the main line.

From the beginning, the Ashton was a strong rival of the Rochdale Canal – with which it connects in Manchester. The two canals were constructed simultaneously, partly to tap the big coal producing area around Oldham (north east of Manchester): in addition the Ashton opened a new trade route from Manchester to the textile mills of Ashton, while the Rochdale served as a broad canal link over the Pennines between the Mersey and the rivers of Yorkshire. Before long, the Ashton Canal was joined by the Peak Forest and Huddersfield canals: both provided useful trade and the latter provided a secondary through route across the Pennines. And in 1831 completion of the narrow Macclesfield Canal gave the Ashton the added bonus of becoming part of a through route from Manchester to the Potteries.

The 1830s saw the peak of the Ashton Canal's prosperity. After this it was seriously threatened by railway competition, and the canal company sold out to the forerunner of the Great Central Railway Company in 1846. This company continued successfully to maintain and operate the canal for many years, but traffic declined in the present century and the branches began to decay.

By 1962 it was unnavigable – however a determined effort by the Peak Forest Canal Society, the IWA, local councils and the BWB resulted in its reopening in 1974.

THE PEAK FOREST CANAL

This canal runs from the Ashton Canal at Ashton through Marple to Whaley Bridge and Buxworth. Its name is misleading, for Peak Forest is only a small village 2½ miles east of Doveholes, and the canal never went to Peak Forest. Its history is similar to, and tied up with, its neighbour the Ashton Canal; authorised by Act of Parliament in 1794, it was aimed at providing an outlet for the great limestone deposits at Doveholes, a few miles south east of Whaley Bridge. However, since Doveholes is over 1000ft above sea level, the canal was terminated in a basin at Buxworth, and the line was continued up to the quarries by a 6½-mile tramroad.

Construction of the canal and tramway and their four short tunnels was carried out by navvies directed by Benjamin Outram, a notable Derbyshire engineer and one of the founders of the famous Butterley Ironworks. The canal was completed in 1800, except for the flight of locks at Marple, which were not built until four years later. (A second, temporary, tramway bridged the gap in the meantime.)

Buxworth soon became a bustling interchange point where the horse-drawn wagons bringing the stone down from Doveholes tipped their load either into canal boats or into limekilns, for burning into lime. This traffic, and the boats bringing coal *up* the canal for firing the kilns at Buxworth, accounted for the greatest proportion of the canal company's revenue.

Like the Ashton Canal, the Peak Forest was greatly boosted by the opening of the Macclesfield Canal to Marple top lock in 1831. This made it (with the Ashton) part of a new through route from Manchester to the Potteries. In 1831 too, the Cromford & High Peak Railway was opened, joining up Whaley Bridge with the Cromford Canal on the far side of the Peak District.

By the early 1840s the Peak Forest Canal was suffering from keen competition on trade between Manchester, the Midlands and London. The competition came not only from the long-established Trent & Mersey Canal Company but also from two new railways. All the companies tried to undercut each other; the Peak Forest came off badly, so in 1846 the company leased the navigation in perpetuity to the Sheffield, Ashton-under-Lyne & Manchester Railway, which later became the Great Central. The canal declined slowly up to the present century. In 1922 the Buxworth traffic finished, while (through) traffic on the 'lower' Peak Forest Canal – from Marple Junction northwards – gradually disappeared by the last war.

Along with the Ashton, full navigation was restored in 1974, with the Buxworth line currently being restored.

New Mills

As one passes from the Macclesfield Canal to the Upper Peak Forest Canal one enters at once dramatic, mountainous scenery. To the north and east, the land falls away sharply, with the Marple flight of locks emphasising the drop. The Upper Peak Forest Canal leads off to the south east; and it rapidly becomes apparent that this is a navigation set in a robust, handsome landscape. Clinging desperately to a wooded mountainside overlooking the steep, wide Goyt Valley, it winds its precarious way to New Mills. The trains that traverse the opposite side of the valley look like tiny models on the distant, massive mountains. There are good moorings at bridge 24, where a public footpath gives easy access to Strines. Near Disley, another railway pops out of the long Disley Tunnel, way below the canal; while yet another line appears above and beside the canal, from High Lane. Thus around New Mills the valley contains fully three operational and very picturesque railways. One of the pleasant features of this terrain is the easy co-existence of woods, fields and a canal on the one hand, and a certain amount of industrial urbanisation on the other. Usually, this mixture would tend to spoil the rural character of the area; but along this canal the steepness of the slope and the grandness of the landscape leaves the canal's charm unimpaired. As you approach New Mills you will notice the smell of sweets in the air – Matlows, the makers of 'Swizzles', have their factory here. From here to Whaley Bridge the cut is very shallow – the slow progress gives time to appreciate the surroundings fully.

New Mills
Derbs. PO, tel, stores, garage, banks, launderette, stations. A mostly stone-built town on the Cheshire/Derbyshire border: its industries include textile printing, engineering and engraving. One can still see the ruins of the extensive canal stables just east of bridge 28.

Disley
Ches. PO, tel, stores, garage, station. On the south bank of the canal. The centre of the village is quite pretty, slightly spoilt by the A6 traffic. The village is up the hill, south west of bridge 26. The attractive church stands among trees above the little village square. It was greatly renovated in the last century but the ancient tower with the griffin leering down at passers-by dates from the 16thC. Vehicular and pedestrian access to Lyme Park (*see page 119*) is from the A6 near Disley, 1½ miles south west of bridge 26.

Strines
Gt Manchester. PO, tel, stores, station. A useful place for supplies.

BOATYARDS

Ⓑ **New Mills Marina** Hibbert Street, New Mills (45000). Ⓡ Ⓢ Ⓦ Ⓓ Pump-out, gas, overnight mooring, long-term mooring, winter storage, boat sales and repairs, chandlery, gifts, provisions, toilets and showers.

British Waterways Marple Yard at Marple Junction, on the Macclesfield Canal. (061-427 1079). Ⓡ Ⓢ Ⓦ Toilet.

BOAT TRIPS

Top Lock Marine 5 Lime Kiln Lane, Marple. (061-427 5712). 12-seater restaurant trip boat for private charter. Also private mooring marina and emergency engine repairs.

PUBS AND RESTAURANTS

◪✗ **Ram's Head Hotel** Disley (62019). Smart hotel with full restaurant.

◪✗ **Dandy Cock** Disley. Bar lunches.

◪✗ **Ring O'Bells** Marple. Near the junction. (On the Macclesfield Canal). Good food: fine children's menu and Robinson's real ale. Garden. Telephone kiosk outside.

The Upper Peak Forest Canal. A very attractive, but shallow, waterway. *Derek Pratt.*

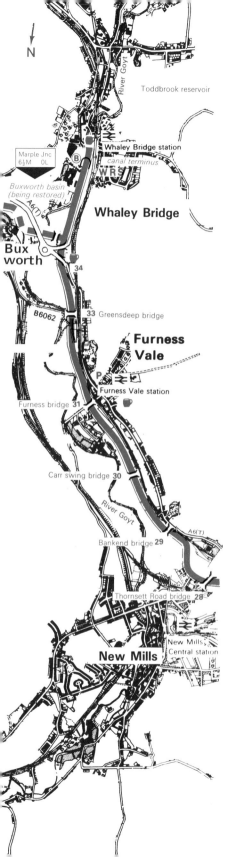

Whaley Bridge

The canal continues south east along the
mountainside towards Whaley Bridge. It is an
enchanting stretch, passing plenty of woods,
pastures and grazing horses. The A6 road and
the railway are always close to the navigation,
but they detract not at all from its isolation.
There are charming stations at New Mills,
Furness Vale and Whaley Bridge: from these
one may take a magnificent railway trip past
two canal-feeding reservoirs and over the hills
to the summit, 1200ft above sea level, then
down to the old Roman town of Buxton, now
unfortunately the end of the line. As the canal
approaches Whaley Bridge, and the River Goyt
comes closer, there is a swing bridge and two
lift bridges to contend with – they can be hard
work. South of bridge 34 the canal splits: the
original main line, at present closed beyond the
bridge, turns east across the Goyt on an
aqueduct to Buxworth (its name changed from
the supposedly less desirable Bugsworth) with
its basin complex. The former Whaley Bridge
Branch continues for a short distance south to
Whaley Bridge, where it terminates in a small
basin, with a boatyard, at the north end of the
town. There is a building at the basin of great
interest to industrial archaeologists: it covers a
dock and was built in 1832 at this, the junction
of the Peak Forest Canal and the Cromford &
High Peak Railway. Here, transhipment
between canal boat and railway wagon could
take place under cover. The former railway's
Whaley Bridge inclined plane (now a footpath)
rises to the south of this historic building.

Coombs Reservoir 1½ miles south of Whaley
Bridge. An 84-acre canal reservoir with public
access from the three highways round it. It is
used extensively as a sailing club and a centre
for angling.
Toddbrook Reservoir Just south of Whaley
Bridge. A very pleasant area for picnicking and
walking. Private sailing club; fishing rights on
this BWB reservoir are exercised by an angling
club.
Whaley Bridge
*Derbs. EC Wed. PO, tel, stores, garage, station,
launderette, fish & chips, banks.* Built on a steep
hill at the end of the canal, with good views
across the Goyt valley, this is now a quiet and
pleasant place, a new by-pass having removed
much of the traffic. The beautiful nearby hills
are, however, more noteworthy than the town.
Cromford & High Peak Railway In the early
1820s a physical connection was planned
between the Peak Forest Canal at Whaley
Bridge and the Cromford Canal, way over to
the south east on the other side of the Peak
District, using a junction canal. However a
canal would have been impracticable through
such mountainous terrain, and so a railway was
constructed. Known as the Cromford & High
Peak Railway, it was opened throughout in
1831, 33 miles long. With a summit level over
1200ft above the sea, this extraordinary
standard-gauge goods line was interesting
chiefly for its numerous slopes and inclined
planes, up which the wagons were hauled by
either stationary or tenacious locomotive steam
engines. (The steepest gradient on the line was
1 in 7.) The C & HPR closed in 1967; much of
the route is now being turned into a public
footpath and bridleway. Around Whaley
Bridge one may still see the remains of the short
inclined plane (now a footpath) which brought
the goods down the hill, then through the town
to the wharf at the terminus of the Peak Forest
Canal.
Buxworth
Derbs. PO, tel, stores. The main feature in
Buxworth is the old terminal basin system.
This used to be a tremendously busy complex,
and is of great interest to industrial
archaeologists. The canal line to Buxworth
(once Bugsworth) was built to bring the canal
as near as possible to the great limestone

quarries at Doveholes, a plate tramway being constructed in 1799 via Chapel Milton to complete the connection. Known as the Peak Forest Tramway, this little line, 6½ miles long, brought the stone down the hills to Buxworth, where it was transhipped into waiting canal boats. Throughout the history of the line, the wagons on the tramway were drawn exclusively by horse power – except for a 500yd inclined plane in Chapel-en-le-Frith, where the trucks were attached to a continuous rope so that the descending trucks pulled empty ones up the 1 in 7½ slope. The tramway was closed by 1926, and the sidings and basins at Buxworth have been disused and overgrown since that time. However the Inland Waterways Protection Society is working towards a complete restoration of the complex by voluntary labour and already part of the basin is cleared and reopened. See the noticeboard by the bridge for the latest information.

Furness Vale
Derbs. PO, tel, stores, garage, station. A main road (A6) village, useful for supplies.

BOATYARDS

Ⓑ **Unicorn Marine** The Wharf, Canal Street, Whaley Bridge (3411). ⓇⒹ Pump-out, gift shop.

BOAT TRIPS

Judith Mary Unicorn Marine, The Wharf, Canal Street, Whaley Bridge (3411). Lovely 70ft-narrowboat available for private charter. Also public trips *at weekends & B. Hols.*

PUBS

Jodrell Arms Whaley Bridge (2164). Wilson's real ale, meals *lunchtime and evenings.*
Railway Whaley Bridge (2245). Robinson's real ale, meals *lunchtime and evenings.*
Navigation Whaley Bridge, near the canal terminus. Boddingtons real ale.
Navigation Buxworth, by the canal terminus. Wilson's real ale.
Dog & Partridge Near the junction to Buxworth Basin.
Soldier Dick Furness Vale.
Station Hotel Furness Vale.

Marple Aqueduct on the Lower Peak Forest Canal. The railway viaduct is in the background.

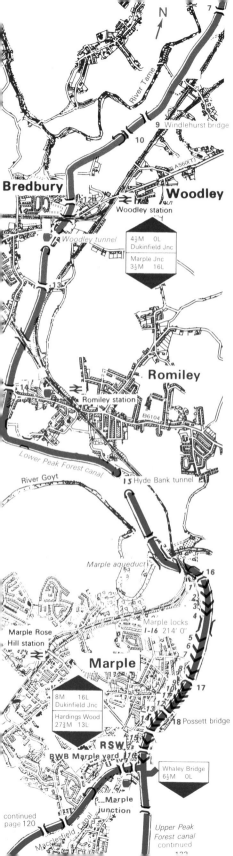

Marple Aqueduct

At Marple Junction the 16 narrow (standard 7ft beam) Marple Locks carry the Peak Forest Canal down 214ft past the Macclesfield Canal towards Manchester. The southernmost 5 miles of the Lower Peak Forest Canal (ie from Marple Junction northwards) are really very beautiful. The locks themselves, which are spaced out over 1 mile, have an unrivalled setting in an excellent combination of built-up area, parkland, tall trees and steep hillside; the River Goyt is hidden down in the wooded valley to the east. Look out for the interesting Possett Bridge, where there is a small tunnel for the towpath (and horse) and an even smaller one for the boatman, leading down to the lock. At the foot of the locks, where the River Goyt is crossed, one is treated to the double joys of a major canal aqueduct with an even bigger railway viaduct alongside. West of here a long narrow stretch was once Rose Hill Tunnel, long since opened out. The canal then traverses a wooded hillside before diving into Hyde Bank Tunnel, 308yds long. The towpath is diverted over the hill, past a farm. On the other side, a couple of minor aqueducts lead the canal northwards, away from the Goyt Valley and past Romiley, Bredbury and Woodley. Here is a narrow 176yd-long tunnel, this time with the towpath continued through it. Beyond these not unattractive outer suburbs of Manchester, the canal runs again along a hillside in unspoilt countryside, overlooking the tiny River Tame. There are plenty of trees and the occasional textile mill to add interest to the rural scenery. One should relish this length of the canal – it is the last one sees of the countryside before entering the vast conurbation of Manchester. The towpath is well used between Woodley and Ashton, and is marked with wooden signposts giving mileages.

Navigational notes
1. There is no mooring on the Marple flight since water levels in the pounds can fall dramatically when the locks are in use.
2. Hyde Bank Tunnel, although appearing wide, does not have sufficient clearance for two boats to pass. Hold back until it is clear.

Romiley
Gt Manchester. All services. A useful place for supplies.

Marple
Gt Manchester. All services. Once a famous hat-making centre, the town is most interesting by the canal. There are shops just downhill from bridge 17.

Marple Aqueduct
Deservedly scheduled as an ancient monument, this three-arched aqueduct over the River Goyt is a very fine structure, in an exquisite setting almost 100ft above the river.

Marple Locks
The 16 locks at Marple were not built until 1804, four years after the rest of the navigation was opened. The 1-mile gap thus left was bridged by a tramway, while the Canal Company sought the cash to pay for the construction of a flight of locks. This was obviously a most unsatisfactory state of affairs, since the limestone from Doveholes had to be shifted from wagon to boat at Buxworth Basin, from boat to wagon at Marple Junction, and back into boat again at the bottom of the tramway. Not surprisingly, a container system was developed – using iron boxes with a 2-ton payload – to ease the triple transhipment. However, this was no long-term solution, and when the necessary £27,000 was forthcoming the company authorised construction of the flight of locks. Today they stand comparison with any flight on the network: note especially Samuel Oldknow's superb warehouse, by lock 9 opposite the lock-keeper's house.

BOATYARDS

British Waterways Marple Yard At Marple
Junction, on the Macclesfield Canal. (061-427
1079). R S W Toilet.

PUBS AND RESTAURANTS

🍺 **Navigation** Woodley. At north end of
tunnel. Robinson's real ale, garden.
🍺 **Spread Eagle** Hatherlow, Romiley.
🍺 **Railway** Romiley.
✕ **Bridge Café** 164 Stockport Road, Romiley.
(061-430 2569). Moor north of bridge 14. A
friendly and welcoming café decorated in canal
style, offering reasonably priced, authentic,
homemade food. Fresh vegetables, Scotch
salmon, hams and turkeys roasted on the
premises. *Open 09.00–15.00 Mon–Sat;
gourmet evening every second Sat in month –*
book for this and bring your own wine.
Swimming pool adjacent and shops and services
close by.
✕🍷 **Waterside Restaurant** Romiley. (061-430
4302). Near bridge 14. Restaurant with a
pleasant canalside patio. Le Bistro downstairs.
W Mooring for patrons. *Open Mon–Sat eves
only. Book Fri & Sat.*
🍺 **Duke of York** 250yds east of bridge 14.
Food, garden.
🍺 **Navigation** By lock 13. Useful for 'lock
wheelers' (no mooring on flight!) Chinese
take-away close by.

The Ashton Canal, with central Manchester being left behind down the locks. *David Perrott.*

Hyde

The canal continues northward through a landscape which becomes less rural, but in some ways more interesting. At bridge 7 the towpath changes sides; the building nearby is the headquarters of the Peak Forest Canal Society. Bridge 6 is a pretty roving bridge, grown wider over the years. Beyond is a wharf with some well-restored buildings and good moorings on either side. To the north the industrial tentacles of Hyde – Greater Manchester – ensnare the canal traveller. Beyond Hyde the canal traverses a great expanse of landscaped wasteland. There used to be two short branches along here; they are both untraceable now. The approach to Dukinfield Junction (Portland Basin) is now very pleasant. The towpath is nice and tidy, with plenty of grass, trees and seats. Below and to the west there is a fine farmhouse, with horses in the paddock. A Llangollen-type lift bridge, an aqueduct over the River Tame and a stone roving bridge provide canal interest. The warehouse which faces you across the junction is being restored as a canal heritage centre and museum. Heading off to the south west, the Ashton Canal takes you into Manchester proper: to the north west is a short restored section of the Huddersfield Narrow Canal, soon to be extended past the first three locks. If you pass this way during *July*, you may see the gay and colourful Ashton Canals Festival, which has been running successfully for over 10 years now.

Heritage Centre and Museum Portland Basin, Ashton-under-Lyne. (Huddersfield 666805). Boat building, canal exhibits, water wheel, and many other things of interest.

BOATYARDS

Ⓑ **Warble Narrowboats** Ashton Old Wharf. (061-330 0228). The following are expected to be available from 1989: R S W D Pump-out, gas, boat building, repairs, restaurant.

PUBS

🍺 **Globe** By bridge 2. Food.
🍺 **Cheshire Ring Hotel** A few yards east of bridge 6. Shops and station nearby.

Droylsden

From start to finish, the Ashton Canal passes
through a densely built-up area in which the
canal is conspicuous as an avenue of escape
from the oppressive townscape that flanks it. Its
clear water, its excellent towpath, its functional
but dignified old bridges and the peace that
surrounds it make it a haven for local
schoolchildren, anglers, walkers and idlers, and
for anyone else who enjoys an environment that
is quite separate from and unrelated to his
ordinary daily life. The rare pleasure, afforded
only by an English canal, stepping out of the
noise and bustle of everyday life in a city
suburb, into the peaceful and unpretentious
atmosphere of the 18thC is once again, with
gradual restoration work, becoming available to
all. Leaving Dukinfield Junction – where
substantial old canal warehouses and docks face
the Peak Forest Canal – one turns west towards
Manchester. Electrified suburban railway lines
jostle the canal, which enters a cutting and
passes Guide Bridge. There are pubs, shops
and a railway station nearby, but it can be
difficult to scramble up the bank out of the
cutting. Droylsden is memorable for the
wonderful smell of a marmalade factory –
Fairfield Junction is the last 'safe' mooring this
side of Manchester – here the 18 locks begin the
descent to the Rochdale Canal. Shops and pubs
are all close to the junction; there is also a
sanitary station. One can see the remains of
several old canal arms along the Ashton Canal:
one of the more important ones was the 5-mile
Stockport Branch, leaving Clayton Junction just below lock 11.

Navigational note
A British Waterways anti-vandal key is needed
for all the locks and moveable bridges on the
Ashton, and for the first lift bridge on the
Lower Peak Forest. Be very careful where you
moor in this area, and do not offer anyone a ride
on your boat.

BOATYARDS

British Waterways Fairfield Junction ⑤Ⓦ
Toilet, mooring. (061-273 4686 from
07.45–16.30, nights 061-330 8599). Anti-vandal
keys for sale.
Ⓑ **Warble Narrowboats** Ashton Old Wharf.
(061-330 0228). The following are expected to
be available from 1989: ⓇⓈⓌⒹ Pump-out,
gas, boat building, repairs, restaurant.

PUBS

🍺 **Bridge Inn** Canalside at Lock 11. Basic
two-room pub offering Chesters real ale and
food at *lunchtime*. Children usually allowed in
(ask). Garden.
🍺 **Church Inn** Canalside at Lock 11.
🍺 **Strawberry Duck** Canalside at Lock 13.
Traditional two room pub which welcomes
children. Wilson's and Holts real ale and
lunchtime food.
🍺 **Friendship** Canalside by Lock 15. Busy
popular local serving Chesters real ale and
lunchtime food. Garden, children welcome.
🍺 **Church Hotel** Ashton Road, Droylsden.
Victoriana in the lounge, and a sparsely
decorated vault. Chesters real ale, *lunchtime*
food and garden. Children welcome *mid-day*.

Manchester

The canal now falls through the remaining
seven locks into Manchester. The surrounding
are brightened by the well-cared-for Beswick
flight, but eventually become industrial until
the canal is totally hemmed in by the back walls
of tall factories – originally built there because
of the canal's very presence – for ½ mile above
the bottom three locks. The necessary but
tiresome chore of unlocking and locking the
paddle gear tends to slow progress. The
Rochdale Canal, which is still privately owned,
used to stretch for 33 miles over the Pennines
from Manchester to Sowerby Bridge – where it
joined the terminus of the Calder & Hebble
Navigation (*see page 25*). It has been closed to
navigation, and in Manchester much of the
canal has been reduced to a shallow, landscaped
water channel. However the bottom mile of the
canal is navigable, from the junction with the
Ashton Canal at Ducie Street down to
Castlefield and the junction with the
Bridgewater Canal. This remaining mile of the
Rochdale Canal is thus a vital link between the
Bridgewater and Ashton canals in the 100-mile
'Cheshire Ring'. A large-scale redevelopment is
underway at Paradise Wharf, by Ducie Street
Junction. Casual moorings have been provided
here – handy if you wish to visit the 'Jolly
Angler' pub. Persons wishing to navigate the
nine wide locks to the Bridgewater Canal
should apply to the Head Office of the
Rochdale Canal Company, 75 Dale Street,
Manchester (061-236 2456) for a separate
licence, if they do not already have one. The
locks can accommodate vessels up to 74ft long
and 14ft wide, drawing up to 14ft, with a height
above water level of up to 9ft. A safe but
isolated mooring can be made by Hulme Lock.
If you've just come from Fairfield Junction in a
day, you'll be too tired to go out, anyway. The
Rochdale passage is described in full on page
35, in the Bridgewater section.

Manchester
See page 35.
Salford
See page 37.

BOATYARDS

British Waterways Section Office Vesta
Street, Ancoats. (061-273 4686). W̅

PUBS

🍺 **Navigation** Near lock 6, Ashton Canal.
🍺 **Jolly Angler** Ducie Street, Manchester, near
the junction. Small pub used by the Ashton
Canal Society, offering Hyde's real ale,
lunchtime meals and snacks *at all times*. Children
welcome.
🍺 **Pollard Inn** Pollard Street, Manchester.
Basic friendly pub serving Lees real ale and
snacks *at all times*.
🍺 **Mitchell Arms** Corner of Every Street and
Ashton New Road, Manchester. Well
renovated pub where children are welcome.
Banks real ale and snacks *at all times*.

RIVER TRENT

Maximum dimensions

Shardlow to Meadow Lane Lock,
Nottingham
Length: 81'
Beam: 14' 6"
Headroom: 8'
Meadow Lane Lock to Gainsborough
Length: 165'
Beam: 18' 6"
Headroom: 13'

Mileage

DERWENT MOUTH to
Cranfleet Lock: 2¾
Beeston Lock: 7
Meadow Lane Lock, Nottingham: 12
Gunthorpe Bridge: 22
Fiskerton: 29¾
Newark Castle: 35½
Cromwell Lock: 40½
Dunham Bridge: 53
TORKSEY Junction: 57
Littleborough: 60½
GAINSBOROUGH Bridge: 67
WEST STOCKWITH: 71¾
KEADBY Junction: 84¼
TRENT FALLS: 93¾

Locks: 12

The River Trent is an historic highway running for about 100 miles from the Midlands to the Humber ports and the North Sea. It has long been of prime economic and social importance to the areas through which it flows.

It is thought that as long ago as the Bronze Age the Trent was part of the trade route from the Continent to the metal-working industry in Ireland. The discovery of two dug-out canoes in the river bed near Nottingham, dating from about 1000BC and complete with bronze weapons, indicates that the Trent was probably being navigated at this time.

The Romans recognised the value of the river as a route to the centre of England from the sea. In about AD120, in the time of Emperor Hadrian, they built the Foss Dyke canal to link the Trent Valley with Lindum Colonia (now Lincoln), the River Witham and the Wash. The Trent later acted as an easy route for the Danish invaders, who got past the guardian Knights of Torksey and penetrated as far as Nottingham. They wintered at Torksey in AD872 and, under King Swein Forkbeard, at Gainsborough in 1013.

In about AD924 Edward the Elder expelled the Danes from Nottingham and built the first bridge there. The second bridge at Nottingham was built in 1156 (some 20 years earlier than Old London Bridge) and lasted 714 years. Its remains can still be seen. The third bridge was built in 1871 and forms the basic structure of today's Trent Bridge. The traditional role of the Trent as a dividing line between one region of the country and another (many people still consider it to be a useful division between north and south England) is strengthened by the existence even today of only seven road bridges in the 80 miles between Nottingham and the sea.

Although the first Act of Parliament to improve the Trent as a navigation was passed in 1699, the first important one was in 1783. This Act authorised the construction of a towpath, thus allowing for the first time the passage of

sail-less barges. Ten years later the Trent Navigation Company's Engineer drew up a comprehensive scheme to build locks and weirs, to increase the depth in certain reaches and build a number of training walls to narrow and thus deepen the channel. Some of these works were carried out, but the scheme was far from complete by 1906, when the Royal Commission on Inland Waterways adopted it as the official future plan. The Act of 1906 authorised for the first time locks at Stoke Bardolph, Gunthorpe, Hazleford and Cromwell; but owing to the shortage of available money caused by the Great War, the works were not completed until 1926. Trade soon increased fourfold.

At its peak in the 19th and early 20thC, the Trent formed the main artery of trade for the East Midlands, being connected with the Sheffield & South Yorkshire navigations, the Chesterfield Canal, the Foss Dyke, the Grantham Canal, the Erewash Canal, the River Soar Navigation and the Trent & Mersey Canal. Although it remains so connected today to all but the Grantham Canal, the large trade between these waterways has dwindled away with railway competition, and in particular as a result of railway ownership of most of those connecting waterways. Today most of the commercial carrying is from the Humber ports to Gainsborough, as well as hundreds of thousands of tons of gravel from Carlton, below Newark. But there is not very much trade now on the non-tidal section, even to Nottingham.

The Trent remains a useful through route for pleasure craft, easy of navigation and with many interesting connections. Although it is notable for the numerous large power stations sited along its banks, the Trent is not otherwise an industrial waterway and has many attractive reaches. The British Waterways has recently improved facilities for pleasure craft with new landing stages at the locks, extra moorings and easier lock operating systems.

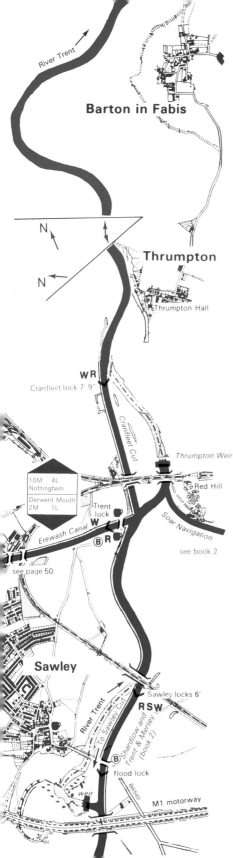

Thrumpton

Downstream from Derwent Mouth (see Book 2), the navigation goes through Sawley Cut, avoiding the weir to the north, by the M1 bridge. Near the head of the Cut is a flood lock, which under most conditions is open. Beyond this lock and the main road bridge is a wide stretch of waterway, where both banks are crowded with moored boats. Just at the tail of Sawley Locks (a pair – one manual, one mechanised with a keeper) is a large railway bridge over the river; this line carries oil and coal trains to Castle Donington and Willington power stations. To the east the cooling towers of the huge Ratcliffe Power Station are clearly visible, but they are discreetly tucked away behind Red Hill and their intrusion into the landscape is thus minimised. Trent Lock marks the junction of the Erewash Canal with the River Trent, while at the wooded Red Hill is the mouth of the River Soar. It is important not to get lost here, for there is a large weir just downstream of the railway bridges. Boats aiming for Nottingham should bear left at the big sailing club house, entering Cranfleet Cut. They will pass a pair of protective flood gates, another railway bridge (the line disappearing into the decorative tunnel through Red Hill), another long line of moored motor cruisers (many belonging to the Nottingham Yacht Club) and an attractive white accommodation bridge. At the end of the Cut is Cranfleet Lock; from here one may enjoy a view of the woods hiding Thrumpton Park. The old lockhouse at Cranfleet is now the headquarters of the Nottingham Yacht Club. Steep wooded slopes rise behind Thrumpton, while the towers of the power station still overlook the whole scene. Below Thrumpton, the river winds through flat land, passing the village of Barton in Fabis.

Barton in Fabis
Notts. Tel. A small and isolated village, composed mainly of modern housing and set well back from the river. The 14thC church seems unbalanced in several respects; it has a great variety of styles. The building has, however, considerable charm; it is light, and attractively irregular. It contains several monuments to the Sacheverell family.

Thrumpton
Notts. PO, tel. This little village beside the Trent is, like so many other places on the river, a dead end. Motorists only go there if they have a good reason to. Hence Thrumpton is a quiet and unspoilt farming village, with new development only up at the far end. Although the impressive Hall is hidden away at the west end of the village, its large uncompromising gateway serves to remind the villagers what they are there for. The tiny church, with its narrow nave and a tower, was built in the 13thC but restored in 1872 by the well-known architect G. E. Street, at the expense of Lady Byron. The single street winds past it down to the river – there used to be a ferry here.

Thrumpton Hall Basically a James I mansion built around a much older manor house. The Hall is famous for its oak staircase, which dates from the time of Charles II. The ground floor rooms are well used, and elegantly decorated; the grounds are delightful, encompassing a backwater off the River Trent. The house is private.

Trent Lock
A busy and unusual boating centre at the southern terminus of the Erewash Canal. (*See page 50*). There is a boatyard and two pubs here.

Sawley
Notts. PO, tel, stores, garage. The tall church spire attracts one across the river to Sawley, and in this respect the promise is fulfilled, for the medieval church is very beautiful and is approached by a formal avenue of lime trees leading to the 600-year-old doorway. But otherwise Sawley is an uninteresting main road village on the outskirts of Long Eaton.

Sawley Cut
In addition to a large marina and a well-patronised BWB mooring site, the Derby Motor Boat Club have a base on the Sawley Cut. All kinds of boats are represented here: canal boats, river boats and even sea-going vessels. It is certainly no place to be passing

through on a summer Sunday late-afternoon, for there will be scores of craft queueing up to pass through the locks after spending the weekend downstream. There are windlasses for sale at Sawley Lock, as well as the more conventional facilities.

BOATYARDS

ⓑ **Davison's Sawley Marina** Above Sawley Locks. (Long Eaton 734278). Ⓡ Ⓢ Ⓦ Ⓓ Pump-out, gas, day hire boats, overnight mooring, long-term mooring, winter storage, chandlery, café, toilet, showers.
ⓑ **Davison's** Trent Lock, Long Eaton (734278). On the Erewash Canal, just above the lock. Ⓔ Overnight mooring, dry dock, boat building, repairs, toilet. *Closed Sat & Sun.*

PUBS

📮✕ **Steamboat Inn** Trent Lock, on the Erewash Canal. (Long Eaton 732606). Built by the canal company in 1791, when it was called the Erewash Navigation Inn, it is now a busy and popular venue. The bars have been handsomely restored and decorated with suitably nautical objects. The real ale is brewed on the premises and includes a dark mild, a bitter and a stronger brew aptly called the 'Destroyer'. Bar and restaurant meals *lunchtime and evenings*. Garden, playground, children welcome.
📮 **Navigation Inn** Trent Lock. Large popular pub with a garden. Home's real ale and *lunchtime* food.
📮 **Nag's Head** Sawley, north of the Flood Lock. Marstons real ale and excellent *lunchtime* food.
📮 **Tiger** Tamworth Road, Long Eaton. North of B6540 bridge. Refurbished Marstons real ale pub. *Lunchtime* food.
📮 **Barge** 200yds east of B6540 bridge. Shipstone's real ale and *lunchtime* meals.

The Nottingham Canal, by the Waterways Museum. *David Perrott.*

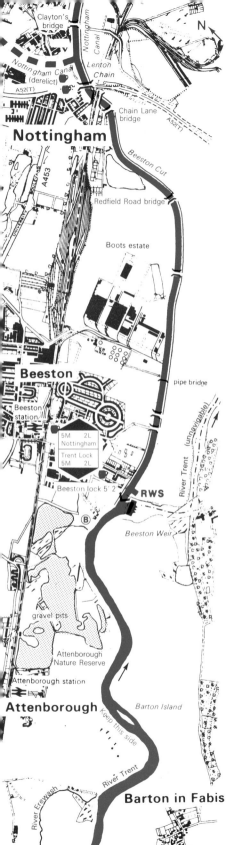

Lenton Chain

The river winds on towards Nottingham, passing the picturesque Barton Island (keep to the west of it), the old gravel pits of the Attenborough Nature Reserve and many sailing boats; this is clearly a popular stretch of the river. To the south runs a ridge of hills on which stands Clifton Hall. At the boatyard one should keep to the north side of the river to avoid the weir and enter Beeston Lock. This introduces the Beeston Canal or Beeston Cut, which bypasses an unnavigable section of the River Trent. The canal passes first a housing estate and then the industrial estate of Boots, followed by Players' Horizon Factory, designed by Arup Associates. East of the A52 bridge, the canal passes Lenton Chain. This marks the end of the short Beeston Canal, for at this point the Nottingham Canal used to flow in from the north. The junction was called Lenton Chain because the Trent Navigation Company used to lock their Beeston Canal (with a chain across it) from Saturday evening until Monday – without fail. The major part of the Nottingham Canal, from Lenton to the Erewash Canal at Langley Mill (see page 53) is now closed, but the rest of it forms the main line of through navigation from the Beeston Canal back to the River Trent at Meadow Lane Lock. The Nottingham Canal leads the traveller towards the town centre.

Beeston Lock
A splendidly kept lock where facilities are available for boats. The pretty cottages and the little backwater off the canal are a hint of its past importance; there used until some years ago to be a lock down into the river here, at right angles to the present lock. The river channel used to be navigable – by shallow-draft vessels – from here down to Trent Bridge, the Beeston Canal being cut to connect with the Nottingham Canal and to afford access into the middle of the town. But now the river is unnavigable as a through route and the canal is the only way.
Attenborough Nature Reserve Worked out gravel pits, once derelict and unsightly, are now providing an interesting habitat for plant and animal life. A comprehensive nature trail has been laid, and a wooden observation hide erected.

BOATYARDS

Ⓑ **Beeston Marina** Riverside, Beeston (223168). Ⓡ Ⓦ Ⓓ Gas, overnight mooring, long-term mooring, winter storage, slipway, chandlery, boat sales, repairs, toilets, café.

PUBS

🍺 **Johnsons Arms** Abbey Street, Nottingham, west of Lenton Chain. Friendly Shipstone's real ale pub serving *lunchtime* food.
🍺 **Boat** Priory Road, Nottingham, west of Lenton Chain. Home's real ale in a single bar pub.
🍺 **Jolly Anglers** Meadow Road, Beeston. North of Beeston Lock. Large pub with two comfortable lounges. Home's real ale and *lunchtime and evening* food.
🍺 **Boat & Horses** Trent Road, Beeston. North of Beeston Lock. Once a change-over station for barge horses. Fine traditional pub serving Home's real ale.

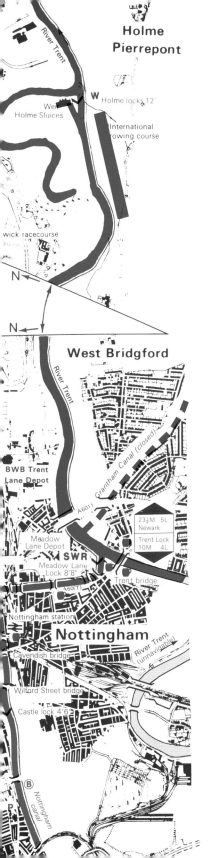

Nottingham

East of Lenton Chain, the Nottingham Canal
continues towards Nottingham Castle, which is
clearly visible on its rocky cliff near the centre
of the city. A large new marina, new houses and
a Sainsbury's superstore brighten what was
once a gloomy aspect. Already the local folk are
using the area for their recreation – when it is
all finished it will be quite an asset to the city.
Beyond the shallow Castle Lock is the
Waterways Museum, situated in the old
Fellows, Morton & Clayton warehouse. Notice
the covered loading bay with a boat and butty
inside. Stop here if you can; the moorings
opposite are excellent, and the new pub and
restaurant adjacent to the museum is very
handy. Now buildings close in as the canal
makes a sharp turn at what was once a junction,
and progresses in a cutting, tidied up and
grassed towards Meadow Lane Lock and the
River Trent. Upstream the river is navigable
for a short distance above Trent Bridge, but the
main navigation is to the west. Near Meadow
Lane Lock is the Notts County football
ground, while on the opposite side of the river
is the Trent Bridge cricket ground, with
Nottingham Forest football stadium next to it.
Below the latter is the entrance to the now
derelict Grantham Canal. Downstream from
the railway bridge, the wide river soon leaves
Nottingham behind and enters pleasant
countryside. On the north bank are many
boating centres and the Colwick racecourse. On
the south side, an exploration of the landscaped
area will reveal the magnificent rowing course
at Holme Pierrepont. Downstream are Holme
Locks and sluices (Nottingham 811197). The
locks are on the south side – there is a small one
for pleasure boats next to the very big one.

Grantham Canal
A long-disused but delightful canal from Trent
Bridge, Nottingham, to Grantham. The canal
was built purely to serve the agricultural
communities of eastern Nottinghamshire, so it
pursues a remarkably circuitous course through
pleasant farmland, including the Vale of
Belvoir (the subject of an inquiry regarding the
vast stocks of coal which lie beneath – to mine
or not to mine?). Belvoir Castle, seat of the
Duke of Rutland, is only about a mile from the
canal at one point, and a tramway was
constructed to connect them in order to carry
coal up to the castle, using wagons drawn by
horses. Traces can still be seen of this, one of
Nottinghamshire's earliest railways. The
Grantham Canal still feeds water down from
secluded reservoirs at Knipton and Denton to
the Trent, and a canal society has been formed
to campaign for its restoration. But it is
unlikely that through navigation could ever be
restored.

Nottingham
Notts. All services. The city's prosperity derives
largely from the coal field to the north, and the
long-established lace industry. John Player &
Son make all their cigarettes here and Raleigh
Industries turn out bicycles for the world. The
city centre is busy and not unattractive – there
is an imposing town hall in Slab Square – but
little of the architecture is of note. Modern
developments are encouraging, however,
notably the superb Playhouse Theatre and the
appearance of the Nottingham Festival in 1970,
which revived in this country the gentle art of
jousting. The Festival is now an annual event,
taking place in the splendid Wollaton Park on
the west side of the town. A big hot air balloon
race starting in the park is one of its most
spectacular features.
Nottingham Castle Nottingham (483504).
William the Conqueror's castle, which was
notorious as the base of Robin Hood's
unfortunate enemies while King Richard I was
away crusading, has been destroyed and rebuilt
many times during its tumultuous history. (It
was a Yorkist stronghold in the Wars of the
Roses and it was here that Charles I raised his
standard in 1642, starting the Civil War.)
Though the original secret caves beneath the
castle still exist and can be visited by
appointment, the present building dates only
from 1674. It now houses the city's museum

and art gallery which include a fine display of English pottery and textiles, and special collections of the works of Bonington and Sandby, artists from the Nottingham area. *Open daily, and Sun afternoons.*

Nottingham Goose Fair The Goose Fair is now a conventional funfair, but on a gigantic scale. It features traditional entertainments like boxing bouts (challengers invited to fight the 'house champ'), as well as the usual mechanical fairground delights. The fair's original site was in the town centre, but now it is out on the Forest Recreation Ground, a mile to the north east (served by buses). The fair takes place in the *first week of Oct* and it is advisable to get there before the Saturday, when the prices are doubled.

Waterways Museum (Nottingham 284602). Below Castle Lock in the Fellows, Morton & Clayton warehouse. An excellent museum assembled around a working boat and butty moored in the covered loading dock. Local waterways history and some beautiful models. A fine crane stands on the wharf, the scene of a tragic accident on the 28 September 1818, when 21 barrels of gunpowder were accidentally ignited by a boatman. Eight men and two boys were killed in the explosion, which destroyed the warehouse and threw one body over 100yds into Tinkers Leen. Nottingham & Beeston Canal Trail book available. *Open daily and Sun afternoons.* Free.

BOATYARDS

British Waterways 24 Meadow Lane, Nottingham (862411). The Nottingham Area Engineer's office is here. Navigation notes for users of the Trent between Nottingham and Gainsborough may also be obtained here.

Ⓑ **Nottingham Castle Marina** Nottingham (412672). R W D Gas, overnight mooring, long-term mooring, winter storage, slipway, chandlery, boat sales, gift shop. Restaurant/café/bar next door.

PUBS

🍺 **T.B.I.** Trent Bridge. Large pub near the cricket ground. Ind Coope Burton real ale.

🍺 **Sportsman** Trent Bridge. Ind Coope Burton real ale in a pub popular with football supporters.

🍺 **Aviary** Trent Bridge. Young persons' pub serving Whitbread Castle Eden real ale.

🍺 **Norfolk Hotel** London Road, Nottingham. Home's real ale in a friendly local.

🍺 **Narrowboat** Castle Boulevard, Nottingham. Friendly pub with canal theme close to the Waterways Museum. Shipstone's real ale, Bulmers real cider and *lunchtime* food.

🍺 **Navigation** Canalside by the moorings. Banks real ale in a refurbished pub.

🍺 **Queen's Hotel** Carrington Street, Nottingham. Shipstone's real ale and accommodation.

🍺 **Loggerheads** Cliff Road, Nottingham. Fine old pub, where caves at the rear were once used for cock fighting. Home's real ale and snacks at *lunchtime.*

🍺 **Trip to Jerusalem** Set into the cliff face below Nottingham Castle, this is allegedly the oldest pub in England. Sam Smith, Marstons and Bass real ales, *lunchtime* food.

🍺 **F.M.C.** Nottingham. Next door to the Waterways Museum in the old Fellows, Morton & Clayton warehouse, this pub has its own real ale brewed around the back, plus Castle Eden real ale and real draught cider. Restaurant for *lunchtime* meals adjoining.

The River Trent. *David Perrott.*

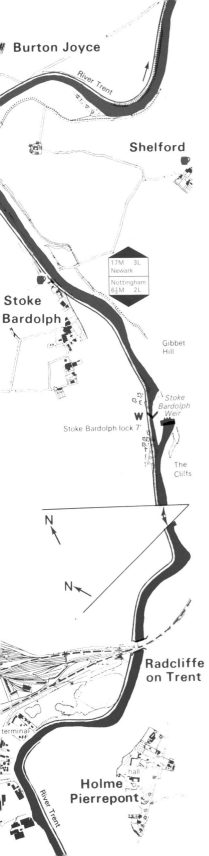

Stoke Bardolph

This section serves to establish the Trent's
attractive rural character as it continues to
sweep along through Nottinghamshire. Passing
under a railway bridge (the Nottingham–
Grantham line), one sees a very steep
escarpment of tree-covered hills, effectively
cliffs, rising out of the water. Radcliffe on
Trent is concealed in the woods by the bend,
but access is difficult. It is better to move on,
down to the delightfully secluded Stoke
Bardolph Lock, (Nottingham 248110), where
there is a water point. The lock island is
covered with trees. Below the lock, the river
bends northwards and crosses over to the other
side of the valley, leaving behind the woods and
cliffs. At Stoke Bardolph there is a sailing club,
an attractive riverside pub and a ferry (a white
rowing boat). At Burton Joyce the river
rebounds from the side of the valley and turns
east again. The water meadows that accompany
the river serve to keep at bay any inroads by
modern housing.

Shelford
Notts. PO, tel, stores. A flood bank protects this
quiet and isolated village from the waters of the
Trent. The old church has a wide
Perpendicular tower which commands the
Trent valley. There is a pub, but there is no
obvious mooring place for boats to be left on
the river. Shelford Manor is 1½ miles north
east of the village. (See next page.)

Burton Joyce
Notts. All services. A long village extending
along the very busy A612. There is a railway
station by the river (Nottingham–Lincoln
line). The cricketer Alfred Shaw – the
'Emperor of Bowlers' – was born here.

Stoke Bardolph
Notts. Tel. Most of the village, which is of little
interest, is away from the river. But the focal
point is the riverside pub, the sailing club is
based here, and it can be a busy spot. This
pub is one of several on the river in
Nottinghamshire which, by their very presence
(invariably on the site of a ferry) have caused
the development of a tiny isolated colony of
houses. They are a magnet for local
day-trippers and anglers.

Radcliffe on Trent
Notts. Access to Radcliffe from the river is
extremely difficult, even from the chic
residential caravan site at the foot of the cliffs.
In fact this caravan site reflects the smart,
suburban atmosphere of Radcliffe.

Holme Pierrepont
Notts. An isolated village east of the Holme
Locks, this is an ancient, strange and virtually
private place, with no surfaced public roads at
all. The hall, once the home of the Pierreponts,
is an extensive stuccoed building with the little
17thC church next to it gently decaying. Inside
the church is a remarkably fine monument
carved from Italian alabaster commemorating
Sir Henry Pierrepont, a champion of Henry
Tudor. Well to the west of the village is the
international rowing course, parallel and close
to, but quite separate from the river. This
award-winning recreational centre, completed
in the summer of 1972, was built from a string
of worked out gravel pits. A lot of wild birds
frequent this area, including yellow wagtails,
sand martins, little winged plover, common
terns, and great crested grebes.

PUBS

🍺 **Earl of Chesterfield** Shelford. Remote pub
serving Bass real ale straight from the barrel.
🍺 **Ferry Boat Inn** Stoke Bardolph riverside.
Good temporary moorings (ask permission) at
this popular venue by the ferry. Shipstone's
real ale and food *lunchtime and evenings.*
🍺 **Manvers Arms** Radcliffe. Real ale and food.

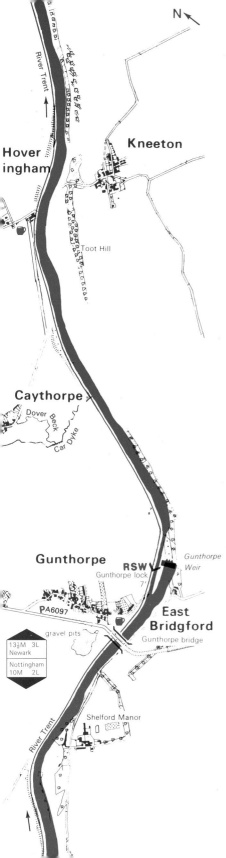

Gunthorpe

This is a stretch in which the presence of big
old riverside pubs has far more effect on the
river scene than do the villages that they
represent. Passing Shelford Manor, one arrives
at the sleek arches of Gunthorpe Bridge – the
only road bridge over the river in the 24 miles
between Nottingham and Newark. To the east
of the bridge are the grand houses up on the
hills of East Bridgford. Boats heading
downstream should keep left to enter the
mechanised Gunthorpe Lock (Lowdham 2621)
and avoid the foaming weir. What looks like a
small boatyard just above the weir is in fact just
a private mooring site. The next 5 or 6 miles
below Gunthorpe are probably the most
beautiful and certainly the most dramatic on
the whole river. On the east side, the wooded
cliffs rise almost sheer from the flat valley floor
to a height of 200ft, allowing here or there the
presence of a strip of fertile land on which cattle
graze. Only at two places does a track manage
to creep down the perilous slope to the river;
otherwise, access is impossible. On the west
side, by contrast, the ground is flat for miles,
across to the other side of the valley. The Elm
Tree, a riverside pub at Hoveringham, is a
popular place from which to launch sailing and
motor boats.

Hoveringham
Notts. PO, tel, stores, garage. The well-known
Hoveringham Gravel Company is based
nearby, although its gravel pits are not easily
seen from the river. Outside the company's
head office is a very striking sheet metal
sculpture representing a mammoth, the
company's symbol. Next to the building is a
superbly landscaped example of what can be
done with worked-out gravel pits.

East Bridgford
Notts. PO, tel, stores, garage. Accessible via a
pleasant shady lane up the hill from the river,
this village has many comfortable Georgian
houses. The church is pleasantly light and has
several monuments of the Hacker family.
Rector Oglethorpe, one time incumbent of this
parish, crowned Queen Elizabeth I.
Margidunum 1½ miles south east of East
Bridgford is the site of Margidunum, a Roman
town on the Fosse Way (the straightest road in
England). Margidunum was probably located
here to guard the ford at East Bridgford, which
in Roman times was one of the very few easy
crossings on the Trent.

Gunthorpe
Notts. PO, tel, stores, garage. Gunthorpe has
been an important river crossing point for over
2000 years. The bridge built in 1875 was
replaced by the present one in 1927. Prior to
this, a ferry operated here. The riverside near
the bridge and the pubs is a pleasant situation,
backed by the hills of East Bridgford, although
often crowded with motorists and trippers,
speed boats buzz about on certain days when
British Waterways relax the speed limit Bylaw
for particular clubs. The vast mechanised lock,
surrounded by trees, seems to lend a tone of
sobering functionalism.

Shelford Manor Near the river just west of
Gunthorpe Bridge. The old manor was burnt
down in 1645 after 2000 Roundheads attacked
this Royalist stronghold. They forced an
entrance and massacred 140 of the 200 men
inside. The manor was rebuilt in 1676. *Not open
to the public.*

PUBS

🍺 **Elm Tree** Hoveringham. Riverside.
🍺 **Marquis of Granby** Hoveringham. Small
village pub with a choice of Ruddles and
Marstons real ale.
🍺 **Anchor Inn** Gunthorpe. Riverside.
🍺 **Black Horse** 1 mile north of Gunthorpe
Bridge. Reputedly once a haunt of Dick
Turpin. Shipstone's real ale, food *lunchtime and
evenings.*

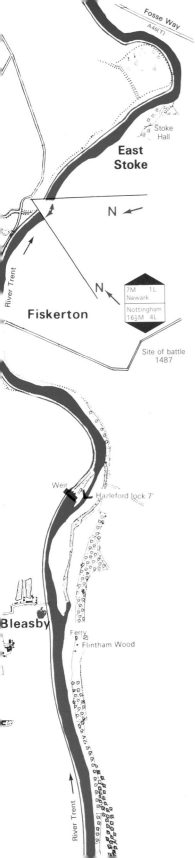

Fiskerton

The river continues along its superb isolated course, with the forested cliffs of the Trent Hills striding along the river's east bank, while on the other side the flat plain of the valley rolls away through green fields and quiet Nottinghamshire villages. Unseen up on the plateau to the east is the big Syerston Airfield, now little used. A solitary hut on the east bank houses a ferryman, who plies across the river at weekends for the fishermen. The Star & Garter pub is on the left bank near an island in the river; boats should keep west of the island to reach Hazelford Lock (Newark 830312). The lock-keeper here lives in isolation on the rabbit-infested lock island, for there is no bridge over the adjacent weir, and his sole access is by boat. Beyond this lock, the steep Trent Hills dwindle away and the river leaves the woods (near the battlefield of East Stoke) for Fiskerton. There is a splendid wharf here – one of the few good places on the whole of this river navigation where it is easy to tie up. Downstream of Fiskerton, the river sweeps round past the parkland at Stoke Hall. The site of a 4-acre Roman fort is on the nearby Fosse Way.

East Stoke
Notts. Tel. The village is nearly a mile from the river, and mooring is difficult. The dark and gloomy lane by the church and hall seems to brood on Stoke's violent past. For in 1487 the concluding battle in the Wars of the Roses was fought here. Two years after the Battle of Bosworth Field (fought on a site near the Ashby Canal), where Henry Tudor defeated King Richard III and was proclaimed King Henry VII, the Earl of Lincoln set up Lambert Simnel – a 10-year-old lad – as the Earl of Warwick and proclaimed him King Edward VI. (The real Earl of Warwick was in fact locked up in the Tower of London.) With a 9000-strong army, comprising mainly German and Irish mercenaries, the rebels engaged the Crown's army at Stoke Field as the Earl of Oxford led Henry's 12,000 men away from Nottingham. The battle was short but sharp. After three hours most of the rebel leaders were dead and their army in total disarray. This effectively terminated the Wars of the Roses, although the last Yorkist claim to the throne was not extinguished until the real Earl of Warwick was executed in 1499. The appropriately named Red Gutter in Stoke is a reminder of the battle, although there is no physical trace.

Fiskerton
Notts. PO, tel, stores, station. A charming riverside village with excellent access for boats. Although the normal river level is well below the wharf, all the buildings along the splendid front are carefully protected from a possible flood by stone walling or a bank of earth. The wharf is definitely the most interesting part of Fiskerton.

Southwell
Notts. 3 miles north west of Fiskerton, this very attractive country town is well worth visiting in order to see its Minster. The Minster was founded at the beginning of the 12thC by the Archbishop of York, and is held by many to be one of the most beautiful Norman ecclesiastical buildings in England. Its scale is vast for Southwell, but it is set well back from the houses and is in a slight dip, so it does not overawe the town centre, in spite of the two western towers and the massive central tower. Chief among the treasures inside the building are the naturalistic stone carvings in the late 13thC chapter house, and the wooden carvings of the choir stalls.

BOATYARDS

Ⓑ **Fiskerton Boats** Trent Side, Fiskerton. (Newark 830695). RWD Pump-out, gas, long-term mooring, winter storage, toilets, grocery shop nearby.

PUBS

🍺 **Bromley Arms** Fiskerton Wharf. An attractive riverside pub serving Kimberley real ale.

🍺 **Star & Garter** Hazelford Ferry, Bleasby. A huge, heavily gabled riverside pub opposite the Trent Hills and the head of the mile-long lock island. Home's real ale, and meals by arrangement. Gnome-filled garden and model village.

🍺 **Waggon & Horses** Bleasby. ½ mile north of Hazelford Ferry, this fine village pub offers Home's real ale.

Newark Castle. *Derek Pratt.*

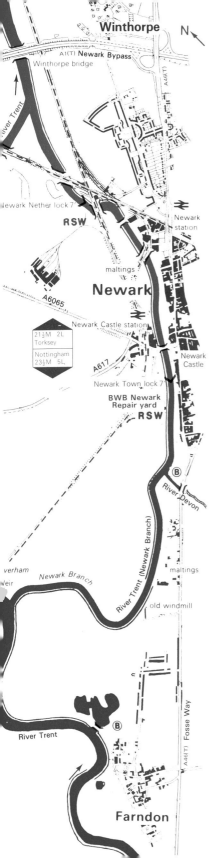

Newark-on-Trent

Farndon is a pleasant riverside village, with
sailing clubs on either side and a small ferry.
The boat population is further increased by the
use of some old gravel pits just north of
Farndon as a mooring site for pleasure boats.
For a mile or two, the flat landscape is
dominated by the great Staythorpe Power
Station, which is beside the river and is visible
for miles; this common feature of the gentle
river landscape will by now be familiar to those
cruising on the Trent. Navigators must be
especially careful to avoid the large Averham
Weir which takes the main channel of the Trent
to Kelham and round the north side of Newark.
Boats heading downstream should keep right,
steering by the 240ft spire of Newark church.
The waterway immediately becomes narrower
east of this weir. This is the Newark Branch
which takes boats straight into the middle of
the town. On the way into Newark, the
navigation passes an old windmill, a boatyard at
the mouth of the River Devon (pronounced
'Deevon'), some extensive old maltings, and a
gently decaying warehouse with the words
'Trent Navigation Company' in faded lettering
on the side. Opposite is the British Waterways
Repair Yard, and just beyond it is Newark
Town Lock (Newark 702226). This is a large,
mechanically operated lock. The remains of the
old one are alongside, half of which is now used
as a mooring for pleasure boats while the rest is
a covered drydock. The townscape at this point
is dominated by the northwest wall of the
ruined Newark Castle. Hard by is a splendid
old five-arched stone bridge. The size of the
arches limits the width of boats which can use
the navigation, but this bridge is listed as an
ancient monument and so cannot be altered to
accommodate bigger vessels. Just through the
bridge is Town Wharf, which is the best
temporary mooring site in Newark. Beyond
here the navigation passes the oldest and most
interesting industrial buildings in Newark – an
old ironworks, a maltings, a brewery and a
glueworks giving off a smell of old leather. A
weir follows this to the left, then a right bend
under a railway bridge, and one arrives at
Newark Nether Lock (Newark 703830) with a
smart new lock keeper's cottage nearby. East of
the lock, the navigation rejoins the main
channel of the River Trent and proceeds
north-eastward under the graceful modern road
bridge carrying the Newark bypass.

Winthorpe
Notts. Tel. Access from the river is not easy.
Winthorpe is an attractive village. Bypassed by
the A1, it is free from all through traffic and the
abundance of mature trees gives it a peaceful
air. The pub is inviting and the church, in an
ostentatious Victorian style, was entirely rebuilt
between 1886 and 1888, at the sole cost of its
patron, the Reverend Edward Hadley.

Newark
Notts. EC Thur. MD Wed, Sat. 2 stations.
Newark is magnificent, easily the most
interesting and attractive town on the Trent,
and it is very appealing from the navigation.
Situated at the junction of two old highways,
the Great North Road and the Fosse Way, the
town is of great historical significance. During
the Civil War it was a Royalist stronghold
which was besieged three times by the
Roundheads between March 1645 and May
1646. The defensive earthworks or 'sconces'
constructed by the Royalists are still visible.
Today Newark, like everywhere else, is large,
busy and surrounded by industry and modern
housing. But the town centre is intact and still
full of charm.
Market Place It is worth making a point of
visiting Newark on market day to view the
scene in the colourful old market. In opposite
corners of the square are two ancient pubs: one
of them, the White Hart, was built in the 15thC
and is the oldest example of domestic
architecture in the town, the other is the
Clinton Arms where W. E. Gladstone made his
first speech in 1832. He later became Prime
Minister.
Church of St Mary Magdalene The enormous
spire is all that one can see of this elegant
church from the market place, for the buildings

on one side of the square hide the body of the structure. Inside, the church is made light and spacious by soaring columns and a magnificent 15thC east window in the chancel. The building was begun in 1160 and completed about 1500. It is rich in carving, both within and without, but one of the church's most interesting features is a brass made in Flanders to commemorate Alan Fleming, a merchant who died in 1375. The monument is made up of 16 pieces of metal and measures 9ft 4in by 5ft 7in – one of the biggest of its type in England.

Newark Castle Only a shell remains, the one intact wall overlooking the river. The first known castle on this site was constructed around 1129, probably for Alexander, Bishop of Lincoln. The present building was started in 1173, with various additions and alterations in the 14th, 15th and 16thC – notably the fine oriel windows. King John died here in October 1216, soon after his traumatic experience in the Wash. The castle was naturally a great bastion during the Civil War sieges and battles that focused on Newark. When the Roundheads eventually took the town in 1646, they dismantled the castle. The ruins and the grounds are *open daily.*

Newark Museum & Art Gallery Appleton Gate, Newark (702358). An historical collection of local items, which includes several Civil War relics, a lead Roman coffin (and its original contents) and W. E. Gladstone's advertisement board ('Gladstone and the Conservative Cause') which he used at elections. During the early part of his career, Gladstone spent 14 years as MP for Newark. Half of the museum is in a schoolroom which is much as it was when built by Archbishop Magnus in 1529. *Open daily except Sun.*

Governor's House Market Place. A late 16th or early 17thC half-timbered house where successive Governors of Newark lived during the Civil War. It is thought that the quarrel between Charles I and Prince Rupert in 1645 took place here. It resulted in Rupert losing his position as Army General and Governor of Newark. It is obvious from the size and style of the house that it was built for someone of distinction, and further evidence of this is the line of cobble paving running from the house across the square to the south porch of the church.

Tourist Information Centre The Offington, Beast Market Hill, Castlegate, Newark (78962).

Farndon
Notts. PO, tel, stores. A pleasant riverside village; with the sailing boats and riverside pub this is a busy place in summer. The 14thC church is tucked away in the trees near the older houses of the village.

BOATYARDS

Ⓑ **British Waterways Newark Repair Yard** Above Newark Town Lock. (Newark 704106). Ⓡ Ⓢ Ⓦ at the lock.

Ⓑ **Newark Marina** Farndon Road, Newark (704022). Ⓦ Gas, overnight mooring, long-term mooring, winter storage, chandlery, boat sales, repairs.

Ⓑ **Farndon Harbour** Farndon, nr Newark (705483). Ⓡ Ⓢ Ⓦ Ⓓ Gas, overnight mooring, long-term mooring, winter storage, slipway, chandlery, boat sales, repairs, salvage, toilets, showers.

PUBS

🍺 **Admiral Nelson** Winthorpe.

🍺 **Castle Barge** Floating pub at Newark Town Wharf, in a 94ft former Spillers grain barge.

🍺 **White Hart** Market Place, Newark. 15thC pub.

🍺✕ **Clinton Arms** Market Place, Newark (72299). Bar meals and restaurant *L & D.*

🍺 **Newcastle Arms** Appleton Gate, Newark. A fine locals' pub serving Home's real ale.

🍺 **Old Kings Arm's** Kirkgate, Newark. Marstons real ale in a popular young persons' pub.

🍺 **Rose & Crown** Farndon. John Smith real ale and snacks.

A 'pusher' tug entering Newark Town Lock.

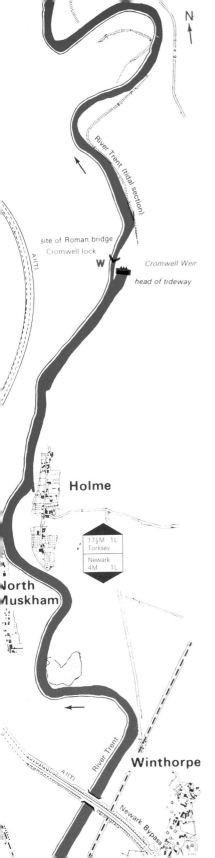

site of Roman bridge
Cromwell lock

W

Cromwell Weir

head of tideway

Holme

17½M 1L
Torksey

Newark
4M 1L

North
Muskham

Winthorpe

Cromwell Lock

From Newark, the Trent follows a generally
northerly course towards the Humber, which is
still over 50 miles away owing to the very
sweeping and tortuous line of the river. The
villages of North Muskham and Holme face
each other across the water; neither has a good
landing stage, but the former has a waterside
pub and thus beckons more strongly. There
used to be a ferry between the two villages. A
mile or more below Holme is Cromwell Lock
and Weir. The weir is the largest on the Trent,
and is thankfully now buoyed and has a safety
boom so all boats should keep to the west side
of the river. The lock too is truly enormous; it
is mechanised, and there is a lock keeper on
duty every day (Newark 821213). Cromwell has
always been a significant place on the river; the
Romans built a bridge across at this point.
More importantly, this lock marks the
beginning of the tidal section of the Trent, so
navigation north of here requires a very
different approach.

Navigating the tidal Trent

A suitable boat is essential: proper navigation
lights (compulsory on all the navigable Trent)
and safety equipment (including an anchor and
cable) is compulsory. Navigation notes are
available from the British Waterways, 24
Meadow Lane, Nottingham (862411).
Deep-draughted boats should beware of shoals
at low water and should avoid the inside of
bends. The river banks are unsuitable for
mooring and there are few wharves. Navigators
who are more used to canals and non-tidal
rivers will be more likely to treat the tidal Trent
as a link route with the Fossdyke & Witham
Navigation, the Chesterfield Canal, the
Sheffield & South Yorkshire Canal or the
Humber estuary. They should plan their trip
with an eye to the tide-table. The best approach
is either to use a Hull tide-table (available from
local boatyards, fishing shops and newsagents)
bearing in mind that the Trent floods for only
about 2¼ hours and ebbs for the remainder of
the 12 hour period or, if in doubt, to ask the
British Waterways lock keepers at the various
junctions along the river. The relevant
telephone numbers are listed below:
Cromwell Lock: Newark 821213
Torksey Lock: Torksey 202
West Stockwith Lock: Gainsborough 890204
Keadby Lock: Scunthorpe 782205
Plan your journey so that the tide is running
with you, and bear in mind the lock operating
times.

Holme

Notts. Tel. Separated from the river by a flood
bank and a line of trees. Holme is really more of
a large farming hamlet than a village. The
church is a delightfully irregular shape; it has a
tiny stub of a spire, and a 15thC porch that
resembles an Elizabethan gatehouse. In fact the
porch has an upper room. During the Great
Plague a woman called Nanny Scott took refuge
in it, but when she emerged to get more food
after a prolonged stay she found that she and
one man were the only people alive in the whole
village, so she returned to the room and spent
the rest of her life there. There is no proper
landing place on the river for this village.

North Muskham

Notts. PO, tel, stores. A small, quiet village
right on the river bank. The church was built
mainly in the 15thC, and has large clerestory
windows. The village used to be in the same
parish as Holme, because previously the two
villages were on the same side of the river.
However in Elizabethan times the river
changed its course and since then it has
separated them. No proper landing place from
the river.

PUBS

Newcastle Arms North Muskham.
Riverside.

Sutton on Trent

This is a typical stretch of the upper section of the tidal Trent. The river meanders along its northward course. It is flanked by flood banks and there are no bridges. There is little to see except the occasional barge. A relatively interesting place is Carlton Wharf, where there are still working barges to be seen, but the moorings here are not for pleasure boats. The village of Sutton on Trent is near this wharf; so is a big derelict windmill. On the east bank is Besthorpe Wharf, which is used for feeding gravel from the adjacent pits into the river barges. These two wharves handle several hundred thousand tons of gravel every year. Mooring along the tidal Trent is not recommended.

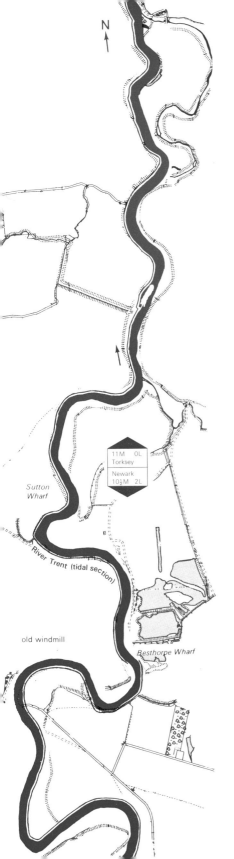

N

11M   0L
Torksey

Newark
10½M   2L

Sutton
Wharf

River Trent (tidal section)

old windmill

Besthorpe Wharf

Dunham Bridge

Passing the nearby villages of High Marnham, Low Marnham and South Clifton, the river reaches the big cooling towers of High Marnham Power Station. There is a footbridge carrying a pipe across the river here; just north of it is the iron railway viaduct that carries the line supplying the power station. Near the viaduct is an isolated church. 1½ miles further, the river describes a sharp S-bend as it passes a welcome little ridge of hills, pleasantly wooded. But the ridge fades away as one reaches Dunham Toll Bridge (built in 1832) and the iron aqueduct that precedes it. The countryside resumes its flat and rather featureless aspect, while the river now forms the border between Nottinghamshire and Lincolnshire (as far downstream as West Stockwith). From Stapleford to Dunham the river is a birdwatcher's paradise of water meadows, pools and marshes. Mooring along the tidal Trent is not recommended.

Dunham

River Trent (tidal section)

Dunham
Toll bridge

pipe bridge

6M	0L
Torksey	
Newark	
15½M	2L

A57(T)

North Clifton

Fledborough

Fledborough Viaduct

A1133

High
Marnham
Power
Station

South Clifton

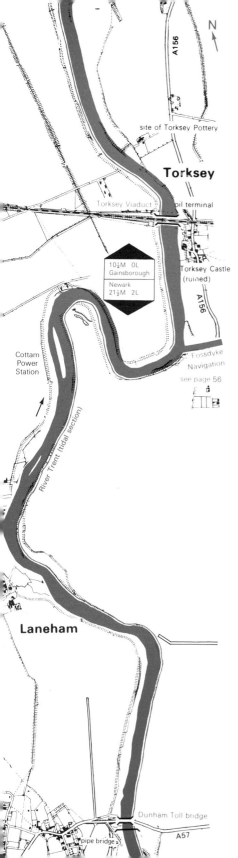

Torksey

At Laneham the traveller will enjoy a little
relief from the Trent's isolation. Here there is a
church and a few houses on a slight rise near the
river. There is also a sailing club. To the north
of the village, yet another power station –
Cottam – appears as the river turns back on
itself to the south before swinging northwards
again at the junction with the Fossdyke
Navigation (marked by a new pumping
station). The lock up into the Fossdyke is just
through the road bridge; there is a small
mooring jetty below the bridge, and a pub,
petrol station and shop are all near the lock.
There is also a good restaurant in the village –
but further information on Torksey can be
found on page 56. Nearing the railway viaduct
at Torksey, one sees the gaunt ruin of Torksey
Castle standing beside the river. As at Newark,
the façade that faces the Trent is the most
complete part of the building, for the rest has
vanished. (The castle has been abandoned since
the 16thC.) For the first 15ft or so from the
ground, the castle is built of stone – above this
it is dark red brick. The railway viaduct at
Torksey is disused, although, curiously
enough, the line on either side is much used;
from the west, coal trains supply Cottam Power
Station, while from the east oil trains bring fuel
from Immingham to an oil terminal on the
river. From here it is taken away by lorries,
mostly to the numerous air bases around
Lincolnshire. Mooring on the tidal Trent is not
recommended.

Littleborough

From Cottam, the river continues to wind
northwards towards Gainsborough. This is not
as dull a stretch as those further south. A
windmill marks the exaggeratedly named Trent
Port, which is in fact the wharf for the small
village of Marton. Speedboats operate from
here, but owners of any larger boats will once
again find it difficult to land. The next place of
interest is Littleborough, a tiny riverside
settlement. Fortunately boats may moor
temporarily at the floating jetty. Below
Littleborough is a beautiful reach, with steep
wooded hills rising from the water's edge on the
Lincolnshire side. The attractive timbered
building set in the parkland is called Burton
Château. A little further downstream, another
clump of trees on the east bank at Knaith
conceals a former nunnery and chapel, but
mooring is only just possible here. On towards
Gainsborough, the cooling towers of West
Burton Power Station stand out prominently in
the flat landscape on the west side of the river.

Knaith
Lincs. Temporary mooring just possible.
Among the trees is the hall and an interesting
old church, with its Jacobean pulpit. Both were
part of a nunnery dissolved in 1539. The hall
was the birthplace of Thomas Sutton, who
founded Charterhouse School and Hospital.
Littleborough
Notts. An attractive hamlet with reasonably
good access from the river. The little church
stands on a slight rise; it is a delightfully simple
Norman structure and incorporates much
herringbone masonry. It is assumed from
various finds, including the perfectly preserved
body of a woman dug up in the graveyard, that
this was the site of the Roman camp
Segelocum. The paved ford dating from the
time of Emperor Hadrian became visible
during a drought in 1933. King Harold's army
crossed this ford on their way to Hastings in
1066.

to West Stockwith, Kneadby
and the Humber

N

Gainsborough

Gainsborough Central
station

A631

4½M   0L
W. Stockwith   Gainsborough Arches

Torksey
10¼M   0L

A156

mills

Gainsborough Lea Road
station

River Trent (tidal section)

Gainsborough

The river moves away from the wooded slopes,
passes the power station (the northernmost on
the river) and heads for Gainsborough, which is
clearly indicated by a group of tall flour mills.
Below the railway bridge, the river bends
sharply before reaching the flour mills, the
bridge at Gainsborough and the busy wharves,
where it is possible to tie up (seek permission
first). The town is set entirely on one side of the
river, and is worth visiting.

Navigational note
Below Gainsborough the river is covered at a
much reduced scale on the general map of the
North East Waterways. The entrance to the
Chesterfield Canal at West Stockwith is just 4½
miles below Gainsborough Bridge; Keadby, the
entrance to the Stainforth & Keadby Canal, is a
further 13 miles downstream from Stockwith.
Those proceeding from Gainsborough to either
of these places are advised to warn the
respective lock keepers of their impending
arrival (*see page 143*).

Gainsborough
*Lincs. EC Wed, MD Tue, Sat. All services, 2
stations*. Gainsborough is best seen from the
river, where the old wharves and warehouses
serve as a reminder of the town's significance as
a port in the 18th and 19thC. Possibly Britain's
furthest inland port, it now handles vessels of
850 tonnes deadweight, carrying animal
feedstuffs, grain, fertilisers and scrap.
Elsewhere industrial sprawl and Victorian red
brick housing tends to obscure the qualities of
the old market town. There are several
Victorian churches, but All Saints retains its
Perpendicular tower. Gainsborough was a
frequent battleground during the Civil War and
George Eliot described it as St Ogg's in 'The
Mill on the Floss'.
The Old Hall Parnell Street, Gainsborough
(2669). An attractive manor house of the 15thC
and 16thC in the centre of the town: it contains
a medieval kitchen and Great Hall. Here Henry
VIII met Catherine Parr, later his sixth wife,
who was the daughter-in-law of the house. The
Pilgrim fathers also met here. Now a folk
museum. *Open weekday afternoons all year; Sun
Easter–Oct only.*

TRENT & MERSEY

Maximum dimensions

Harding's Wood to Middlewich
Length: 72'
Beam: 7'
Headroom: 5' 9"
Middlewich to Anderton
Length: 72'
Beam: 14' 6"
Headroom: 7'
Anderton to Preston Brook
Length: 72'
Beam: 7'
Headroom: 7'

Mileage

HARDING'S WOOD, junction with
Macclesfield Canal to King's Lock,
Middlewich, junction with Middlewich
Branch: 10½
Anderton Lift, for River Weaver: 22¾
PRESTON BROOK, north end of tunnel and
Bridgewater Canal: 29¾

Locks: 36

This early canal was originally conceived partly as a roundabout link between the ports of Liverpool and Hull, while passing through the busy area of the Potteries and mid-Cheshire, and terminating either in the River Weaver or in the Mersey. One of its prime movers was the famous potter Josiah Wedgwood (1730–1795). Like the Duke of Bridgewater a few years previously, he saw the obvious enormous advantages to his – and others' – industry of cheap, safe and rapid transport which a navigation would offer compared with packhorse carriage (the only alternative then available). Wedgwood was greatly assisted in the promotion of the canal by his friends, notably Thomas Bentley and Erasmus Darwin. Pamphlets were published, influential support was marshalled; and in 1766 the Trent & Mersey Canal Act was passed by Parliament, authorising the building of a navigation from the River Trent to Runcorn Gap, where it would join the proposed extension of the Bridgewater Canal from Manchester.

The ageing James Brindley was – of course – appointed engineer of the new canal. Construction began at once and much public interest was excited in this remarkable project, especially in the great 2900yd tunnel under Harecastle Hill.

Once opened in 1777 the Trent & Mersey Canal was a great success, attracting much trade in all kinds of commodities. Vast tonnages of china clay and flints for the pottery industry were brought by sea from Devon and Cornwall, then transhipped into canal boats on the Mersey

and brought straight to the factories around Burslem, taking finished goods away again. Everyone near the canal benefited: much lower freight costs meant cheaper goods, healthier industries and more jobs. Agriculture gained greatly from the new supply of water, and of stable manure from the cities.

The Trent & Mersey soon earned its other name (suggested by Brindley) as the Grand Trunk Canal – in the 67 miles between Fradley Junction and Preston Brook Junction, the Trent & Mersey gained connection with no less than eight other canals or significant branches.

By the 1820s the Trent & Mersey was so busy that the narrow and slowly-sinking tunnel at Harecastle had become a serious bottleneck for traffic. Thomas Telford was called in; he recommended building a second tunnel beside Brindley's old one. His recommendation was eventually accepted by the company, and a tremendous burst of energy saw the whole tunnel completed in under three years, in 1827. A much-needed towpath was included in this tunnel although this has now been removed so that boats can use the headroom in the centre of the channel.

Although the Trent & Mersey was taken over in 1845 by the new North Staffordshire Railway Company, the canal flourished until the Great War as a most important trading route. The complete canal is covered in Book 2 – this section, Harding's Wood to Preston Brook, is included to complete the coverage of the 'Cheshire Ring' canal circuit within this volume.

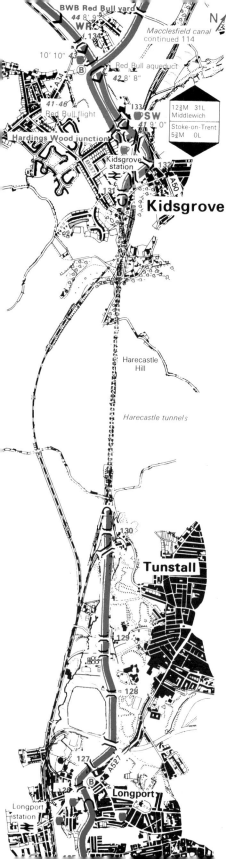

Harding's Wood Junction

The Trent & Mersey from Harding's Wood to
Preston Brook Tunnel is included in this book
to complete the coverage of the 'Cheshire
Ring'. Those on the ring with time to spare may
wish to have a look at the northern entrance of
the Harecastle Tunnel, only a short walk from
Harding's Wood Junction, or even make a
'through and back' journey, winding at
Longport Wharf (bridge 126). Operating times
for the tunnel are given on a board at the
entrance. Those who make the passage will not
regret it. Coal and Calor gas are available at a
yard by bridge 132. The Trent & Mersey
proceeds to descend from the summit level
through a flight of paired narrow locks. Just
below the second lock, the Macclesfield Canal
crosses the T & M on Red Bull Aqueduct.

Kidsgrove
Staffs. All services. Originally a big iron and
coal producing town, Kidsgrove was much
helped in its growing size and prosperity by the
completion of the Trent & Mersey Canal,
which gave the town an outlet for these goods.
James Brindley is buried in the town in a
churchyard at Newchapel.
St Saviour's Church Butt Lane. This building
is unusual in looking quite unlike a church.
Built in 1878, it was designed in black and
white Tudor style.
Harecastle Tunnels There are altogether three
parallel tunnels through Harecastle Hill. The
first, built by James Brindley, was completed in
1777, after 11 years work. To build a 9ft wide
tunnel 1¾ miles long represented engineering
on a scale quite unknown at that time, and
everyone was duly impressed.
Since there was no towpath in the tunnel the
boats – which were of course all towed from the
bank by horses in those days – had to be
'legged' through by men lying on the boat's
cabin roof and propelling the boat by 'walking'
along the tunnel roof. (The towing horse would
have to be walked in the meantime over the top
of the hill.) This very slow means of
propulsion, combined with the great length of
the narrow tunnel and the large amount of
traffic on the navigation, made Harecastle a
major bottleneck for canal boats. So in 1822 the
Trent & Mersey Canal Company called in
Thomas Telford, who recommended that a
second tunnel be constructed alongside the first
one. This was done: the new tunnel was
completed in 1827, with a towpath, after only
three years work. Each tunnel then became
one-way until in the 20thC Mr Brindley's bore
had sunk so much from mining subsidence that
it had to be abandoned. An electric tug was
introduced in 1914 to speed up traffic through
Telford's tunnel; this service was continued
until 1954. Subsidence has necessitated the
complete removal of the towpath, allowing the
use of the full height of the centre of the arch.
The third tunnel through Harecastle Hill was
built years after the other two, and carried the
Stoke–Kidsgrove railway line. It runs 40ft
above the canal tunnels and is slightly shorter.
This tunnel was closed in the 1960s: the railway
line now goes round the hill and through a
much shorter tunnel. Thus two out of the three
Harecastle tunnels are disused.

BOATYARDS

British Waterways Red Bull Yard North of bridge 134. (Kidsgrove 5703). R W.

Ⓑ **David Piper** Red Bull Basin, Church Lawton, Kidsgrove (4754). D Pump-out, gas, slipway up to 60ft, winter storage, chandlery, shop. Boat and engine sales and service. Steel boats built and fitted out. Useful source of information regarding tunnel opening times.

Ⓑ **Stoke-on-Trent Boat Building** Longport Wharf, Longport, Stoke-on-Trent (813831). R W D Pump-out, gas, overnight mooring, long-term mooring, winter storage, slipway, chandlery, boat building and repairs, gift shop, toilet.

PUBS

🍺 **Red Bull** Canalside, in the Red Bull flight of locks. Robinson's real ale. Garden, food.

🍺 **Blue Bell** at junction with Macclesfield Canal. Real ale.

🍺 **Canal Tavern** opposite the Blue Bell.

🍺 **Duke of Bridgewater** near bridge 126. The lounge is full of narrowboat parts. Bass real ale.

🍺 **Pack Horse** Station Street. Near bridge 126. Ansells and Ind Coope real ale.

The northern entrance to the Harecastle Tunnel – Brindley's disused bore is to the right. *David Perrott.*

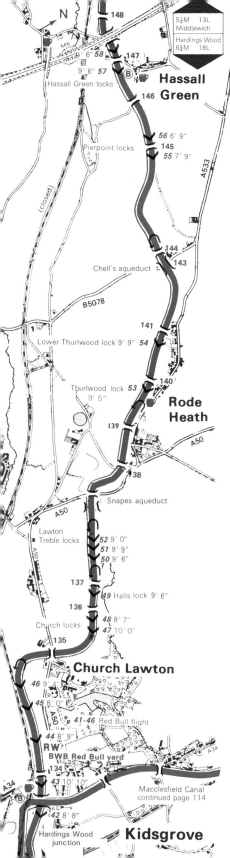

Rode Heath

Leaving behind the spire of Church Lawton,
the canal continues to fall through a heavily
locked stretch sometimes called, unfairly,
'heartbreak hill'. The countryside is entirely
rural and pleasant, slightly hilly and wooded.
Two minor aqueducts are encountered, but the
locks are more interesting: they are all pairs of
narrow locks, side by side. Some of the
duplicate locks are unusable or even filled in,
but many of them are in good condition, so that
a boatman can choose whichever lock is set for
him. There are good moorings above Church
Locks, and above Hassall Green Locks. The
duplicate lock at Thurlwood, alongside the
existing lock, used to be one of the strangest
structures on the waterways network. Known
as Thurlwood Steel Lock, it was built in 1957
to overcome subsidence caused by local brine
pumping, and was a massive and complicated
affair, with a huge steel superstructure. Unused
for many years, it was dismantled in 1988. At
Hassall Green a *PO, tel and stores* incorporating
a canal shop and boatyard services can be found
just by the new concrete bridge. The M6
motorway crosses noisily nearby.

Rode Heath
Ches. PO, tel, stores. A useful shopping area
right by bridge 139.

BOATYARDS

Vistra Marina Hassall Green. (Crewe
762266). W D Pump-out, mooring, gas, post
office, general store, off-licence, lunches, coffee
and tea.
British Waterways Red Bull Yard North of
bridge 134. (Kidsgrove 5703). R W.
B **David Piper** Red Bull Basin, Church
Lawton, Kidsgrove. (4754). By Red Bull
Aqueduct. D Pump-out, gas, slipway up to
60ft, winter storage, chandlery, shop. Boat and
engine sales and service. Steel boats built and
fitted out. Useful source of information
regarding tunnel opening times.

PUBS

Romping Donkey Hassall Green. A pretty
country pub, offering real ale, and bar meals
and snacks *lunchtime and evenings*. Children
welcome, garden.
Broughton Arms Canalside at Rode Heath.
Friendly and popular pub with good moorings.
Snacks, garden.

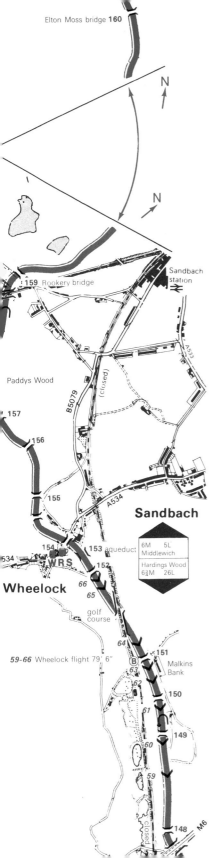

Wheelock

The canal now descends the Wheelock flight of eight locks, which are the last paired locks one sees when travelling northwards. The countryside continues to be quiet and unspoilt but unspectacular. The pair of locks halfway down the flight has a curious situation in the little settlement of Malkin's Bank: overlooked by terraced houses (one of which used to be the boatman's Co-op), the boatman can get the distinct feeling that his lock operating routine is a very public performance. At the bottom of the flight is the village of Wheelock (good moorings after bridge 152); west of here the navigation curls round the side of a hill before entering the very long-established salt-producing area that is based on Middlewich. The 'wild' brine pumping and rock-salt mining that has gone on hereabouts has resulted in severe local subsidence: the effect on the canal has been to necessitate the constant raising of the banks as lengths of the canal bed sink. This of course means that the affected lengths tend to be much deeper than ordinary canals. Non-swimmers beware of falling overboard.

Sandbach
Ches. EC Tue. MD Thur. PO, tel, stores, garage, bank, station. 1½ miles north of Wheelock. An old market town that has maintained its charm despite the steady growth of its salt and chemical industries.
Ancient crosses In the cobbled market place on a massive base stand two superb Saxon crosses, believed to commemorate the conversion of the area to Christianity in the 7thC. They suffered severely in the 17thC when the Puritans broke them up and scattered the fragments for miles. After years of searching for the parts, George Ormerod succeeded in re-erecting the crosses in 1816, with new stone replacing the missing fragments.
St Mary's Church High Street. A large, 16thC church with a handsome battlemented tower. The most interesting features of the interior are the 17thC carved roof and the fine chancel screen.
Old Hall Hotel An outstanding example of Elizabethan half-timbered architecture, which was formerly the home of the lord of the manor, but is now used as an hotel.
Wheelock
Ches. EC Tue. PO, tel, stores, garage, fish & chips, Chinese takeaway. Busy little main road village on the canal.

BOATYARDS
ⓑ **Malkins Bank Canal Services** (Crewe 764595). Long-term mooring, winter storage, slipway, boat building and repairs.

PUBS
🍺 **Cheshire Cheese** Wheelock. Canalside pub serving Tetley's real ale and food. Garden with children's play area.
🍺 **Nag's Head** Wheelock.
🍺 **Commercial Hotel** Wheelock.
🍺 **Market Tavern** The Square, Sandbach. Opposite the crosses. Food, garden.

Elton Moss bridge **160**

N

N

159 Rookery bridge

Sandbach station

Paddys Wood

157

156

155

Sandbach

154

153 aqueduct

WRS

152

Wheelock

66

65

golf course

64

59-66 Wheelock flight 79' 6"

151

Malkins Bank

63

62

150

61

149

60

59

148 M6

	6M	5L
Middlewich		
Hardings Wood	6¾M	26L

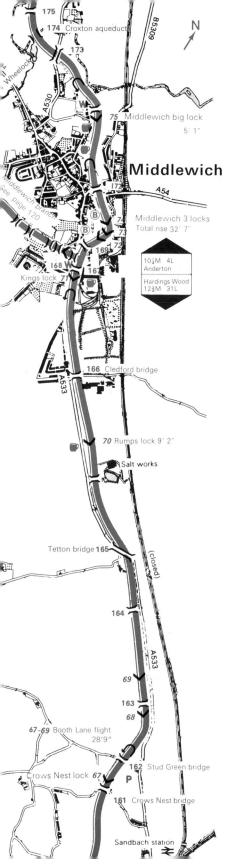

Middlewich

The navigation now begins to lose the rural
character it has enjoyed since Kidsgrove.
Falling through yet more locks, the canal is
joined by a busy main road (useful for fish &
chips and Chinese take-away) which crosses at a
very low bridge and accompanies it into
increasingly flat and industrialised landscape,
past several salt works and into Middlewich,
where a branch of the Shropshire Union leads
off westwards towards that canal at Barbridge.
The Trent & Mersey skirts the centre of the
town, passing lots of moored narrowboats and
through three consecutive narrow locks,
arriving at a wide (14ft) lock (which has
suffered from subsidence) with a pub beside it.
This used to represent the beginning of a wide,
almost lock-free navigation right through to
Preston Brook, Manchester and Wigan (very
convenient for the salt industry when it shipped
most of its goods by boat), but Croxton
Aqueduct had to be replaced many years ago,
and is now a steel structure only 8ft 2ins wide.
The aqueduct crosses the River Dane, which
flows alongside the navigation as both water
courses leave industrial Middlewich and move
out into fine open country.

Middlewich
Ches. EC Wed. PO, tel, stores, bank, garage.
A town that since Roman times has been
dedicated to salt extraction. Most of the salt
produced here goes to various chemical
industries. Subsidence from salt extraction has
prevented redevelopment for many years, but a
big new renewal scheme is now in progress.
The canalside area is a haven of peace below the
busy streets. The Tourist Information Centre is
by bridge 172.
St Michael's Church A handsome medieval
church which was a place of refuge for the
Royalists during the Civil War. It has a fine
interior with richly carved woodwork.

BOATYARDS

Ⓑ **Anderson Boats** Wych House, St Anne's
Road, Middlewich (3668). Ⓡ Pump-out, boat
hire, gas, groceries, gifts.
Ⓑ **Middlewich Narrowboats** Canal Terrace,
Middlewich (2460). Ⓡ Ⓢ Ⓦ Ⓓ Pump-out, gas,
hire craft, gift shop, provisions, launderette,
dry dock, repairs and alterations, breakdown
service, toilets. Useful tool-hire shop nearby.

PUBS AND RESTAURANTS

🍺 **Big Lock** Middlewich. Canalside. Food.
🍺 **Newton Brewery Inn** Canalside above big
lock. Garden with children's play area.
🍺 **Cheshire Cheese** Lewin Street,
Middlewich. Food.
🍺 **Kings Lock** Middlewich. Canalside. *Fish &
chips* opposite.
🍽 **Tempters Wine Bar** 11 Wheelock Street,
Middlewich (5175). *L & D Tue–Sat.*
🍺 **Kinderton Arms** Close to canal 1 mile south
of Middlewich, by lock 70.

Dane Valley

Initially, this is a stretch of canal as beautiful as any in the country. Often overhung by trees, the navigation winds along the side of a hill as it follows the delightful valley of the River Dane. The parkland on the other side of the valley encompasses Bostock Hall, a school for subnormal children.

At Whatcroft Hall (privately owned), the canal circles around to the east, passing under a derelict railway before heading for the industrial outskirts of Northwich and shedding its beauty and solitude once again. The outlying canal settlement of Broken Cross acts as a buffer between these two very different lengths of canal.

Navigational note
There are several privately-owned wide 'lagoons' caused by subsidence along this section of the Trent & Mersey, in some of which repose the hulks of abandoned barges and narrowboats, lately being salvaged. Navigators should be wary of straying off the main line, since the offside canal bank is often submerged and invisible just below the water level.

Northwich
Ches. EC Wed, MD Fri, Sat. All services (see page 162). Regular buses from Barnton (see page 156). A rather attractive town at the junction of the rivers Weaver and Dane. (The latter brings large quantities of sand down into the Weaver Navigation, necessitating a heavy expenditure on dredging.) As in every other town in this area, salt has for centuries been responsible for the continued prosperity of Northwich. (The Brine Baths in Victoria Road are still open throughout the year for the benefit of salt-water enthusiasts.) The Weaver Navigation has of course been another very prominent factor in the town's history, and the building and repairing of barges, narrowboats, and small seagoing ships has been carried on here for over 200 years. Nowadays this industry has been almost forced out of business by foreign competition, and the last private shipyard on the river closed down in 1971. (This yard – Isaac Pimblott's – used to be between Hunt's locks and Hartford bridge. Their last contract was a tug for Aden.) However the big British Waterways yard in the town continues to thrive; some very large maintenance craft are built and repaired here. The wharves by Town Bridge are empty, and are an excellent temporary mooring site for anyone wishing to visit the place. The town centre is very close, much of it has been completely rebuilt very recently. There is now an extensive shopping precinct. Although the large number of pubs has been whittled down in the rebuilding process, there are still some pleasant old streets. The Weaver and the big swing bridges across it remain a dominant part of the background.

Salt Museum Weaver Hall, London Road, Northwich (41331). The history of the salt industry from Roman times to the present day, housed in the town's former workhouse. Look out for the remarkable model ship, made from salt of course. *Open daily, except Mon.*

PUBS

🍺 **Old Broken Cross** Canalside, at bridge 184. An attractive old canal pub. Shops and launderette a short way past the pub.

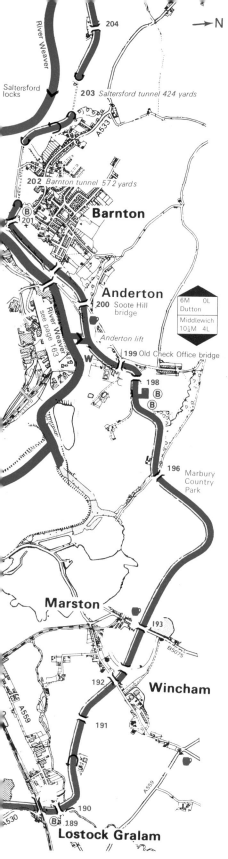

Anderton Lift

This is another length in which salt mining has determined the nature of the scenery. Part of it is heavily industrial, much of it is devastated but rural (just), some of it is nondescript, and some of it is superb countryside. Donkey engines can still be seen in surrounding fields pumping brine. Leaving the vicinity of Lostock Gralam and the outskirts of Northwich, one passes Marston and Wincham (*PO, tel, stores*). Just west of the village, one travels along a ½ mile stretch of canal that was only cut in 1958, as the old route was about to collapse into – needless to say – underground salt workings. Beyond the woods of Marbury Country Park (attractive short stay mooring) is Anderton (*PO, tel, stores*) – the famous boat lift down into the Weaver Navigation is on the left. The main line continues westward, winding along what is now a steep hill and into Barnton Tunnel. At the west end one emerges onto a hillside overlooking the River Weaver, with a marvellous view straight down the huge Saltersford Locks. Now Saltersford Tunnel is entered: beyond it, one is in completely open country again.

Navigational note
Both Barnton and Saltersford Tunnels are crooked; two boats cannot pass in the tunnel so take care they are clear before proceeding.

Anderton Lift
An amazing and enormous piece of machinery built in 1875 by Leader Williams (later engineer of the Manchester Ship Canal) to connect the Trent & Mersey to the flourishing Weaver Navigation, 50ft below. As built, the lift consisted of two water-filled tanks counterbalancing each other in a vertical slide, resting on massive hydraulic rams. It worked on the very straightforward principle that making the ascending tank slightly lighter – by pumping a little water out – would assist the hydraulic rams (which were operated by a steam engine and pump) in moving both tanks, with boats in them, up or down.
In 1908 the lift had to have major repairs, so it was modernised at the same time. Electricity replaced steam as the motive power. One of the most fascinating individual features of the canal system, it draws thousands of sightseers every year although it is now undergoing extensive repairs, and out of use as we go to press. If you plan to use it, ring Northwich 74321 and check beforehand.

Marston
Ches. Tel. A salt-producing village, suffering badly from its own industry. The numerous gaps in this village are presumably caused by the demolition or collapse of houses affected by subsidence. Waste ground abounds.

BOATYARDS

Ⓑ **I.M.L. Waterways Cruising** Anderton Marina, Uplands Road, Anderton. (Northwich 79642). ⓇⓈⓌⒹ Pump-out, gas, hire craft, overnight mooring, long-term mooring, slipway, repairs, café, grocery shop. *Closed Mon & winter weekends*.
Ⓑ **Clare Cruisers** Uplands Basin, Uplands Road, Northwich (77199). ⓇⓌⒹ Pump-out, hire craft, gas, repairs.
Ⓑ **Colliery Narrow Boat Co** Wincham Wharf (bridge 189), Lostock Gralam, Northwich (44672). ⓌⒹ Pump-out, day hire craft, overnight mooring, long-term mooring, crane hire, slipway, dry dock, chandlery, boat building, repairs, 48-seater trip boat.

PUBS

🍺 **Red Lion** Barnton, just east of bridge 201. Food, garden, children's room.
🍺 **Stanley Arms** Canalside, right opposite the Anderton Lift. A friendly real ale pub with a lovely family room, where children are welcome. Food *lunchtime and evenings*. Putting green.
🍺 **New Inn** Marston.
🍺 **Black Greyhound** ½ mile north east of bridge 192. Good food, garden, children welcome lunchtime.

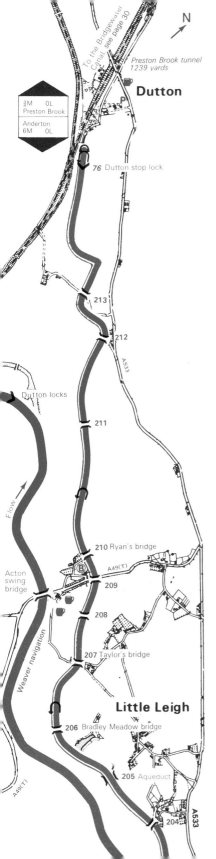

Dutton

This, the northernmost stretch of the Trent &
Mersey, is a very pleasant one and delightfully
rural. Most of the way the navigation follows
the south side of the hills that overlook the
River Weaver. From about 60ft up, one is often
rewarded with excellent views of this splendid
valley and the large vessels that ply up and
down it. At one point one can see the elegant
Dutton railway viaduct in the distance; then the
two waterways diverge as the Trent & Mersey
enters the woods preceding Preston Brook
Tunnel. There is a stop lock just south of the
tunnel, it has only one gate. At the north end of
the tunnel a notice announces that from here
onwards one is on the Bridgewater Canal.

Dutton
Ches. PO, tel, stores, garage. Small settlement
on top of Preston Brook Tunnel, at the end of
the lane uphill from the south end of the
tunnel. There is a large hospital up the road,
and a pub.
Preston Brook Tunnel
1239yds long and forbidden to unpowered
craft. No towpath. *On summer weekends & B.
Hols* entry is as posted on the notices at each
end. It is crooked, like Barnton and Saltersford
tunnels, and two boats cannot pass, so at other
times, make sure it is clear before entering.

BOATYARDS

Ⓑ **Black Prince Holidays** Bartington Wharf,
Acton Bridge, Northwich (852945). ⓦⒹ
Pump-out, gas, hire craft, overnight mooring,
boat sales, repairs, toilets, shop.

PUBS

🍺 **Talbot Arms** Dutton. Food, garden.
🍺 **Horns** 200yds south of bridge 209 on A49.
Food *lunchtime and evenings.*
🍺 **Leigh Arms** 1/4 mile south of bridge 209,
beside the Weaver. Sandwiches.

Mellow riverside architecture at Northwich, on the Weaver. *Derek Pratt.*

WEAVER NAVIGATION

Maximum dimensions

Winsford to Winnington
Length: 150'
Beam: 30'
Headroom: 29'
Winnington to Weston Point
Length: 176'
Beam: 30'
Headroom: 56'

Mileage

WINSFORD BRIDGE to
Northwich: 5½
Anderton Lift (Trent & Mersey Canal): 7
Acton Bridge: 11
Sutton Bridge: 17
WESTON POINT DOCKS (Manchester Ship Canal) 20

Locks: 5

The Weaver Navigation still carries a large amount of commercial traffic. In general terms, this must be due to its fortunate position in the centre of the salt and chemical industries, its endless supply of water, and the enterprising attitude of its past (and present) administrators.

The river itself, which rises in the Peckforton Hills and proceeds via Wrenbury, Audlem, Nantwich, Church Minshull and Winsford to Northwich and Frodsham, is just over 50 miles long. Originally a shallow and tidal stream, it was long used for carrying salt away from the Cheshire salt area. The mineral was carried down by men and horses to meet the incoming tide. The sailing barges would load at high water, then depart with the ebbing tide. It was a somewhat unsatisfactory means of transport.

In the 17thC the expansion of the salt industry around Northwich, Middlewich and Winsford gave rise to an increasing demand for a navigation right up to Winsford. In 1721, three gentlemen of Cheshire obtained an Act of Parliament to make and maintain the river as a navigation from Frodsham to Winsford, 20 miles upstream. Plans were drawn up, labourers were organised, and by 1732 the Weaver was fully navigable for 40-ton barges up to Winsford. It was naturally a great boost to the salt industry near Winsford, which now exported salt and imported coal via this splendid new navigation. And clay was also brought upstream to Winsford: it was then carted up to the Potteries by land.

When the Trent & Mersey was planned in 1765 to pass along the River Weaver the trustees of the Weaver were understandably alarmed; but in the event the new canal provided much traffic for the river, for although the two waterways did not join, they were so close at Anderton that in 1793 chutes were constructed on the Trent & Mersey directly above a specially built dock on the River Weaver, 50ft below. There-after salt was transhipped in ever increasing quantities by dropping it down the chutes from canal boats into 'Weaver flats' (barges) on the river. This system continued until 1871, when it was decided to construct the great iron boat lift beside the chutes at Anderton. This remarkable structure (which still operates) thus effected a proper junction between the two waterways. Trade improved accordingly.

The Weaver Navigation did well throughout the 19thC, mainly because continual and vigorous programmes of modernisation kept it thoroughly attractive to carriers, especially when compared to the rapidly dating narrow canals. The Weaver locks were constantly reduced in number and increased in size; the river was made deeper, and the channel wider; the docks at Weston Point (built in 1806 along with the canal from Frodsham Cut to the docks) were duplicated and enlarged. Eventually coasters were able to navigate the river right up to Winsford. Much of this progress was due to the efforts of Edward Leader Williams, who was the engineer of the Weaver Navigation from 1856 to 1872, when he left to become engineer of the new Manchester Ship Canal.

In spite of this constant improvement of the navigation, the Weaver's traditional salt trade was affected by 19thC competition from railways and the new pipelines. However the chemical industry began to sprout around the Northwich area at the same time, so the salt and clay traffic was gradually replaced by chemicals. Today, ICI's chemical works at Winnington and British Waterways' Anderton Depot supply all the traffic on the river: coasters up to 1000 tonnes deadweight capacity ship cargoes through the Manchester Ship Canal and to various ports in the UK and Europe. Meanwhile Weston Point Docks profit from being beside the Manchester Ship Canal (opened in the 1890s) and continue to flourish.

N

Vale Royal cut

Newbridge swing bridge
6' 8" headroom

(closed)

7M   2L
Anderton

A5018

Winsford

A54

Winsford bridge
10' 8" headroom

A54

Winsford station

tocks Hill

Winsford bottom flash

Top flash

Shropshire Union Canal (Middlewich branch) see book 2

Winsford

Although Winsford Bridge (fixed at 10ft 8in) is the upper limit of navigation for shipping and the limit of British Waterways jurisdiction, canal boats can easily slip under the bridge and round the bend into the vast, wonderful and deceptively shallow Winsford Bottom Flash. Navigation upstream of the Bottom Flash is unreliable, for the channel is shallow and winding, but can apparently be done by adventurous persons with small craft. The Top Flash is situated just beside and below the Middlewich Branch of the Shropshire Union Canal; but there is no junction between them here. Downstream of Winsford Bridge, there are some disused wharves – a good place to tie up. Further down is a winding stretch of little interest: each bank is piled high with the industrial leftovers of chemical industries. But soon the horizon clears as one arrives at Newbridge, beyond which is the superb stretch known as Vale Royal Cut.

Navigational note
Boats with a headroom greater than 6ft 8in will not clear the swing bridge known as Newbridge. Crews of such boats which are proceeding downstream should first telephone the British Waterways office (Northwich 74321) to arrange for the bridge to be opened.

Winsford
Ches. MD Sat. All services. A busy salt-mining town astride the Weaver. The centre of town used to be very close to the river, but now a huge new shopping precinct has shifted the heart of the town well away from it.

Winsford Bottom Flash
This very large expanse of water in an attractive setting among wooded slopes, was created by subsidence following salt extraction in the vicinity. It is a unique asset for the town, whose citizens obviously appreciate it to the full. Three caravan sites and a sailing club are based along its banks, anglers crouch in the waterside bushes, and at the northern end (nearest to Winsford) one may hire dinghies and runabouts by the hour. It is, however, quite shallow in places – those in canal craft beware!

PUBS

🍺 **Red Lion** Winsford. Riverside, at Winsford Bridge.
🍺 **The Ark** Winsford.
🍺 **Bees Knees** Winsford. Riverside, above Winsford Bridge.

Navigating the Weaver

The Weaver is a river navigation that carries a substantial traffic – transported not in canal boats or barges, but in small seagoing ships displacing up to 1000 tonnes, which use the navigation at all times of day or night. The locks are correspondingly large and often paired. The locks and bridges are all operated by keepers, and are open to pleasure craft *08.00–16.30 Mon–Thur (to 15.30 Fri), with a break for lunch 12.00–13.00. They are not open B. Hols. They also operate on summer weekends but times vary* – contact the area office on Northwich 74321 for details. Remember to arrive at the locks 30 minutes before closing, to allow sufficient time for the passage through. The bridges are either very high, or are big swing bridges operated by British Waterways staff. With the exception of Town Bridge in Northwich and Newbridge below Winsford (6ft 9in) none of these bridges needs to be swung for any boat with a height above water of less than 8ft. Those craft which do require the bridges to be opened should give prior notice to the British Waterways Area Office. Unless there has been heavy rain, the current is quite gentle – however, as on any river navigation, an anchor and rope should be carried, and the set rules should be adhered to. There are few facilities for pleasure craft.

Winsford Bottom Flash, at the head of the Weaver Navigation.

Northwich

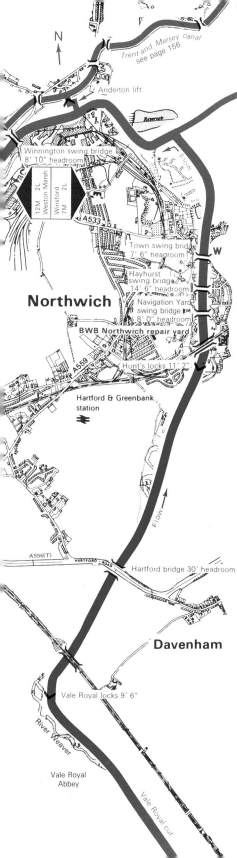

The Vale Royal Cut typifies the Weaver at its most attractive. The river flows along a closely-defined flat green valley floor, flanked by mature woods climbing the steep hillsides that enclose the valley. No buildings or roads intrude upon this very pleasant scene. Vale Royal Locks are at the far end of the cut; the remains of the old Vale Royal Abbey (believed to have been founded by Edward I and dissolved by Henry VIII) is just up the hill nearby. It is now much changed, and is a summer school for an electronics firm. Beyond is a tall stone railway viaduct, then Hartford Road Bridge, a steel girder construction offering to ships a headroom of only 30ft – by far the lowest fixed bridge between Winsford and the Mersey. Another stretch of pleasant water meadows leads to Hunts Locks, another railway viaduct and the three swing bridges that are so much a feature of the town of Northwich. The trip through Northwich is pleasant enough, but north of the town the river twists and turns through a repetition of the industrial landscape that predominates outside Winsford. This stretch does not last long, and as the Anderton Lift (see page 156) comes into view one rounds the bend to be confronted by the shipping tied up at the Winnington wharves.

Northwich
Ches. EC Wed. MD Fri, Sat. All services. A rather attractive town at the junction of the rivers Weaver and Dane. (The latter brings large quantities of sand down into the Weaver Navigation, necessitating a heavy expenditure on dredging.) As in every town in this area, salt has for centuries been responsible for the continued prosperity of Northwich. The town's motto is *Sal est Vita*, Salt is Life, and there is a salt museum in London Road. The Brine Baths in Victoria Road are still open throughout the year for the benefit of salt-water enthusiasts. The Weaver Navigation has of course been another very prominent factor in the town's history, and the building and repairing of barges, narrowboats, and small seagoing ships has been carried on here for over 200 years. Nowadays this industry has been almost forced out of business by foreign competition, and the last private shipyard on the river closed down in 1971. (This yard – Isaac Pimblott's – used to be between Hunt's Locks and Hartford Bridge. Their last contract was a tug for Aden.) However the big British Waterways yard in the town continues to thrive; some very large maintenance craft are built and repaired here. The wharves by Town Bridge are empty, and are an excellent temporary mooring site for anyone wishing to visit the place. The town centre is very close; much of it has been completely rebuilt very recently. There is now an extensive shopping precinct. Although the large number of pubs has been whittled down in the rebuilding process, there are still some pleasant old streets. The Weaver and the big swing bridges across it remain a dominant part of the background.
Salt Museum Weaver Hall, London Road, Northwich (41331). The history of the salt industry from Roman times to the present day, housed in the town's former workhouse. Look out for the remarkable model ship, made from salt of course. *Open daily, except Mon.*
Tourist Information Centre Northwich 557651.

BOATYARDS

British Waterways Northwich Area Offices and Repair Yard (Northwich 74321). Alongside the extensive workshops is the Area Engineer's office – formerly the Weaver Navigation Trustee's offices. From here are controlled the Weaver Navigation, the Trent & Mersey Canal and a string of other canals in the north west. Wet and dry docks for hire. As usual, this yard contains many mellow 18thC buildings. There is also an elegant clock tower on the office block.

PUBS

Northwich pubs include:
- Beehive.
- Crown Hotel.
- Sportsman.

Barnton Cut

North of Northwich, the river begins to
meander extravagantly in a generally westerly
direction. The amazing structure that is
Anderton Lift is on one side of the river: this is
on the way up to the Trent & Mersey Canal (see
page 156), which runs along the Weaver Valley
as far as Dutton Locks. Beside the lift is the
thriving Anderton Depot, which can handle
ships of up to 1000 tonnes deadweight capacity.
Opposite Anderton Lift is Winnington. Here
are a large ICI chemical works and extensive
wharves, where several ships are usually to be
seen. These ships take their cargoes of
potassium, caustic soda and soda ash (used for
making glass) to many countries around Europe
– and to Israel. With these ships about,
pleasure boats should keep a good lookout from
Winnington onwards to Weston Point,
especially on the bends. (The rule of the road is
of course 'keep to the right' and out of the
deep-water channel.) It is also important to give
correct sound signals. Below Winnington, the
river runs again along a peaceful green valley,
lined by hills on its north side, and is
inaccessible to motor cars. Part of the route is
canalised, leading to Saltersford Locks. The
town of Weaverham is on the hills to the south.

Weaverham
Ches. PO, tel, stores, garage. The heart of this
town contains many old timbered houses and
thatched cottages – but these are now heavily
outnumbered by council housing estates. The
church of St Mary is an imposing Norman
building containing several items of interest.

PUBS
🍺 **Red Lion** Barnton. Between the river and
canal.

Acton Bridge

The A49 joins the river for a while, crossing at
Acton Bridge. A backwater here houses a boat
club; pubs and a riverside restaurant are
nearby. A mile further on, Dutton Locks lead
to the Dutton railway viaduct, whose elegant
stone arches carry the main electrified West
Coast line. Beyond the viaduct one comes to
Pickering's Wharf, the site of a swing bridge
long gone. From here down to Frodsham, the
Weaver Valley is a beautiful green, narrow
cutting reminiscent of Vale Royal. Woods are
ranged along the hills on either side. There are
no roads, and no houses except for one farm. It
is a delightfully secluded rural setting. As the
valley gradually widens out to reveal the
impending industrialism that stretches along
the river from Sutton Bridge, one may notice a
branch off to the left. This is where a cut from
the navigation leaves to fall through a shallow
lock before rejoining the river course. This was
the old line of navigation until 1827, when the
Weston Canal was constructed to take the main
line of the Weaver Navigation to Weston Point.
One may still venture down the old cut to a
swing bridge, now fixed, and the derelict lock.
(The size of the lock reveals how much the
navigation has been improved and enlarged in
the past 100 years.)

Acton Swing Bridge
An impressive structure weighing 650 tons,
which uses a very small amount of electricity to
open it; 560 tons of its weight is borne by a
floating pontoon. It was built in 1933.

PUBS AND RESTAURANTS
🍺 **Horns** Acton Bridge. Between the bridge
and the Trent & Mersey Canal. Food *lunchtime
and evenings*.
🍺 **Leigh Arms** Acton Bridge. Riverside, at the
bridge. Food. Note the 'painted' windows.
✗🍷 **Rheingold Restaurant** Acton Bridge
(Weaverham 852310). Riverside, on south side
of the river. *Evenings*.

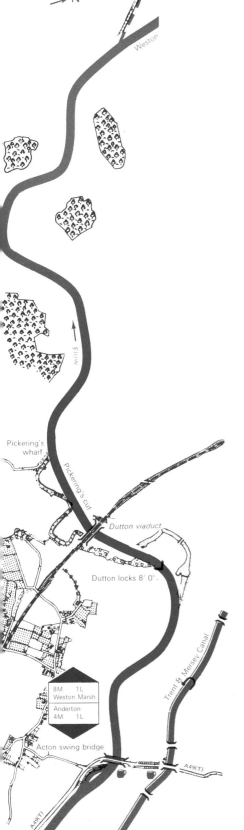

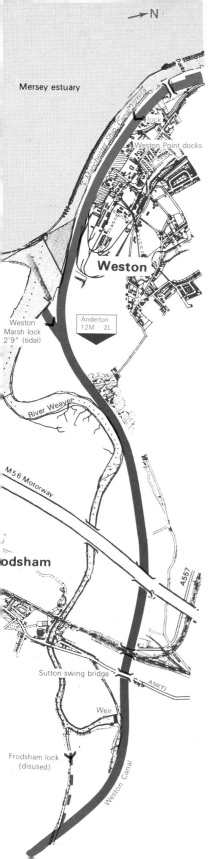

Weston Point

Passing the former Sutton Flood Lock, now
completely disused, the Weston Canal section
of the Weaver Navigation now runs along the
side of the valley, while the river follows its own
twisting course down towards the Mersey. By
Sutton (Frodsham) swing bridge one leaves for
good the charming pastures that flank the
Weaver; chemical works line one side of the
canal all the way from here to Weston Point.
The wooded hills and grassy fields of the
Weaver suddenly seem very distant. At Weston
Marsh there is a lock down into the Manchester
Ship Canal (see navigational note below).
Beyond here the navigation goes right alongside
the Ship Canal from which it is separated by a
tall bank. Eventually, after passing the entrance
lock up into the abandoned Runcorn & Weston
Canal one arrives at a low (about 5ft) swing
bridge. Beyond it are the Weston Point Docks
and another lock into the Ship Canal. There are
shops, fish & chips and pubs at Weston Point,
through the dock gates.

Navigational note
Those wishing to pass through Weston Marsh
Lock should give the British Waterways
advance notice (Northwich 74321) and get
clearance from the Manchester Ship Canal
Company (061-872 2411).

Weston Point Docks
The docks, at the junction of the Weaver
Navigation's Weston Canal and the Manchester
Ship Canal, are an industrial centre. The docks
have been modernised and their facilities
expanded to handle ships up to 2500 tonnes.
Christ Church Situated between Weston Point
Docks and the Manchester Ship Canal, this
church was built by the Weaver Navigation
Commissioners. Known as 'the island church',
its tall spire is a distinctive landmark.

PUBS
Netherton Hall Chester Road, Frodsham.
Ind Coope and Tetley's real ales in a converted
farmhouse. Food *lunchtime and evenings*.
Garden.

Turnbridge Loco Lift Bridge: Huddersfield Broad Canal. *David Perrott*.

NORTH EAST WATERWAYS

River Derwent

A navigation since 1701, the River Derwent joins the Ouse near Barmby-on-the-Marsh and is navigable at present to Stamford Bridge, with isolated stretches between the as yet unusable locks above here carrying some craft. There are launching and mooring facilities at Malton. The Yorkshire Derwent Trust has been busy restoring the disused locks, but it may be some time before this work is completed.

Maximum dimensions
Length: 55'
Beam: 14'
Headroom: 10'
Mileage
BARMBY-ON-THE-MARSH to
East Cottingwith, junction with
Pocklington Canal: 11½
STAMFORD BRIDGE: 18½
Locks: 1 in use.

Navigation authority
There is no *navigation* authority as such, but the river is controlled by the Yorkshire Water Authority, and their Recreation and Amenities Division can supply information to prospective navigators (67 Albion Street, Leeds. Leeds 448201). No licence is required, but powered craft, and those with sea toilets, must register with the YWA (£5) in the interests of pollution control. Those intending to navigate the Derwent from Selby Lock should take advice from the lock keeper (Selby 703182) and also inform the lock keeper at Barmby (Selby 638579).

River Ouse

In 1462 the city of York was granted responsibility for the River Ouse and the first navigation works were started, which led to the river navigation reaching Swale Nab and beyond. The Ure, which together with the Swale, forms the Ouse, was made navigable to Ripon by an Act of 1767, the last 2 miles of this route being canal. Today only half of this remains, terminating near Littlethorpe. The Ouse is tidal to Naburn Lock, and commercial traffic still reaches York.

Although remote from the main cruising network, the reaches above York are much used by local pleasure craft. Below Naburn the tidal river, and commercial traffic, should be treated with the greatest respect.

Maximum dimensions
Naburn to York
Length: 150'
Beam: 25' 6"
Headroom: 25' 6"
York to Swale Nab
Length: 60'
Beam: 15' 4"
Headroom: 16' 4"

Mileage
TRENT FALLS to
Goole, junction with Aire & Calder: 8
Barmby-on-the-Marsh, junction with River
Derwent: 17¼
Junction with River Wharfe: 32¾
York: 43
SWALE NAB: 60¾
Locks: 2

Navigation authority
The Ouse and Foss Navigation Trustees control the river from 2 miles south of Linton Lock to 100yds short of Skelton Railway Bridge, Goole. Those who require information should contact The River Manager, Captain W. C. Rimmer, Naburn Lock, Naburn, N. Yorks (Escrick 229 or Selby 708949). There is no licence fee but craft are charged for passage through Naburn Lock.

RIVER URE & RIPON CANAL
Maximum dimensions
Ure Navigation
Length: 59'
Beam: 15'
Headroom: 10'
Ripon Canal (navigable section)
Length: 57'
Beam: 14' 3"
Headroom: 8' 6"
Mileage
SWALE NAB to
Boroughbridge: 2¾
Oxclose Lock: 8
LITTLETHORPE LOCK: 9
Locks: 3

Navigation authority
British Waterways

Pocklington Canal

By the end of the 18thC, prosperous local farmers were in need of a cheap means of transporting their produce to the rapidly expanding industrial towns of the West Riding. In 1814 a bill was put forward to build a canal from the River Derwent at East Cottingwith to Street Bridge on the York to Hull turnpike, 1 mile from Pocklington. George Leather jnr of Leeds drafted the plans, and the canal was opened in 1818, having been completed for less than the estimated cost. For 30 years the canal prospered, but with its sale to the York & North Midland Railway Company in 1847, trade began to decline. Tolls increased and maintenance was neglected. By the turn of the century the upper reaches of the canal were becoming unnavigable, and in 1932 the last traffic used the canal. Local support for the upkeep of the canal has always been strong, and proposals in 1954 to use it as a dumping ground for chalk sludge were happily suppressed. The Pocklington

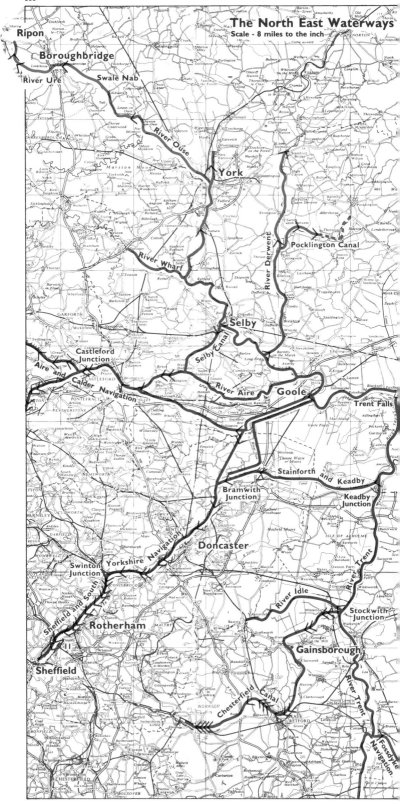

The North East Waterways
Scale - 8 miles to the inch

Canal Amenity Society are aiming for complete restoration of the canal with the cooperation of the British Waterways.

Maximum dimensions
Navigable section
Length: 57'
Beam: 14'
Headroom: 9'
Mileage
RIVER DERWENT to
Melbourne: 5
Bielby: 7
CANAL HEAD: 9½
Locks: 9

Navigation authority
British Waterways

Sheffield & South Yorkshire Navigation

First attempts in 1697 to make the River Don navigable were unsuccessful. But following Acts passed in 1726 and 1727, work began, and in 1731 boats reached Aldewarke, below Rotherham. They had access to Rotherham in 1740, and in 1751 the uppermost section to Tinsley was opened. From here a toll road connected with Sheffield. The Navigation prospered, and in 1793 two independent canals were joined to it – the Dearne & Dove and the Stainforth & Keadby. After the Napoleonic Wars, the Sheffield Canal was built from Tinsley to Sheffield but it was financially unsuccessful. The coming of the railways brought an amalgamation in 1850, and ownership by the new Manchester, Sheffield and Lincolnshire Railway Company in 1864. Later the Sheffield and South Yorkshire Navigation Company was established to remove the entire Don-based waterway system from railway interests, but it was never able to raise sufficient capital to purchase majority interest in the waterways, and improvement was not possible. In 1905 however, the New Junction Canal was built to connect with the Aire & Calder, and provide access to the port of Goole.

Between Bramwith and Rotherham the waterway has been the subject of a £16 million improvement scheme. Seven locks have been improved, bridges have been underpinned and in one case removed, and extensive bank protection has taken place. The maximum size craft able to use the navigation is 700 tonnes, with lock mechanisation halving transit times.

Maximum dimensions
SHEFFIELD & SOUTH YORKSHIRE BELOW ROTHERHAM
Length: 232'
Beam: 21'7"
Draught: 8'
ROTHERHAM TO SHEFFIELD
Length: 61'6"
Beam: 15'6"
Draught: 3'
Headroom: 10'
STAINFORTH & KEADBY
Length: 61'6"
Beam: 17'6"
Headroom: 10'
Mileage
KEADBY to
Thorne Lock: 10¼
Swinton Junction: 31
SHEFFIELD Basin: 43
Locks: 28

Navigation authority
British Waterways

BRITISH WATERWAYS

Head Office
Melbury House, Melbury Terrace, London NW1 6JX. (071-262 6711). For general and official enquiries and the canal bookshop.

Regional offices
For general enquiries, and other enquiries regarding licences, stoppages, long-term moorings and any problems on a particular canal in their area.

North West British Waterways, Navigation Road, Northwich, Cheshire CW8 1BH. (Northwich 74321).

North East British Waterways, PO Box 9, 1 Dock Street, Leeds LS1 1HH. (Leeds 436741).

Stoppages
For the latest information regarding stoppages, phone 071-723 8486 for recorded information

Help outside working hours
For assistance from operational staff outside of normal office hours and at weekends, dial 100 and ask for FREEPHONE CANALS.

Other navigation authorities are listed in the appropriate places in the text.

A BRIEF HISTORY OF BRITISH CANALS

River navigations, that is rivers widened and deepened to take large boats, had existed in England since the Middle Ages: some can even be traced back to Roman times. In 1600 there were 700 miles of navigable river in England, and by 1760, the dawn of the canal age, this number had been increased to 1300. This extensive network had prompted many developments later used by the canal engineers, for example, the lock system. But there were severe limitations; generally the routes were determined by the rivers and the features of the landscape and so were rarely direct. Also there were no east–west, or north–south connections.

Thus the demand for a direct inland waterway system increased steadily through the first half of the 18thC with the expansion of internal trade. Road improvements could not cope with this expansion, and so engineers and merchants turned to canals, used extensively on the Continent.

One of the earliest pure canals, cut independently of existing rivers, was opened in 1745, at Newry in Northern Ireland, although some authorities consider the Fossdyke, cut by the Romans to link the rivers Trent and Witham, to be the first. However, the Newry is more important because it established the cardinal rule of all canals, the maintenance of an adequate water supply, a feature too often ignored by later engineers. The Newry canal established the principle of a long summit level, fed by a reservoir to keep the locks at either end well supplied. Ten years later, in England, the Duke of Bridgewater decided to build a canal to provide an adequate transport outlet for his coal mines at Worsley. He employed the self-taught James Brindley as his engineer, and John Gilbert as surveyor, and launched the canal age in England. The Bridgewater canal was opened in 1761. Its route, all on one level, was independent of all rivers; its scale of operations reflected the new power of engineering and the foresight of its creators. Although there were no locks, the engineering problems were huge; an aqueduct was built at Barton over the River Irwell, preceded by an embankment 900yds long; 15 miles of canal were built underground, so that boats could approach the coal face for loading – eventually there were 42 miles underground, including an inclined plane – the puddled clay method was used by Brindley to make the canal bed watertight. Perhaps most important of all, the canal was a success financially. Bridgewater invested the equivalent of £3 million of his own money in the project, and still made a profit.

Having shown that canals were both practical and financially sound, the Bridgewater aroused great interest throughout Britain. Plans were drawn up for a trunk canal, to link the four major rivers of England: the Thames, Severn, Mersey and Trent. This plan was eventually brought to fruition, but many years later than its sponsors imagined. Brindley was employed as engineer for the scheme, his reputation ensuring that he would always have more work than he could handle. The Trent & Mersey, and the Staffordshire & Worcestershire Canals received the Royal Assent in 1766, and the canal age began in earnest.

Canals, like the railways later, were built entirely by hand. Gangs of itinerant workmen were gathered together, drawn by the comparatively high pay. Once formed these armies of 'navigators' – hence 'navvies' – moved through the countryside as the canal was built, in many cases living off the land. All engineering problems had to be solved by manpower alone, aided by the horse and the occasional steam pump. Embankments, tunnels, aqueducts, all were built by these labouring armies kept under control only by the power of the section engineers and contractors.

The Staffordshire & Worcestershire Canal opened in 1770. In its design Brindley determined the size of the standard Midlands canal, which of course had direct influence on the rest of the English system as it was built. He chose a narrow canal, with locks 72ft 7in by 7ft 6in, partly for reasons of economy, and partly because he realised that the problems of an adequate water supply were far greater than most canal sponsors realised. This standard, which was also adopted for the Trent and Mersey, prompted the development of a special vessel, the narrowboat with its 30-ton payload. Ironically this decision by Brindley in 1766 ensured the failure of the canals as a commercial venture 200 years later, for by the middle of this century a 30-ton payload could no longer be worked economically.

The Trent & Mersey was opened in 1777; 93 miles long, the canal included five tunnels, the original one at Harecastle taking 11 years to build. In 1790 Oxford was finally reached and the junction with the Thames brought the four great rivers together. From the very start English canal companies were characterised by their intense rivalries; water supplies were jealously guarded, and constant wars were waged over toll prices. Many canals receiving the Royal Assent were never built, while others staggered towards conclusion, hampered by doubtful engineering, inaccurate estimates, and loans that they could never hope to pay off. Yet for a period canal mania gripped British speculators, as railway mania was to grip them 50 years later. The peak of British canal development came between 1791 and 1794, a period that gave rise to the opening of the major routes, the rise of the great canal engineers, Telford, Rennie and Jessop, and the greatest prosperity of those companies already operating. At this time the canal system had an effective monopoly over inland transport: the old trunk roads could not compete, coastal traffic was uncertain and hazardous, and the railways were still a future dream. This period also saw some of the greatest feats of engineering.

A contemporary view of canal promoters. Eric de Maré.

The turn of the century saw the opening of the last major cross-country routes; the Pennines were crossed by the Leeds & Liverpool Canal between 1770 and 1816, while the Kennet & Avon (opened in 1810) linked London and Bristol via the Thames. These two canals were built as broad navigations: already the realisation was dawning on canal operators that the limits imposed by the Brindley standard were too restrictive, a suspicion that was to be brutally confirmed by the coming of the railways. The Kennet & Avon, along with its rival the Thames & Severn, also marks the introduction of fine architecture to canals. Up till now canal architecture had been functional, often impressive, but clearly conceived by engineers. As a result, the Kennet & Avon has an architectural unity lacking in earlier canals. The appearance of architectural quality was matched by another significant change, canals became straighter, their engineers choosing as direct a route as possible, arguing that greater construction costs would be outweighed by smoother, quicker operation, whereas the early canals had followed the landscape. The Oxford is the prime example of a contour canal, meandering across the Midlands as though there were all the time in the world. It looks beautiful, its close marriage with the landscape makes it ideal as a pleasure waterway, but it was commercial folly.

The shortcomings of the early canals were exploited all too easily by the new railways. At first there was sharp competition by canals. Tolls were lowered, money was poured into route improvements; 14 miles of the Oxford's windings were cut out between 1829 and 1834; schemes were prepared to widen the narrow canals; the Harecastle tunnel was doubled in 1827, the new tunnel taking three years to build (as opposed to 11 years for the old). But the race was lost from the start. The 19thC marks the rise of the railways and the decline of the canals. With the exception of the Manchester Ship Canal, the last major canal was the Birmingham & Liverpool Junction, opened in 1835. The system survived until this century, but the 1914–18 war brought the first closures, and through the 1930s the canal map adopted the shape it has today. Effective commercial carrying on narrow canals ceased in the early 1960s, although a few companies managed to survive until recently. However, with the end of commercial operation, a new role was seen for the waterways as a pleasure amenity, a 'linear national park 2000 miles long'.

Water supply has always been the cardinal element in both the running and the survival of any canal system. Locks need a constant supply of water – every boat passing through a wide lock on the Grand Union uses 96,000 gallons of

The rudimentary tools of the early 'navvies'. *Hugh McKnight.*

Worcester and Birmingham Canal Company toll ticket, dated 1816. *Hugh McKnight.*

water. Generally two methods of supply were used: direct feed by rivers and streams, and feed by reservoirs sited along the summit level. The first suffered greatly from silting, and meant that the canal was dependent on the level of water in the river; the regular floods from the River Soar that overtake the Grand Union's Leicester line shows the dangers of this. The second was more reliable, but many engineers were short-sighted in their provision of an adequate summit level. The otherwise well-planned Kennet & Avon always suffered from water shortage. Where shortages occurred, steam pumping engines were used to pump water taken down locks back up to the summit level. The Kennet & Avon was dependent upon pumped supplies, while the Birmingham Canal Navigations were fed by 6 reservoirs and 17 pumping engines. Some companies adopted side ponds alongside locks to save water, but this put the onus on the boatman and so had limited success. Likewise the stop locks still to be seen at junctions are a good example of 18thC company rivalry; an established canal would ensure that any proposed canal wishing to join it would have to lock *down* into the older canal, which thus gained a lock of water each time a boat passed through.

Where long flights or staircase locks existed there was always great wastage of water, and so throughout canal history alternative mechanical means of raising boats have been tried out. The inclined plane or the vertical lift were the favoured forms. Both worked on the counterbalance principle, the weight of the descending boat helping to raise the ascending. The first inclined plane was built at Ketley in 1788, and they were a feature of the west country Bude and Chard canals. The most famous plane was built in Foxton, and operated from 1900–10. Mechanical failure and excessive running costs ended the application of the inclined plane in England, although modern examples work very efficiently on the continent, notably in Belgium. The vertical lift was more unusual although there were eight on the Grand Western

Canal. The most famous, built at Anderton in 1875 (and currently being re-built) stands as a monument to the ingenuity shown in the attempts to overcome the problems of water shortage.

Engineering features are the greatest legacy of the canal age, and of these, tunnels are the most impressive. The longest tunnel is at Standedge, on the Huddersfield Narrow Canal (not navigable throughout, but restored in part). This tunnel runs for 5716yds through the Pennines, at times 638ft below the surface. It is also on the highest summit level, 644ft above sea level. The longest navigable tunnel is now Blisworth, at 3056yds long. Others of interest include the Dudley Tunnel, 3154yds, which can be seen from the electric trip boat which operates from the Black Country Museum; the twin Harecastle Tunnels on the Trent and Mersey Canal – the first 2897yds long and now disused, the second 2919yds and still in use; Sapperton, which carried the Thames & Severn Canal through the Cotswolds and Netherton on the Birmingham Canal navigations. This last, built 1855–58, was the last in England, and was lit throughout by gas lights, and at a later date by electricity.

The Netherton Tunnel was built wide enough to allow for a towing path on both sides. Most tunnels have no towing path at all, and so boats had to be 'legged', or walked through.

The slowness and relative danger of legging in tunnels led to various attempts at mechanical propulsion. An endless rope pulled by a stationary steam engine at the tunnel mouth was tried out at Blisworth and Braunston between 1869 and 1871. Steam tugs were employed, an early application of mechanical power to canal boats, but their performance was greatly limited by lack of ventilation, not to mention the danger of suffocating the crew.

An electric tug was used at Harecastle from 1914 to 1954. The diesel engine made tunnel tug services much more practical, but diesel-powered narrowboats soon put the tugs out of business: by the 1930s most tunnels had to be

Islington Tunnel during construction. *Hugh McKnight.*

navigated by whatever means the boatman chose to use. Legging continued at Crick, Husbands, Bosworth and Saddington until 1939.

Until the coming of the diesel boats, the horse reigned supreme as a source of canal power. The first canals had used gangs of men to bow-haul the boats, a left over from the river navigations where 50–80 men, or 12 horses, would pull a 200-ton barge. By 1800 the horse had taken over, and was used throughout the heyday of the canal system. In fact horse towage survived as long as large-scale commercial operation. Generally one horse or mule was used per boat, a system unmatched for cheapness and simplicity. The towing path was carried from one side of the canal to the other by turnover bridges, a common feature that reveals the total dominance of the horse. Attempts to introduce self-propelled canal boats date from 1793, although most early experiments concerned tugs towing dumb barges. Development was limited by the damage caused by wash, a problem that still applies today, and the first fleets of self-propelled steam narrowboats were not in service until the last quarter of the 19thC. Fellows, Morton & Clayton, and the Leeds & Liverpool Carrying Co ran large fleets of steam boats between 1880 and 1931, by which time most had been converted to diesel operation. With the coming of mechanical power the butty boat principle was developed: a powered narrowboat would tow a dumb 'butty' boat, thereby doubling the load without doubling the running costs. This system became standard until the virtual ending by the 1960s of carrying on the narrow canals. Before the coming of railways, passenger services were run on the canals; packet boats, specially built narrow-

boats with passenger accommodation, ran express services, commanding the best horses and the unquestioned right of way over all other traffic. Although the railways killed this traffic, the last scheduled passenger service survived on the Gloucester & Berkeley Canal until 1935.

The traditional narrowboat with its colourful decoration and meticulous interior has become a symbol of English canals. However this was in fact a late development. The shape of the narrow boat was determined by Brindley's original narrow canal specification, but until the late 19thC boats were unpainted, and carried all-male crews. Wages were sufficient for the crews to maintain their families at home. The increase in railway competition brought a reduction in wages, and so bit by bit the crews were forced to take their families with them, becoming almost water gipsies. The confines of a narrowboat cabin presented the same problems as a gipsy caravan, and so the families found a similar answer. Their eternally wandering home achieved individuality by extravagant and colourful decoration, and the traditional narrowboat painting was born. The extensive symbolic vocabulary available to the painters produced a sign language that only these families could understand, and the canal world became far more enclosed, although outwardly it was more decorative. As the canals have turned from commerce to pleasure, so the traditions of the families have died out, and the families themselves have faded away. But their language survives, although its meaning has mostly vanished with them. This survival gives the canals their characteristic decorative qualities, which make them so attractive to the pleasure boater and to the casual visitor.

INDEX

Abbey House Museum 112
Abram 91
Acton Bridge 164
Adlington 94
Adlington Hall 119
Aire, River 15, 16, 18, 104,
  105, 107, 108, 109, 111,
  112
Aire & Calder Canal 15–21,
  112, 169
Airedale 104, 105, 108
Aldcliffe Basin 76
Aldewarke 169
Allerton Bywater 18
Altofts 19
Altrincham 34
Anderton Lift 156, 159, 163,
  172
Anton's Gowt 66
Apperley Bridge 111
Appley Bridge 90
Appley Lock 89
Ashton Basin 70
Ashton Canal 35, 121, 127,
  128, 129–130
Ashton Memorial 76
Aspley Basin 28
Astbury 115
Astley Green 39
Astley Hall 95
Attenborough Nature
  Reserve Wood 134
Averham Weir 141

Baildon 109
Bank Newton Locks 104
Bardney 61
Barmby-on-the-Marsh 167
Barnby Wharf Bridge 46
Barnoldswick 103
Barnton Cut 163
Barnton Tunnel 156
Barrowford 101, 102
Barton in Fabis 132
Barton Island 134
Barton Swing Aqueduct 29,
  37, 170
Barton upon Irwell 37
Bassetlaw Museum 46
Battyeford 25
Beeston Canal 134
Beeston Lock 134
Bentley, Thomas 149
Besthorpe Wharf 144
Beswick Locks 130
Bilsborrow 72
Bingley 109
Bingley Five Rise Locks 109,
  110
Birkwood Lock 20
Birmingham & Liverpool
  Junction Canal 113, 171
Blackburn 97
Boat Trips
  Bollington Packet Boat
    Co 117
  Calder Lady 23
  Calder Valley Cruising
    27
  Castlefield & Tiller 38
  Cromford Canal Society
    53
  Duke of Lancaster 77
  Judith Mary 125
  Kiveton Park Station 48
  Lorenz & Co 38
  Norwood Packet 44
  Pennine Cruisers 106

The Princess Mary 23
Top Lock Marine 120,
  122
Waterbus, Abram 91
Boatyards
  Adventure Cruisers 71
  Anderson Boats 154
  Apollo Canal Carriers
    109
  Aspley Wharf Marina 28
  Beeston Marina 134
  Belle Isle Marina 64
  Black Prince Holidays,
    Bartington Wharf 157
  Black Prince Holidays,
    Silsden Boats 107
  Boston Marina 68
  Bridge House Marina 73
  Brinks Boats 38
  Canal Cruises 77
  Clare Cruisers 156
  Claymore Navigation 30
  Colliery Narrow Boat Co
    156
  Constellation Cruises
    119
  David Piper 114, 151,
    152
  Davisons 51, 133
  Davisons Sawley Marina
    51, 133
  Doug Moore
    (Boatbuilders) 103
  Farndon Harbour 142
  Fiskerton Boats 139
  Glasson Basin 75
  Hainsworths Boatyard
    109
  Hapton Boatyard 99
  Heritage Narrow Boats
    114
  Hesford Marine 33
  I.M.L. Waterways
    Cruising 156
  James Mayor 87, 88
  Kerridge Dry Dock 117
  L & L Cruisers 94
  Langley Mill Boat Co 54
  Latham Marina 86
  Lincoln Marina, James
    Kendall & Co 59
  Lorenz & Co 38
  Lymm Marina 33
  Macclesfield Marina 118
  Malkins Bank Canal
    Services 153
  Marina Park 74, 75
  Middlewich
    Narrowboats 154
  Milethorne Marine 43
  Mills Dockyard 51
  Mirfield Boatyard 23
  New Mills Marina 122
  Newark Marina 142
  Nottingham Castle
    Marina 136
  Nu-Way Acorn 79
  Peak Forest Cruisers 117
  Pennine Cruisers 106
  Preston Brook Marina 30
  Preston Hire Cruisers 71
  Robinson's Hire
    Cruisers 23
  Rodley Boat Centre 111
  Shire Cruisers, Sowerby
    Bridge 27
  Snaygill Boats 107
  Sowerby Marine 27

Stanley Ferry Marina 21
Stoke-on-Trent Boat
  Building 151
Thorn Marine 31
Unicorn Marine 125
Vistra Marina 152
Warble Narrowboats
  128, 129
Wayfarer Narrow Boats
  91, 93
West Riding Marine 21
Wharfage Boat Co 32
White Bear Marina 94
Worsley Dry Docks 38
Wyvern Marine 51
Yorkshire Hire Cruisers
  17, 112
Bollin Aqueduct 33
Bollington 33, 117
Bolton-le-Sands 78
Borwick 79
Bosley Locks 113, 116, 118
Boston 55, 67–68
Bradford Canal 109
Bramwith 169
Branston Island 61
Brayford Pool 58, 59
Bridgewater, Duke of 29, 37,
  170
Bridgewater Canal 29–39, 81,
  91, 92, 96, 130, 149, 157,
  170
Brierfield 101
Brighouse 25
Brindley, James 29, 41, 149,
  150, 170, 171, 173
British Waterways
  Ancoats Section 130
  Anderton Depot 159,
    163
  Apperley Bridge 111
  Burnley Yard 100
  Burscough Yard 86, 89
  Castleford Area 169
  Fairfield Junction 129
  Headquarters, London
    169
  Lancaster Yard 77
  Lincoln Yard 59
  Marple Yard 120, 122,
    127
  Newark Repair Yard
    142
  Northwich Area 162,
    169
  Nottingham Area 136,
    169
  Red Bull Yard 151, 152
  Shepley Bridge 23
  Torksey Yard 56
  Wigan Yard 91, 93, 169
  Worksop Yard 48
Broad Cut Low Lock 22
Broadreach Flood Lock 20
Burnley 100
Burscough 86
Burton Joyce 137
Buxworth 121, 124–125

Calder, River 19, 20, 22
Calder & Hebble Canal
  20–27, 130
Calderdale Industrial
  Museum 26
Carlton Wharf 144
Carnforth 79
Castle Lock 135, 136
Castlefield Junction 35, 130

Castleford 19
Catforth 71
Chapel Hill 64
Chapel Milton 124
Chesterfield Canal 41–48,
  131, 143, 148
Chorley 95
Church Locks 152
Churchtown 73
Clarborough 45
Claughton Hall 72
Clayton Junction 129
Clayworth 40, 44
Cliffe Castle 108
Clumber Park 48
Cobblers Locks 64
Conder Valley 75
Congleton 115
Coombs Reservoir 124
Cooper Bridge 25, 28
Cossall 52
Cowbridge Lock 66
Cranfleet Cut & Lock 132
Cromford & High Peak
  Railway 121, 124
Cromford Canal 49, 53, 121
Cromwell Bottom 25
Cromwell Lock 131, 143
Crosley, William 113
Croxton Aqueduct 154

Dane, River 116, 154, 155,
  162
Daresbury 31
Dean Locks 90
Dearne & Dove Canal 169
Derby Canal 49, 50
Derwent, River 50, 167
Derwent Mouth 132
Devon, River 141
Dewsbury 23
Dewsbury Arm 23
Disley 122
Dobson's Locks 111
Dogdyke 64
Don, River 169
Double Bridge 74
Douglas, River 81, 88, 89
Douglas Navigation 89, 90
Doveholes 121, 124
Dowley Gap 109
Drakeholes Tunnel 44
Droylsden 129
Dukinfield Junction 128, 129
Dunham Bridge 145
Dunham Massey Hall 33
Dunham Town 33
Dunkenhalgh Hall 98
Dutton 157
Dutton Locks 164

East Bridgford 138
East Cottingwith 167
East Marton 103
East Retford 46
East Riddlesden Hall 108
East Stoke 139
Eastwood 53
Eccles 37
Egerton, Francis 29
Elland 26
Ellel Grange 74
Erewash, River 53
Erewash Canal 49–54, 131,
  132

Fairfield Junction 35, 129
Fall Ing Lock 20, 21
Farndon 141, 142
Field Locks 111
Figure of Three Locks 22
Fishpond Lock 16
Fiskerton (Lincs) 60
Fiskerton (Notts) 139–140

Fleet Lock 18
Fly-boats 69, 70
Forest Locks 46
Foss Dyke Canal 131, 170
Fossdyke & Witham Canal
  55–68, 143, 146
Foster's Swing Bridge 99
Foulridge 102
Frith Bank Drain 66
Frodsham Cut 159
Furness Vale 124, 125
The Fylde 71, 73

Gainsborough 148
Galgate 74
Gallows Inn Lock 52
Gannow Tunnel 100
Gargrave 104
Garstang 73
Gathurst 89
Gawsworth 116
Gilbert, John 29, 37, 170
Glasson 75
Glasson Branch 69, 74, 75
Glory Hole 55, 58
Goole 15, 167, 169
Goyt, River 124, 126
Goyt Mill 120
Grand Sluice, Boston 55,
  67–68
Grantham Canal 131, 135
Grappenhall 32
Great Northern Basin 53
Greenberfield Top Lock 103
Greenhalgh Castle 73
Greenwood Lock 23
Gringley on the Hill 42
Gunthorpe 131, 138

Haigh Hall 94
Halifax 26
Hall Green 113, 114
Hall Green Branch 113
Halsall 85
Hapton 99
Harding's Wood Junction
  150–151
Harecastle Tunnels 149, 150,
  151, 170, 171, 172
Haskayne 85
Hassall Green Locks 152
Hayton 45
Hazlehurst Lock 131, 139
Heath Village 21
Hebden Bridge 27
Henshall, Hugh 41
Hest Bank 78
High Lane 120
Higher Poynton 119
Higher Walton 31
Higherland Lock 104
Hirst Lock 109
Holme 143
Holme Locks 135
Holme Pierrepont 135, 137
Horbury 22
Horncastle Tunnel 64
Hoveringham 138
Huddersfield 28
Huddersfield Broad Canal 25,
  28, 121
Huddersfield Narrow Canal
  15, 28, 121, 128, 172
Hulme Lock 130
Hulme Lock Branch 35
Humber 55
Hunts Locks 162
Hyde 128
Hyde Bank Tunnel 126

Idle, River 42
Ilkeston 52
Irwell, River 29, 170

Johnson's Hill Locks 81, 96

Keadby Lock 143, 148
Keighley 108
Keighley & Worth Valley
  Railway 108
Kent Green 114
Kidsgrove 150
Kildwick 107
King's Road Lock 19
Kippax Lock 16, 18
Kirklees Park 25
Kirkstall Abbey 112
Kirkstead Abbey 63
Knaith 147
Knostrop Fall Lock 16
Knostrop Flood Lock 16
Kyme Eau 64

Lancaster 76–77
Lancaster Canal 69–80, 81,
  93, 96
Lancaster Pool 94
Langley Mill 53–54
Langrick 69
Leather, George 20, 167
Ledgard Bridge Flood Lock
  23
Leeds 16–17, 112
Leeds & Liverpool Canal 16,
  17, 29, 35, 39, 69, 81–112,
  171
Leeds-Settle-Carlisle Railway
  17
Leigh 29, 39, 92
Leigh Branch 37–38, 91–92
Lenton Chain 134
Lewis Textile Museum 97
Lincoln 55, 58–59
Linton Lock 167
Litherland 83
Little Moreton Hall 114
Littleborough 147
Liverpool 82
Long Eaton 50–51
Longbotham, John 81
Longport Wharf 150
Lune, River 69, 78
Lune Aqueduct 78
Lyme Park 119
Lymm 32

Macclesfield 117
Macclesfield Canal 113–120,
  121, 122, 126, 150
Maggoty's Wood 116
Maghull 84
Manchester 35–36, 130
Manchester Ship Canal 30,
  32, 35–36, 37, 156, 165,
  171
Margidunum 138
Marple 120, 126
Marple Aqueduct 125, 126
Marple Junction & Locks
  120, 121, 122, 126
Marston 156
Maud Foster Drain 66
Meadow Lane Lock 134, 135
Melling 84
Mersey, River 30, 36, 82, 170
Mickleton 18
Middleton Railway 17
Middlewich 154
Middlewich Branch 160
Mill Bank Lock 23
Mirfield 23
Misterton 42
Moore 31
Mow Cop 114

Naburn Lock 167
Nelson 101
New Junction Canal 15, 169

New Mills 122
Newark Branch 141
Newark Nether Lock 141
Newark-on-Trent 141–142
Newark Town Lock 141, 142
Newbridge 160, 161
Nocton Delph 62
North East Waterways 167–169
North Muskham 143
Northwich 155, 158, 159, 161, 162
Norton Priory 30
Nottingham 131, 135–136
Nottingham Canal 49, 52, 53, 134, 135–136
Nutbrook Canal 49, 52

Oakgrove 116
Office Lock 17, 112
Osberton Park 47
Oughtrington 33
Ouse, River 167
Outram, Benjamin 121

Pagefield Locks 90
Paradise Mill 117
Parbold 89
Park Nook Lock 26
Pasture Lock 50
Patricroft 37
Peak Forest Canal 113, 120, 121–128
Peak Forest Tramway 124–125
Peaks & Plains Discovery Centre 117
Pendle Heritage Centre 102
Pennine Way 103
Pickering's Wharf 164
Plank Lane Swing Bridge 92
Pocklington Canal 167–169
Portland Basin 128
Possett Bridge 126
Potters Brook Bridge 74
Preston 70, 96
Preston Brook 29, 30
Preston Brook Tunnel 30, 157

Queen Street Mill Museum, Burnley 100

Radcliffe on Trent 137
Rain Hall Rock Branch 103
Ramsden's Swing Bridge 20
Ranby 47
Red Bull Aqueduct 114, 150
Red Doles Lock 28
Rennie, John 69, 78, 170
Retford 46
Ribble, River 69, 96
Ripon Canal 167
Rishton 98
River Lock 16, 112
Rochdale Canal 26, 27, 35–36, 121, 129, 130
Rode Heath 152
Rodley 111
Romiley 126
Rose Hill Tunnel 126
Round House Farm 65
Royal Oak Swing Bridge 116
Rufford 87
Rufford Branch 86, 87, 88, 89
Runcorn 29, 30
Runcorn & Weston Canal 165

Sale 34
Salford 37
Salt Museum 155, 162
Saltaire 109
Salterforth 102
Salterhebble Branch 26
Saltersford Locks & Tunnel 156, 163
Salwick 70
Salwick Wharf 71
Sandbach 153
Sandiacre 50, 52
Savile Town Basin 23
Sawley 132
Sawley Cut 132–133
Saxilby 57
Scofton 47
Selby 15
Selby Lock 167
Sheet Stores Basin 50
Sheffield & South Yorkshire Navigation 131, 143, 169
Shelford 137
Shelford Manor 138
Shepley Bridge Flood Lock 23
Shibden Hall Folk Museum 26
Shipley 109
Shipley Lock 53
Shropshire Union Canal 36, 154, 160
Silk Museum, Macclesfield 117
Silsden 107
Skipton 105
Sleaford Navigation 64
Soar, River 131, 132, 172
Southrey 62
Southwell 139
Sowerby Bridge 26–27
Springs Branch 81, 105, 106
Stainforth & Keadby Canal 148, 169
Stamford Bridge 167
Stamp End Lock 58
Standedge 28, 172
Stanley Dock Branch 82
Stanley Ferry Aqueduct 20
Steetley Chapel 48
Stockport Branch 129
Stockton Heath 31
Stockton Quay 31
Stoke Bardolph 131, 137
Strines 122
Sutton Flood Lock 165
Sutton on Trent 144
Sutton Reservoir 116
Swale, River 167

Tame, River 126, 128
Tarleton 87, 88
Tattershall Castle 64
Telford, Thomas 113, 116, 149, 150, 170
Temple Newsam House 18
Tewitfield Locks 69, 79
Thelwall 32
Thornes Flood Lock 20, 22
Thornhill 23, 24
Thrumpton 132–133
Thrumpton Hall 132
Thrumpton Weir 51
Thurlwood Steel Lock 152
Thurnham Hall 75
Thwaite Mills Industrial Museum 17

Toddbrook Reservoir 124
Torksey 56, 146
Torksey Lock 143
Townley Hall 100
Trencherfield Mill 80, 91
Trent, River 42, 50, 55, 56, 131–148, 170
Trent & Mersey Canal 29, 50, 113, 114, 131, 149–158, 159, 163
Trent Falls 167
Trent Lock 50, 51, 132, 133
Trent Port 147
Turnbridge Loco Lift Bridge 28

Ure, River 167

Vale Royal Cut & Locks 160, 162
Varley, John 41, 49

Wakefield 20–21
Walton Summit Branch 81, 96
Warton 79
Washingborough 60
Waters Meeting 35
Waterways Museum 135
The Way We Were 91
Weaver, River 156, 158, 159, 162
Weaver Navigation 36, 155, 156, 159–165
Weaverham 163
The Weavers' Triangle 100
Wedgwood, Josiah 149
West Park Museum 117
West Stockwith 42–43, 148
West Stockwith Lock 143
Weston Canal 164, 165
Weston Marsh Lock 165
Weston Point 159, 164, 165
Whaley Bridge 124–125
Whaley Bridge Branch 124
Wheelock 153
Wheelton 96
Whitsunday Pie Lock 45
Whitworth, Robert 81
Wigan 80, 93
Wigan Locks 93
Wigan Pier & Heritage Centre 91
Wigan Top Lock 81, 96
Williams, Sir Edward Leader 37, 156
Winsford 159, 160, 161
Winthorpe 141
Wiseton 44
Witham, River 55, 170
Witham Navigable Drains 66
Witham Navigation 58–68
Withnell Fold 96
Witton Park 97
Woodhall Spa 63
Woodlesford 18
Woodnock Lock 19
Worksop 41, 48
Worsley 37–38
Worsley Delph 29, 37

Yorkshire Dales National Park 104
Yorkshire Dales Railway 106
Yorkshire Mining Museum 22